MAELER'S REGARD

Images of adult learning

By the same author:

Adult Education and Community Action (Writers and Readers
    Publishing Cooperative, London, 1975)
The Poor Cousin: A Study of Adult Education (George Allen and
    Unwin, London, 1979)
Tutoring Adults (Council of Adult Education, Melbourne, 1986)
*The Third Contract: Theory and Practice in Trade Union Train-
    ing* (Stewart Victor Publishing, Sydney, 1993)
Defining the Enemy: Adult Education in Social Action (Stewart
    Victor Publishing, Sydney, 1994)

MAELER'S REGARD

Images of adult learning

by MICHAEL NEWMAN

STEWART VICTOR PUBLISHING
Sydney

Maeler's Regard: Images of Adult Learning
© Michael Newman, 1999

Published by Stewart Victor Publishing
PO Box 51, Paddington, NSW 2021, Australia.
publisher@svp.com.au
www.svp.com.au

ISBN 0 9577057 0 0

First printing March, 1999
Second printing August, 1999
Printed in Australia by Wild and Woolley
Glebe, NSW 2037
Member: Australian Publishers Association/Publish Australia

National Library of Australia Cataloguing-in-Publication entry

Newman, Michael, 1939- .
Maeler's regard : images of adult learning

Bibliography.
Includes index.
ISBN 0 9577057 0 0.

1. Educational sociology. 2. Adult education - Social
aspects. 3. Adult education - Moral and ethical aspects.
4. Adult learning - Social aspects. 5. Adult learning -
Moral and ethical aspects. I. Title.

374.001

Contents

Introduction

The major part of the title of this book—*Maeler's Regard*—is explained in the first few pages, and there is no need to elaborate here. However I would like to comment briefly on the second part of the title—*Images of Adult Learning*. Then I want to acknowledge the help I have received.

In some of the literature of adult education, theoretical writing is divorced from practice. This probably arises from the fact that people like myself who are given the time to write are often working in universities where we coordinate and teach courses for adult educators. The participants in our courses are community workers, health educators, industrial trainers, diversional therapists, teachers in technical colleges, training officers in the armed services, and so on. These people are directly engaged in helping adults learn in the daily business of their lives. We, on the other hand, are in a meta-profession. We educate educators. We *talk* about what our participants *do*; and this means that when we come to write we may, out of habit or as a defence, engage in a purely theoretical form of discourse. In this book I have tried to counter this tendency by linking theory with image. Sometimes these images have a direct association with adult education and learning but sometimes they do not. So I have taken time out in the text to describe a surfer, a painting, a climb, a night in a jazz club, and pieces of theatre. I have described recent and distant events from my own past. I have described other people's experiences. I have placed case studies at various points in the text. And I have described people in a number of different contexts: on a picket line in South Africa, in the brick kilns of north Pakistan, in a women's refuge in Sydney, on an oil tanker in the Persian Gulf. I have not privileged practice over theoretical discussion but, by peppering the book with images, I have tried to place practice at the *centre* of theoretical discussion.

A number of people have helped me in a variety of ways to write this book. I want to thank Joelle Battestini and our son Frank Newman and our daughter Alicia Newman, from whose activism I have drawn a number of examples. I want to thank the people who advised me on the text itself. These include Astrid von Kotze, Kate Collier, Steven Segal, Yolande Munn and Peter Willis, all of whom read a draft of the full text and gave me encouragement and comment; and Lann Dawes, Sallie Saunders, Clive Chappell, Rennie Johnston, Alex Nelson, and Liz Hill who read sections of the text and made comments. Thanks also to Glen Morris who formatted the text in preparation for publication.

I would like to thank all the people, old friends and new ones, whom I met while on study leave in the second half of 1996. These include Heather and Gordon McColl for their welcome in Singapore; Shele Pepane, Bobby Marie, Susan Westcott and Chris Bonner in Johannesburg, who welcomed me and shared their expertise and experience as union educators with me; Jillian Nicholson and Christopher Nicholson who offered accommodation and friendship to me in Durban; Jillian Nicholson, who arranged for me to be an associate of the Trade Union Research Project at the University of Natal, and her colleagues at TURP; Astrid von Kotze who welcomed me to the Department of Adult Education at the University of Natal; Sithando Ntshingila who took me into Cato Crest Camp and told me of his work there; Deena Soliar of Umtapo in Durban; Tony Morphet, Linda Cooper and Janice McMillan who welcomed me at the Department of Adult Education in the University of Capetown; Budd Hall, who arranged for me to be a visiting scholar in the Department of Adult Education, Ontario Institute for Studies in Education, and his colleagues there for their welcome; and Budd Hall and Darlene Clover for the friendship and accommodation they offered me while I was in Toronto.

I would like to thank all those people who have allowed me to name them in the text.

I would also like to thank all those others—colleagues and participants in courses at the University of Technology, Sydney, and in union seminars I have conducted—for their ideas and advice and comments as I developed or tried out some of the ideas that now appear in this book. In particular I would like to acknowledge the support of colleagues involved in the Centre for Popular Education at UTS, including Tony Brown, Rick Flowers and Griff Foley. And I need also to thank the University of Technology, Sydney where I work for providing the conditions (including that study leave) which enabled me to write.

Of course, having mentioned the help I have received, I need to say that I take sole responsibility for the final form of the text.

MN
Sydney,
March, 1999

Section 1: Experience

1: Self-help for the blind

In the nineteen seventies I was an outreach worker for an adult education institute in London. My job was to respond to the educational needs of community groups within the area served by the institute. These groups were defined by their social class, or some shared history, interest, disadvantage or neighbourhood. One such neighbourhood, I remember, was marked off by a cemetery, railway lines and Wormwood Scrubs stretching away to the prison in the distance. I am back in Australia now, living in Sydney with its beaches, the sun, the harbour, and the smell of vegetation in the back lanes on humid nights. Wormwood Scrubs made a bleak prospect in London's mid-winter.

My institute's patch included the inner London districts of Hammersmith and Shepherds Bush, and through contacts on Hammersmith Council I heard of an organisation of blind people who had been given a lease on a house. The director of the organisation was a tall Scot, a former journalist, about forty I would say, and now completely blind. He had talked money out of various authorities, talked the house out of the council and, with the help of other blind and partially sighted people, set up the centre.

He was immediately interested when I made contact. Through me he could get a couple more braillers for their braille classes, and payment for their volunteer tutor. I put the braille classes on the institute's list.

I liked the centre and the people there. Their discourse was one of resistance. They were disillusioned by the longstanding providers for the blind and partially sighted in London, and had gone ahead and set up their own centre and, as far as possible, their own support mechanisms. Their position was necessarily ambivalent because they still needed the established providers for services such as education in blind mobility; but they had

3

challenged and effectively reduced the pervasive institutional control they felt these providers had exercised over their lives.

I mentioned my institute's relationship with the centre at one or two meetings of adult educators, and was contacted by an inspector from the Department of Education and Science who said she would like to pay the centre a visit. Together with the director we set up the visit for a late afternoon and evening, so that the inspector could see a braille class in progress, attend a discussion, and then join some people for a drink in the basement.

The centre was a fairly down-at-heel terrace house on three levels. The rooms on the two upper levels were small and the general standard of decoration poor. I felt ill at ease during the inspector's visit—we can react to familiar places and people with another kind of awareness when seeing them through someone else's eyes—but the inspector, observant, amiable and unpretentious, seemed genuinely impressed. She lingered in the class and the discussion, and we went downstairs to the basement at about eight.

The basement was the biggest single space in the building, the floor area comprising the full width and depth of the main structure of the house. There were six or seven people present, conversing with a young man who was putting the final touches to a mural.

The mural covered one of the party walls. It was multi-coloured and multi-textured. The colours were strong in places, and subtle and light in others. The texture consisted of fabrics of differing qualities, from silk to hessian, plastics, polystyrene, cardboard and moulded plaster. The artist, Maeler, worked at the mural energetically, with his back to us for most of the time, swinging round every now and then and looking down for a brush or a piece of material or a pot of paste, talking enthusiastically and explaining how he wanted the mural to work as a tactile or visual experience, or both, for the blind, the sighted, and people with every kind and degree of sight in between.

The director explained that Maeler had been an art student.

I am not sure how the next piece of information came out. My memory, if I work on it, can summon up a good deal, but in this case it fails me on a significant detail. Did the Inspector comment on the urgency with which Maeler appeared to be

4

working. Did I? Did the director, unprompted, explain? I do remember Maeler turning and looking at us—at me, because I felt isolated in his regard at that moment whether he looked directly at me or not—and my understanding that there was something wrong about his eyes and my being told that, yes, he was eager to get the job finished because he was going blind.

I remember seeing a film years ago called *La Guerre est Finie* (Resnais, 1966) about people in the nineteen fifties and sixties still fighting the lost cause of the Spanish civil war, moving between Spain and France, engaged in clandestine activities against Franco's regime which also put them at odds with the French authorities. The central character was weary but relentless, obsessed, in his commitment to his cause; and the film-maker used a technique to demonstrate this preoccupation. At moments, with no clear trigger, a single image of a group of his comrades gathered round a table would appear instantaneously on the screen. Even during a lovemaking scene, at the moment when the character seeks to lose himself in sensation, the image of the meeting flashes onto the screen. Thoughts are not always like images, so the analogy with the film may be a loose one, but over the years, without any trigger that I can understand, the 'image' of Maeler has come into my mind.

The inspector and I left the centre after nine. She drove away and I walked to a telephone box and rang my partner. She had just got in from teaching an evening class but she walked out of the house again, got back into our car and picked me up. We went to a pub in West Kensington.

Whether it be Sartre's reflective consciousness, or Freire's *conscientization*, thinkers of one sort and another seem to have wanted to define, describe and make available a heightened form of consciousness, which the rest of us may sometimes want to avoid. Alcohol can provide an escape, but not always. The speech may slow, but an undisciplined kind of reflection rattles the mind. To stop thinking, I need a bad movie or loud music.

The Kensington Tavern in Elsham Road was a straightforward drinking house at the time, bare floor boards, and a venue for talented rock bands. We walked through the door and into a wall of sound. I ordered our drinks by mouthing the words, and we moved through the crowd towards the band.

If this were fiction, a short story, I would describe the hero standing, his wife's arm linked with his, holding his beer, staring at the rock band, surrounded by sound, tears running down his cheeks as he wept publicly but unnoticed for Maeler, and for what he had seen in Maeler's regard. We have no control over our past. We can use it, interpret it, learn from it and even rewrite it but the fact of it mockingly remains. Maeler had been an art student. We have no guaranteed control over our future. We can try to influence it by learning, planning and taking action, but events happen that can divert the whole course of our lives. Maeler's sight began failing. Our futures are there to haunt us. We may grow old. We will die. In this case, in a few months' time Maeler was going to be blind. Our pasts direct us forward, while obvious futures rush back to meet us, and others wait unseen to waylay us. All we have is the present, a moment in which we can make choices, in which we can either give in to our pasts or face up to some, at least, of our futures. Maeler, in an act of defiance, constructed a mural!

In the real life version, however, the memory I have is of standing completely engaged in the sight and the sound. The band was good. The drummer laid down a careering thunder of rhythms, stating the structures. The bass guitarist offered background comment in rich single notes, linking the drumming to the melodies and counter melodies of the lead and support guitars. Through a series of solos, instrumental duets and songs, the lead and support guitarists told their stories. After one particular song the lead guitarist stepped away from the microphone and, with the rest of the group in support, began a long, rising, silvery solo. He played with no extraneous dramatics, moving a pace forward on the small stage, head bowed over the guitar, a professional in full control of his moment.

2: Kinds of experience

Recently I spent five weeks in South Africa. My reasons for going were clear to me but difficult to explain. On the surface I wanted to understand some of the educational challenges in a country undergoing rapid and radical social change, and to witness some of the adult educational responses. To do this I met and worked with union educators and with adult educators who shared my interests in learning in social action. One friend in particular was eager to give me material to read and organise people to meet, and asked continually what I was really interested in. I could not reply with any clarity because I was interested in nothing in particular, and in everything. I had chosen the context, but within that context I was simply in search of experience. I was there to be there.

Experience recalled

Experience is complex, made up of sight, sound, the feeling of someone's arm against yours, the other senses, emotions, thoughts, events and other people. Experience is true in the moment but immediately falsified as it banks away into the past and becomes a recollection. In recalling experience we construct it, giving it a beginning and an end, making it *an* experience, an episode, and so lifting it artificially out of the continuous flow of our being. In each recalling of an experience we reconstruct it. Reconstructing experience is a reflexive activity. We add to ourselves in the process of experiencing; and in the process of recalling and reconstructing our experience, we add further to ourselves and further to the experience.

How 'true' is my story of Maeler and the evening at the Kensington Tavern? Well, the centre, the director, the inspector, the mural and Maeler existed. My memory tells me that the account of Maeler at the mural is accurate. The Kensington Tavern existed and I went there the same evening and listened to some excellent, very loud rock music. But other things must have happened on that day which I, or my memory, have edited out. The story has a beginning and an end and those are arbitrary points in my passage through that day, chosen by me in the telling. I am not sure of the year. Locating the events that took place at the terrace house and the events that took place in the pub within the same experience is an artifice. But the experience, once I recognised it as an experience, began to take shape and become important to me. As that importance grew, so certain details became fixed, others probably elaborated, in my mind's eye: going down the stairs into the basement and seeing the mural for the first time; the moment I really looked into Maeler's eyes; that searing guitar solo. There have been moments over the years when I have thought of using the experience as the basis for a short story. For how long did I reconstruct the experience in my mind with the freedom of a writer rather than the precision of *rapporteur*? What changes had been wrought by the time I abandoned the idea of the short story and sensed the value of the experience as it 'really' happened?

The story is true in that it disturbs me and moves me and makes me think. It is true in that it is now written down, is there. It is true in that I am changed, that I understand more, as a result of having written it: the significance of the touch of my partner's arm, of her companionship at a moment when I sought isolation, for example. And because I have constructed the story and chosen the words, because I have used the devices of writing, I would like to think that the story might have achieved what Aldous Huxley somewhere describes as 'supertruth': that veracity, that accurate echo of human experience, which writing can have even when it is fiction. In a piece of writing that achieves supertruth the experiences described may not have happened but they are nonetheless true.

Experience 'forgotten'
The experience of Maeler and the Kensington Tavern has been with me in a way from the moment it happened but sometimes an experience affects our lives long after the event. The experience does not linger in our consciousness or revisit us from time to time but suddenly sweeps up upon us from a distant past: was long forgotten but is abruptly and vividly there. A while ago I was required to present a paper as part of an application, and in the

nature of these things had to explain certain aspects of my own practice and writing. In the paper I paid tribute to my friend and former adult education colleague, David Head. I described how, by working alongside Head on a number of community adult education projects in the nineteen seventies, I had learnt about dialogue, 'about listening and learning and asking questions that led not so much to answers but to further and more interesting questions'. I wrote about watching how he engaged with people, how he shared his own curiosity, and inspired them to learn. In the written paper I went on:

> And I watched David display an uncomplicated kind of public intimacy. David and I were co-presenting a session. A few days earlier a participant in a community education project we were both connected with had climbed the scaffolding of a tower building under construction in Shepherds Bush and thrown himself off it. I had chosen not to make mention of our friend's death, but David did, weeping for his loss.

I had recalled and recounted the incident to portray the way an adult educator of Head's generosity could share his grief, but the death of the 'participant in a community education project' took over in my mind. I had not thought of the participant for twenty years but now I remembered his name, I remembered the name of his partner, I remembered attending his funeral. Andrew was a photographer. He had a history of schizophrenia but had been apparently well for some time. I recalled learning from other friends that his partner had thought nothing of it when Andrew told her mid-evening that he was going out for a walk. I imagined the change that must have come over him, his entry on to the darkened building site, the climb through the web of steel piping, arm over arm...

When I came to present the paper, I found myself speaking about the sudden and extraordinary energy Andrew must have found to make the climb. In some respects recognising the energy in the event of Andrew's death had become more important than the paper, the presentation, and the application of which they were parts.

Twenty years passed before the experience of Andrew's death and David's public grief became part of my reflected consciousness. When it did, it became a significant aspect of the intensely

9

present experience of presenting a formalised account of my writings for critical scrutiny by my colleagues. I remember talking with a senior colleague in the corridor a day or two after my presentation. He had reservations about the form in which I had written and presented my paper but I found myself not really listening and, as soon as he gave me a chance, telling him again about this friend's death which I had forgotten or ignored or rejected for twenty years.

Immediate experience

Sometimes experiences are change-making in the moment of their happening. We find ourselves in a place, time, context and event of extraordinary intensity. Meaning flows immediately from the experience without our having to exercise memory or reflection. Later we may construct and reconstruct the experience, trying to extend or counteract the changes the experience has effected in us; but at the moment of the experience we are there and there is no construction. In South Africa I spent a day visiting picket lines. If I try to get back as close to the experience itself, it can only be to the first time I recounted it. Three weeks after the event, on a Saturday afternoon in an internet cafe in Capetown, with a coffee and then a couple of glasses of wine beside the keyboard, I sent a progress report of my time in South Africa to my friends and colleagues at my university in Sydney. I had just described meeting a community activist in a squatter camp who expressed disillusionment in the new South Africa:

> I spent a day on the picket lines of a clothing trades strike in Jo'burg and saw the other side of the country, full of optimism and energy and excitement. Hundreds of women, toi-toying (dancing in rhythmic unison almost as if one person, singing in rich, close harmonies) full of the joy of striking for a ten percent rise across the board and likely to get it. I went round with a wonderful organiser. We would arrive at the pickets, and she would raise her arms and jog towards the crowd, and they would immediately burst into song. Amazing. A country that can get 80,000 wonderful women dressed in their best gear (berets, hats, jackets) into the street for more than two weeks and hold the clothing trade to ransom like that has a lot going for it. They are paid so little and giving up even that pay meant more hardship and yet they struck because of the justice of their claim. ... On one of the picket lines—actually hundreds of people in a huge factory canteen—the

10

shop steward, a woman of huge energy and with a megaphone, asked me to address the crowd. I refused, saying I was not part of this, I supported it, but really it was not my place etc., etc. She dragged me to a set of portable steps in front of the singing, dancing crowd and said: 'We have a comrade who has come from Australia!' Deafening roars of applause. 'And,' she added 'he's too frightened to speak to you!' Even more deafening roars of laughter and applause.

Sight, sound, a welter of thoughts and emotions, joy, hope, inspiration. Other things happened on that day that did not get into this first account. A factory manager, male and white, appeared before hundreds of toi-toying women, all of whom were black. He asked for a moment's silence, and told them that the pay office was open for another half hour for those who had not yet collected their pay for the week before the strike. The encounter was conducted with civility, respect and goodwill on both sides. The singing in the canteen had a difference to it, a slightly wider range of harmonies, and I was told afterwards that there had been some twenty or thirty male workers at the very back of the crowd. I watched a white woman, clearly one of the administrative staff, cross a picket line of about forty toi-toying workers. On their invitation she paused for a minute or two and toi-toyed with them. The women at another factory toi-toyed towards us, singing a song composed for the occasion. It was in Zulu but each line ended with the very recognisable words in English: 'Ten percent'.

Of course I have constructed and reconstructed this experience and used it in several ways, giving it a range of meanings. In conversation with an English feminist friend, for example, I described the women and the way they sang and danced, and we compared this with a particular kind of picket line in England where a group of men equipped with placards stand gloomily round a brazier and hurl four letter words at the occasional passing lorry. In conversation with another friend, I offset this example of solidarity and good humour against the violence reported daily in the South African press. But these interpretations came afterwards. The experience itself, in the moment of its happening and before I had any chance of reflecting and drawing conclusions, changed the way I saw South Africa, changed the rest of my stay in the country and, I think, changed me.

Vicarious experience
At other times influential experiences are vicarious. We live them through others. We read, see a television documentary, or listen to friends; the primary experience is someone else's, but it becomes our experience through our thoughts and emotions as we read, watch or listen. I was sitting with four other people at a table on the edge of the field of a cricket club in Singapore as night fell. We came from a number of different countries but all of us were connected in some way with the union movement. We ate together and chatted and one of the group talked of her encounter with women in a Sri Lankan tea plantation. She described a course she had organised which liberated the women workers to the point where in negotiations with the plant manager they would sit on chairs rather than on the floor. In South Africa, late one evening after eating together, two friends and I sat talking quietly. Both had been long-time activists against the apartheid regime. They told me of the night someone—they assumed from the secret police—had rung the husband to tell him they were coming to burn the house down and to kill him. The couple had waited through the night until the light came and the police did not. Their fear was not unfounded. Rick Turner, a philosopher, political analyst and friend of theirs, had been gunned down one evening when he went to see who was at his front door.

In each of these cases I listened to the stories being told, asked questions, and was moved. In each case the experiences had been constructed by the tellers, the essences of each experience distilled through the telling so that I could all the more rapidly understand and absorb them. In each case I was given enough to be able to imagine the mixture of trepidation and exultation those women must have felt the first time they took their seats opposite the manager; and the fear as the couple waited through the night, and their relief in the morning. Recalling experience—one's own and those of others—involves both memory and imagination. I remember Andrew, but am required to imagine the climb.

3: Experience as conflict

By recalling an experience we immediately create a conflict of interests. The person recalling the event prescribes for her or himself the character of subject and for the others in the event the character of object. He or she is central to the story, the person who has feelings, makes choices and is changed, while the others swirl around this central person playing out their parts as actors in what can seem like preordained roles; as actors in a story already constructed and now several times told.

I quickly formed the greatest admiration for the clothing trades union organiser who took me round the picket lines in Johannesburg, to the extent that I have mythologised her, constructing her in my mind into the archetype of a good union organiser. It was clear that she was known and liked by the strikers. As we drove up to each factory, she would sound the car horn and be greeted by high pitched ululations. She would get out of the car, raise both her arms high and stamp towards the crowd, establishing or answering the rhythm of the toi-toying. For a time she would dance with the crowd, but at some stage she would move to one side and consult with the shop stewards. The whole exercise was deftly and genuinely done. She established her presence as the union official, encouraged the crowd to demonstrate their solidarity with her and with each other, and then checked for any problems. This done, she would get back into the car and we would drive on to the next picket line. For her there seemed to be no doubts, no need to make choices, simply a path along which to progress. My memory of my own role in the events is very different. I was beset by doubts about the correctness of my presence. As we approached the first picket line I was unsure whether I should get out of the car or not. Once out, I did not know where to stand, how to react. I was quickly caught up in the excitement but felt unsure how to show it. Throughout the day I had to make choices, throughout the day I was encountering new people, new situations, new sensations. Throughout the day I was learning and changing.

In my turn I was objectified, briefly mythologised, by the shop steward who asked me to address the crowd. I was 'a comrade from Australia' and then a comrade from Australia 'who is too frightened to speak to you'. She used me, brilliantly. For my part I can only imagine her feelings: of surprise and irritation at my refusal, perhaps, and then satisfaction and glee when she realised that she could still exploit my presence to motivate the crowd. She was the one experiencing emotions and making choices whilst I, in this instance, was very much an object that did nothing in itself but was there to be reacted to.

She used me, but then we use everyone around us. This produces the conflict of interests. Each time we exercise our own freedom of choice we impinge on someone's else's freedom. Each time people who are objects in my existence behave as subjects in theirs, they force choices upon me and delimit my own actions.

Hell, as Jean-Paul Sartre (1947) said, is other people. This aphorism presents the phenomenon of one person's actions delimiting the actions of others as negative; but Turner, whose thinking owes much to Sartre, uses the phenomenon positively, as the starting point from which he goes on to construct his analysis of a free society:

> The criterion for freedom cannot be whether or not other people limit what I can do, since this occurs in all societies. Rather we must define a free society as one in which (a) the limits are as wide a possible; (b) all individuals have a say in deciding where it is necessary for those limits to be; and (c) all individuals know how and why they are being limited (Turner, 1980: 53).

By recalling an experience we also produce a conflict of perceptions. If ever the shop steward recalls the incident, the way she does will be different from the way I do, because in my recollection I am subject and she is object, while in her recollection the reverse would be the case. This conflict of perceptions will be further exacerbated because in the process of recalling the experience each of us will reconstruct the story, giving it particular 'truths' for ourselves and falsifying it for others. If we were to meet and share our recollections, talk to each other about our emotions at that moment, 'attend,' as they say in the literature, 'to our feelings', we would be talking to each other from our two separate existences. Of course we could reach some kind of understanding, we could communicate. She and I exchanged glances that I believe contained messages of amusement and solidarity. We were after all two unionists at a strike, the justice of which we both believed in. But in another sense, in any efforts to communicate, we would be from such separate and entirely difference consciousnesses that, even with a 'common language', established communication would only be at a superficial level. But this should come as no surprise. The nature of consciousness means that we cannot be someone else. Despite injunctions to do so, putting ourselves into someone else's shoes, seeing something through someone else's eyes, is an impossibility. Alfred Schutz (1967: 106) argues that if the opposite were the case, that if I could be aware of another person's whole experience, then I and the other person would become the same. Schutz maintains that he and another person engaged in 'a single intentional Act' can experience a 'synchronism' or 'simultaneity' of streams of consciousness, but that:

> The simultaneity of our two streams of consciousness... does not mean that the same experience is given to each of us. My lived experience of you, as well as the environment I ascribe to you, bears the mark of my own subjective Here and Now, and not the mark of yours (pp. 104-105).

Schutz goes in pursuit of a theory of intersubjective understanding, and so concentrates on the proximities or 'intersections' of consciousness we can achieve with others through shared space, time and social relations. I would argue, however, that since conflicts of interest and perception will always be there, a better way forward towards fuller communication will be in an examination of the *conflicts* of consciousness, and of what mediates these conflicts. When showing that inspector over the self-help centre for the blind all those years ago in London I did not see the centre through her eyes. I saw the centre more vividly, differently, through my own eyes. My perception was of a place in which resistance occurred, while hers may have been of a place where educational events occurred. Would she advocate continued support for the centre for her purposes, so that I could continue my support for mine? The experiences the South

African shop steward and I 'shared' took place within a strike, and that strike took place within the turbulent industrial and political climate of post-apartheid South Africa. The strike brought us together. The strike was the occasion of our conflict of interests and perceptions. And in examining the strike we may be able to find some meaningful common ground. Indeed, there is just a chance that in that exchange of glances, mediated by the noise and the movement of the singing and dancing, mediated by the strike, mediated by post apartheid South Africa, a white Australian on leave from a university in Sydney and a black South African shop steward in the midst of orchestrating a hugely successful picket line in Johannesburg were partners in complicity, partners in a moment of solidarity. Ironically, and Schutz notwithstanding, perhaps for just that instant we came reasonably close to being subjects together in an identical experience.

Section 2: Thinking

4: Critical thinking

Experience is complex, and reflection on experience is complex also. We construct and reconstruct our experience, falsify it, break it up into episodes, allocate to each episode particular truths of our own, and so set ourselves in conflict with others. By reflecting on experience we give ourselves at least two roles: that of participant in the experience and that of observer-commentator. And we set up a process in which the act of reflecting becomes a consciously conducted experience in itself, upon which we reflect, observe and comment again. Here lies potential madness, disorientation, a kind of intellectual vertigo. In theory the roles of actor and observer-commentator could spiral away into infinity.

Three points arise from this conundrum. The first is that reflection on experience is too reflexive, too confusingly human to be represented in diagrams or formulae or sets of procedures to follow. It would be wise to remain in the ambiguous and metaphorical realm of language when discussing the process. The second point is that most of us do not go mad. We are pragmatic beings. We know we have a limited time, and at some point in the process we stop, deciding that we have learnt as much as we want or as much as we can bear. At some stage we will decide that a particular truth will do for a particular experience, and leave it at that. And the third point is that some human beings seem able to break free from the trap of reflecting on their own experience and engage in critical thinking. Critical thinking may take a person's own experience into account but will include much else besides. Critical thinking is reflection on experience of another order altogether.

We can find evidence of critical thinking in particular people's actions, speech and writing. Here are three examples.

Nelson Mandela
On 20 April, 1964 Nelson Mandela, who twenty years later was

19

to become President of the Republic of South Africa, made a statement from the dock in the Pretoria High Court at the opening of the defence case in what was known as the Rivonia trial. Mandela stood accused with nine others on charges of sabotage, and in his statement he describes how he and others departed from the African National Congress's (ANC) longstanding policies of constitutional struggle and non-violent protest, and in 1961 formed *Umkhonto we Sizwe*, an organisation whose policies included the use of violence against the government.

The statement has been published and republished, and more than thirty years after the event still has the power to move, and to make one think. Here are some possible reasons why.

There is an unambiguous sense of agency in the statement. Mandela takes responsibility for his own decisions and actions. He speaks about going into hiding to organise a national strike, about travelling abroad to seek political and financial support for the struggle against the government, about organising training for future potential guerrillas, and about his role in intensifying the struggle.

> I admit immediately that I was one of the persons who helped to form Umkhonto we Sizwe... (Mandela, 1994:162)

He affirms his full share of responsibility for decisions and actions he took with others, and for the arguments that informed those decisions.

> We of the ANC had always stood for a non-racial democracy, and we shrank from any action which might drive the races further apart than they already were. But the hard facts were that more than fifty years of non-violence had brought the African people nothing but more and more repressive legislation, and fewer and fewer rights (p. 165).

And he has a vision which is his and which he wants to share.

> I have fought against white domination, and I have fought against black domination. I have cherished the ideal of a democratic and free society in which all people live together in harmony and with equal opportunities (p. 181).

Values are made explicit in the statement. These are justice, equity, dignity, and harmony. Mandela describes various sources from which he derived these values, including traditional lore, socialism, Marxism, British political and legal practices, American constitutional law, and the writings, thinking and action of other African leaders. And he engages in self-reflection, analysing changes in his values and attitudes that had taken place as a result of his involvement in the struggle against apartheid. He traces, for example, the way he shifted from advocating the exclusion of the Communist Party from the affairs of the ANC to his acceptance of close cooperation.

The statement is constructed on an analysis of conflicts of interest and perception. Mandela identifies and attacks the mean-spirited politics, the pseudo-legalities, and the repressive violence which made up the government's policy of apartheid, and which mediated the conflicts. Remove the policy, he argues, and the conflicts it creates and promotes will disappear:

> Political division, based on colour, is entirely artificial and, when it disappears, so will the domination of one colour group by another (p. 181).

There is a strong sense of moment in the statement. The past and various futures meet. Mandela explains his actions by drawing on his personal story, the history of the African people's struggle for equality in South Africa, and the history of the struggle for independence from colonialism on the African continent. He presents two starkly divergent but possible futures available to South Africa: that of a non-racial democracy and that of escalating violence and potential civil war.

Above all, the statement examines choice. Mandela explains his decision to commit himself to the struggle:

> In my youth in the Transkei I listened to the elders of my tribe telling stories of the old days. Amongst the tales they related to me were those of wars fought by our ancestors in defence of the fatherland. The names of Dingane and Bambata, Hintsa and Makana, Squngthi and Dalasile, Moshoeshoe and Sekhukhuni, were praised as the glory of the entire African nation. I hoped then that life might offer me the opportunity to serve my people and make my own humble contribution to their freedom struggle. This is what has motivated me in all that I have done in relation to the charges made against me in this case (p. 161).

He recounts how he and others made the momentous decision to endorse violence:

All lawful modes of expressing opposition to this principle [of white supremacy] had been closed by legislation, and we were placed in a position in which we had either to accept a permanent state of inferiority, or to defy the government. We chose to defy the law. We first broke the law in a way which avoided any recourse to violence; when this form was legislated against, and then the government resorted to a show of force to crush opposition to its policies, only then did we decide to answer violence with violence (p. 162).

And he explains how he and others chose from amongst different kinds of violence:

Four forms of violence were possible. There is sabotage, there is guerrilla warfare, there is terrorism, and there is open revolution. We chose to adopt the first method and to exhaust it before taking any other decision. In the light of our political background the choice was a logical one. Sabotage did not involve any loss of life (p. 167).

It is this frank endorsement of violent action which helps me clarify some of my own thinking. To contemplate the use of violence raises profound moral issues. In 1994 I published *Defining the Enemy*, a book examining adult education in the context of social action. In it I identified and discussed the work of certain writers and practitioners who examined the world in terms of conflicts of interest and whose ideas, I believed, could help adult educators and learners engage in learning that took full account of these conflicts; and I proposed a framework for adult educators and their learners to use in translating their learning into action. Rather than examine ourselves, as is the way in much adult education theory and practice, I argued, we should examine our enemies.

Hugely influential in the book is the story of Myles Horton and the death of Barney Graham (Horton, 1990: 39-41). Horton was an activist educator in the south of the United States, and in 1933 was present at a strike of mineworkers in Wilder, Tennessee. Graham was the president of the mineworkers local. Professional killers came to the town to kill Graham, and Horton found himself 'facilitating' a group of mineworkers who had to make decisions that would result in one or more people dying. The mineworkers could expect no help from the authorities so the question they had to address was: should they kill the killers to prevent them killing Barney Graham?

The story presented a challenge to me and my ideas about learning through defining our enemies, and when I had finished writing the main text of the book I knew I had ducked the issue of the possibility of learning in social action leading to violent action. What would I do, or what would I recommend another educator should do, if caught in a dilemma such as Horton's. And more, what would I do, or recommend, if the learners *initiated* the violence? To try and address these questions I wrote an afterword in which I rejected the 'conventional' pacifist's view of no violence at any price, and opted for what I saw as Horton's brand of realism.

Horton retained a strong commitment to non-violence, but understood that in the fluid affairs of women and men struggling against others' uses and abuses of power, those others could be violent. Sometimes, as in the case of the miners at Wilder, our hands are forced.

> Of course anyone in their right mind would be for non-violence over violence if it were a simple choice, but that's not the problem the world has to face (Horton, 1990: 41).

On a number of occasions in Horton's life he and his learners were on the receiving end of violence, or forced into situations of violence or potential violence. In recounting these events Horton constructed a challenging discourse on learning and violence. However, I am unaware of any incident where he and his learners took the initiative, that is, made the considered choice, to escalate their action from non-violence to violence. In a television interview Horton envisaged this happening:

> And I am also sure in my own mind that there are times come when you've exhausted every avenue of change in a revolutionary situation, if the people won't get off your back and give you leeway to grow, then you've got to push them off. And that's violence (Moyer, 1981).

In South Africa in the early nineteen sixties the government would not get off the black majority's back and give them leeway to grow. In his statement at the Rivonia trial, Mandela, activist, leader, and later adult educator (Robben Island where he was to spend many years of imprisonment became known as the Mandela university) explains how he and others decided to escalate their action from non-violent protest to violent protest in the form of sabotage, and how he envisaged a possible further escalation to guerrilla warfare.

Mandela's statement is constructed around real, not envisaged, decisions to engage in violence. Violence is repugnant. Most advocates of violence are repugnant. Mandela advocates violence, but is not repugnant. This, as I have tried to demonstrate in the selection of the quotations above, is because the statement and the arguments for the escalation to violence contained in it are made from a carefully examined, overtly articulated and personally owned, moral standpoint.

Rick Turner

The second example of critical thinking is about choice. This time, however, it does not so much demonstrate choice as advocate it. Again the context is apartheid South Africa, that is, one of repression; but the time is 1972, eight years on from the Rivonia trial. The example is a small book called *The Eye of the Needle: Towards Participatory Democracy in South Africa* by Richard Turner.

I first heard of Turner during my visit to South Africa. He had been assassinated in 1978, yet in 1996 people talked about him, and did so with affection and sometimes still evident grief. I began asking questions about his life and work, and found former colleagues and friends of his ready to talk of his clarity of thinking, his teaching, his integrity. People were proud to have known him. When I was looking for a copy of *The Eye of the Needle* in a bookshop in a suburban shopping centre in Durban, the bookseller told me he had attended Turner's funeral. Two people I encountered offered me copies of his lecture notes, which they had kept as mementoes of the man and his teaching and thinking. The education officer of a large union talked of the book as a major influence on his own life, on the lives and work of fellow activists, and on the life and politics of South Africa.

Turner was a philosopher. In an introduction to the 1980 edition of Turner's book, Tony Morphet describes how Turner had been banned by government order—that is prevented from working, meeting more than one person at a time, or visiting town centres and workplaces; and he speculates on why this thirty-six

24

year old philosopher who had of necessity spent the past few years in reclusive writing should have been murdered. Morphet describes Turner's philosophical work as 'the act of an extremely strong-willed autonomous individual'. He notes that while the intellectual climate within which Turner was working 'was narrowing all the time and permeated with pessimism and despair', Turner's critical range was increasing. Morphet argues that Turner was opposed to 'the concept and practice of a small vanguard group' and so was 'constitutionally incapable' of leading any 'communist' or other conspiracy the Security Police and the Bureau of State Security might have believed existed. Morphet goes on:

> Yet it is possible to understand why the security police should have seen Turner as a figure of major importance.... It is likely that in their understanding he figured as a man who had the potential to draw together a new formation of opposition groups—a formation which might include the whole spectrum of opposition from exiled organisation, to the 'homeland' leadership and rank and file, to white activists and even some elements of the Progressive Federal Party. In this they were probably, ironically, right (Morphet in Turner, 1980: xxxii).

Turner's power, then, was in his critical thinking. And while he left lecture notes, articles, and the uncompleted draft of a major philosophical inquiry, that thinking is most easily accessed in *The Eye of the Needle*.

The book has a single central message that informs all its detailed reasoning.

> Human beings can choose. They are not sucked into the future by stimuli to which they have to respond in specific ways. Rather, human beings are continually making choices. They can stand back and look at alternatives. Theoretically they can choose about anything. They can choose whether to live or to die; they can choose celibacy or promiscuity, voluntary poverty or the pursuit of wealth, ice cream or jelly (Turner, 1980: 8).

From this flows his argument that a society and its institutions, no matter how permanent or powerful or removed they may seem, are constructed by human beings. Here is Turner describing market forces:

25

But in fact the market is not a force of nature. It is other people going about their business. When there is a slump and a rise in unemployment the limitations placed on people thereby are a result of investment decisions and other commercial decisions made by other people. When I send my apples to market and find there is a glut, it is because other people have been planting, growing, picking and packing too many apples for the needs of yet other people, who will not buy any more apples because they have had enough. The force of the market is what I call a hidden social force. It is other people telling me what to do (p. 53).

A society such as South Africa, any society then, no matter how fixed or 'natural' or removed from our control it may seem, has been constructed on choices made by people. This being the case, it can be *understood* by people. And this being the case it can be unmade and remade by people. For Turner's contemporaries in the South African struggle, dispirited by the apartheid regime's success in the nineteen sixties in crushing opposition, this was an argument to reinvigorate them.

If society can be made, Turner argued, then we must examine the utopia towards which we should strive. In his book, over a number of chapters, he mounts an attack on the distribution of power and wealth that marks capitalist societies and the South African capitalist society in particular. He then describes an alternative society, based on universal suffrage, participatory democracy, and socialist institutions. The roots of this democracy would be in workplace democracy and worker control, and there would be 'a rich variety of intermediate institutions between the individual and the government'.

Turner's writing is both parochial and universal. In opening his argument he says:

Let us, for once, stop asking what the whites can be persuaded to do, and instead explore the absolute limits of possibility by sketching an ideally just society (p. 1).

As well as providing a goal to strive for, Turner argues, the model of an ideal society serves as a tool for analysing social reality.

Turner uses various modes of argument. He employs formal, analytical logic. He appeals to good, grounded common sense, letting certain points become obvious simply by stating them. He uses paradox, constructing, for example, a case for a certain kind of economic management upon the assertion that freedom for oneself and others requires planning and limitations. He exploits the belief systems of the reader: Morphet describes him as 'a wholly secular man', yet Turner uses the Christianity espoused by many of his compatriots as a basis from which to mount an attack on capitalism and to discuss alternative 'human models'. He employs to great effect argument *via negativa*, demonstrating the practicality of his utopianism by showing the impracticality of the 'realism' proffered by those who would oppose him. Again and again he pushes beyond the constraints of formal, conventional discourse in search of a deeper truth.

Turner uses history, at times with crushing irony, in a number of ways: to disprove the 'realists' who base their racial prejudice on terrible misconceptions about human nature and history; to demonstrate that human beings do have choice; to argue that we must 'grasp the present as history' (that is, as a moment of continuing change); and to plan an alternative future.

Turner is ready to critically evaluate the thinking and actions of friends as well as enemies, frankly weighing advantages against disadvantages, merits against demerits. He was in close contact with the leaders of the black consciousness movement at the time and, in the course of a long postscript to *The Eye of the Needle*, written a year after the book was first published, he subjects black consciousness in South Africa to sympathetic but unflinching scrutiny, arguing that the movement's predominantly middle-class and American origin meant it was more concerned with cultural rights than economic rights. It is clear from several passages in the text that Turner sees the black South African trade unions as the most appropriate bodies to help bring about the far-reaching economic and social changes he proposes, and he spends time examining the particular nature of this newly developing industrial working class.

Turner argues from a clearly articulated moral standpoint: love of others. And in discussing this kind of love, he offers what amounts to a definition of critical thinking:

> We have seen that love requires understanding of oneself and of the other. But it is not possible to understand myself or the other without the use of reason, without thinking about myself and

society. Unless I can see the way in which social forces impinge on me and structure my relationships with other people, I cannot escape from mere role-playing, from patterned responses to the other. The stereotypical reaction of white to black is only the most obvious expression of a society in which all relationships, from courtship to commuting, become stereotyped. All relations become rituals (p. 92).

Love and the freedom from role, ritual and stereotype that comes with it, form the basis for people-in-community as opposed to people-in-competition. 'Community is a good in itself and not a way of attaining other goods,' Turner maintains. 'It is the basic mode of human fulfilment' (p. 20).

Turner writes in an uncluttered, simple, inclusive style that suits the nature and purpose of his project. He often chooses straightforward examples. He can talk about growing and selling apples. There are jolting juxtapositions. He offers us the choices of life or death, and jelly or ice cream in the same sentence. There are flashes of sardonic humour, including a brief but scathing depiction of the conversation at a middle-class tea party as the paradigm for human relationships in white South Africa: 'Not an idea, not a moment of communication, troubles the smooth, empty atmosphere' (p. 92). And despite one or two long quotations where he lets someone else—Julius Nyere, for example—make a point for him, Turner only occasionally provides 'academic' references.

Turner's ideas are his, yet they are also clearly and openly the distillation of years of study. The matter-of-fact offer of the alternative of suicide to illustrate his discussions of choice signals his interest in the existentialists. His analysis of the limits and freedoms of that choice in his utopian society owes much to Sartre. His argument that society can be unmade and remade echoes Antonio Gramsci's comparison of 'social and state laws' with natural laws. And his analysis of the capitalist system in South Africa, and the fear, suspicion and intellectual emptiness in which he maintains most white South Africans at that time were living, draws upon Marxist concepts of materialism, commodification and alienation. He, as he argues Marx does, is analysing society from the point of view of changing it, and as such the book is not only straightforward in style but polemical. (Morphet tells us that Turner readily acknowledged the polemical nature of the book.) But, then, perhaps that is a feature of all really critical thinking: that it is analysis of society from the point of view of changing it, and therefore polemical.

Alfred Temba Qabula

The third example of critical thinking consists of two poems by Alfred Temba Qabula, a black South African worker poet. They are polemical, and more besides. One was composed in 1986 when the apartheid regime was entering its final vicious stage, with violence, torture, repression and murder by security forces commonplace. The other was composed in 1995, after the abandonment of apartheid, the establishment of universal suffrage, and the election of Nelson Mandela as president. Both poems are angry.

Qabula is an oral poet. In the nineteen eighties he was a fork-lift driver in a factory, a union militant and a shop steward. When he began composing poetry and performing it to fellow workers and activists, others quickly followed his lead, and he is now recognised as having released a flood of cultural initiatives in the black trade union movement. He went from the factory to work for a while in a cultural project located in a university. At the time of the second poem he was unemployed.

I have only seen Qabula's verse on the page and can only transmit excerpts to you in the same way, but we need to remember that the verse is composed to be recited with all the emphases, the pauses, the variations of pace and rhythm, and the disconnections of the spoken language. We need also to remember that it is composed to be recited, shouted perhaps, at strikes, at political events, in moments of crisis, excitement, fear, disillusion or developing hope. The 1986 poem is called 'The wheel is turning—the struggle moves forward' and is a composition that carries many subtleties. The phrase

    The struggle moves forward
        backwards never

is repeated at irregular intervals throughout the twenty nine verses, but with the phrasing in the second line altered slightly from time to time to prevent it becoming an empty litany.

The phrase

>The wheel is turning

recurs, at first as a metaphor for the progress of the struggle, but just once it is varied and joined with the other chorus to become

>But the wagon-wheel turns
>>the struggle moves forward
>>>backwards never

in ironic reference to the treks that marked the history of Afrikaner conquest in southern Africa.

Qabula uses allusion, but always closely associated with the harsh realities of South African oppression.

>... we die on the one side
>we rise on the other
>and continue
>on and on with our struggle
>until you become mad
>a lunatic oppressor
>wearing garlands of tree leaves on your head...

Images as diverse as white soldiers with blacked-out faces in battle dress and camouflage, and the mad, dispossessed Lear come to mind.

Qabula draws on the past as history.

>The English arrived—
>and we were made ministers of religion
>>teachers and clerks
>taught to be kind
>>humble, trusting and full of respect
>but ignorant of the ways our country was governed...

He vividly depicts the present as history.

>The struggle continues
>>and your Saracens
>>>your machine-guns and sten-guns
>>>your aeroplanes

> your Casspirs and your kwela-kwelas
> your teargas
> shall not break our strength...

And in what at that period must have been an outright act of courage, he contemptuously names names:

> And you—Special Branch
> Who will help you?...

In late 1995, nine years later, Qabula published a poem in the *South African Labour Bulletin*. The poem expresses another kind of anger, and for those former activists now engaged in the managerial and bureaucratic complexities of creating a new South Africa, dealing with international pressures, trying to finance new housing, new schools and new hospitals, trying to plan in a way that might gradually make an extraordinarily unjust society into an equitable one, it made—as several people told me—very distressing reading.

Qabula opens his poem with an image of rejection.

> It has been a long road here
> with me, marking the same rhythms
> everyday.
> Gentlemen, pass me by.
> Ladies, pass me by.
> Each one greets me, "eita!"
> and adds
> "comrade, I will see you on my return
> as you see I am in a hurry... "
>
> "What is your phone number comrade?
> I will call you after I have finished with the planning
> committee on this or that of the legislature
> and then we will work something out for you... "

In the central part of the poem Qabula remembers the old days when

> ... we had become used to calling them
>   from the other side of the river.
> Some of them were in the caves and crevices

hiding when we called
but we hollered loud
until they heard and responded to our voice.

But

When the dust of our struggle settled, there was no one there.

Now, he says,

... we, the abominations, spook them...

Towards the end of the poem, in tones that have echoes of a Greek chorus, he describes the common folk in the struggle.

Although you don't know us, we know ourselves:
we are the movable ladders that take people up towards the skies
left out in the open for the rain
left with the memories of teargas...

And he ends with this cynical salutation:

It has been a long road here
see you again my friends
when you really need us
when the sun clears the fog from your eyes.

Qabula makes no effort to see both sides, to put himself into the other person's shoes, to be detached, balanced and objective. He composes emotionally, angrily. Yet both poems are wonderful examples of critical thinking. Qabula makes judgements, thought out with passion and stated with uncompromising clarity. In both poems he reads and understands a present moment in social history, and scathingly, bitterly marks out the moment as it hovers between one kind of history and several—some of them unwelcome—futures. He challenges, and in doing so presents the listener or reader with choices. He expresses emotion, yes, but he uses it as an analytical tool, freeing his critical analysis from the constraints so often imposed on us by so called 'fair-minded' liberal humanism. Qabula is angry and he sheets home the blame.

In each of these three examples of critical thinking, the writers or speakers are clear-sighted and frank about their own values, assumptions and ideologies. They assume responsibility for what they say and the actions implied by or associated with what they say. They make judgements. They analyse, state a case, and lay the blame. They locate their analyses within social and political contexts. They see these contexts in terms of conflicts of interests and perceptions, and they examine the conditions, people, institutions, and emotions that mediate these conflicts. They communicate the sense of being at the meeting point of the past and a number of possible and significantly different futures, at a moment intensely of the present. If the listeners or readers want to go forward as anything other than objects in someone else's world, Mandela, Turner and Qabula each say, then they must make choices.

5: Uncritical thinking

In a country like South Africa with its forty lost years of apartheid there will also be examples of uncritical thinking. I was lent a wonderful book while I was there called *Ink in the Porridge* in which the author, Arthur Goldstuck, delights in pointing out the uncritical thinking of his compatriots. The book is in fact a very clever and detailed history of the events leading up to the 1994 elections in which the apartheid regime was finally laid to rest, but it is done by examining the disinformation, misinformation and urban legends that proliferated during those four years between Mandela's release from prison and his inauguration as president. Goldstuck tells many entertaining and disturbing stories, describing the circumstances in which they circulated and analysing how and why they came into existence. He recounts urban legends of the purest kind, such as the rumour which spread like wildfire in 1993 and almost destroyed the citrus industry. This rumour had it that oranges had been infected with HIV-positive blood, injected into them by a right wing Natal farmer. Or the story of the black maid borrowing a tape measure from the white mistress of the house in order to measure the windows for the new curtains which the maid intended fitting when the ANC handed the house over to her after the elections. In this story, the maid had been paying ten rand a month to the ANC and they had already registered the house in her name. Goldstuck also examines the way the media both constructed legends and spread rumours and how some journalists valiantly debunked them. And he examines and analyses instances of deliberate misinformation. It is a wild piece of disinformation put around by a prominent black politician in the lead-up to the election which gives rise to the title for the book. On election day people who voted were to be marked by an indelible ink. The pap—a kind of porridge—which the National Party was offering to black voters who came to their rallies, the black politician announced at a rally of his own, was laced with invisible ink. This ink would show up under the ultraviolet lamps on election day and anyone who had eaten the pap would be disqualified from voting.

The ink in the porridge story is ludicrous and while it caused official outrage in the National Party, and anger and probably embarrassment in the black politician's own party, I cannot imagine that anyone would claim that it had the remotest effect on the final result. On the other hand I read an apparently light-hearted column in the Cape Times newspaper on 16 August 1996 which, paradoxically, I believe, could have quite serious ramifications on the thinking of at least some people in the new South Africa. The column appeared at a time when there was a noticeable concern, evident in media stories and people's conversations, about illegal immigration into the new South Africa. An academic described this phenomenon to me as the identification of new demons now that the old divisions were less clear.

The newspaper column was by Dianne Cassere and recounted her overnight stay in a cheap hotel in Johannesburg. It contained a joke about the poor quality of the loo, a description of how that evening at dinner her companions' eyes 'started to round with horror' when she told them where she was staying, and an incident in which she left her room late at night and, on returning, tried to enter the wrong room, arousing the occupant in the process. I read the column because it carried the name Hillbrow, an inner Johannesburg suburb, in its title. I had stayed in a hotel in the neighbouring suburb of Braamfontein three weeks earlier, and had been told that Hillbrow was a violent area and that I should not walk there even in full daylight. In fact I had walked there without incident, and had attended a National Union of Mineworker's seminar held in a hotel there. Was it the same hotel, I wondered?

Cassere's column opened with this sentence:

> I've found myself in some pretty tight situations down the years as has any South African journalist, but none could equal my night surrounded by illegal aliens and Nigerian drug dealers in Hillbrow.

Cassere states her authority as an experienced reporter who has been in 'tight situations' but gives no details. She then claims that others staying in her hotel were engaged in illegal activities but produces no evidence for this allegation, beyond the fact that some of them used a telephone in the corridor to receive calls and carry on conversations. She does say that they were speaking 'what seems to be French', had scars and were wearing nose rings. 'God knows,' she adds, 'where else they were wearing rings'. Of these fellow hotel guests she says:

> These were not our people. These were people from other African countries, and since they were using R100 phone cards, you can be pretty sure they weren't phoning out for pizza.

The exchange rates published in the same paper on the same day indicate that R100 was equal to $22 US, or 14 British pounds, and so would have been about $30 Australian.

Despite Cassere's claim that none of the tight situations she had been in could equal her night in Hillbrow, beyond her mistaking a room and rousing its occupant, *nothing happened*. Even in the mistaken room incident the rightful occupant said nothing, although Cassere does say he was large and bald and that he stared out at her 'in a rage' (as I imagine most people would have done). Most extraordinary, however, is the question of the location of the hotel. The newspaper carried a front page announcement 'Sleepless in Hillbrow: Di Cassere's hotel nightmare' and the heading over the column itself read: 'Visit Hillbrow, and spend a night in an alien environment', yet in describing how she booked the hotel Cassere says (slightly ungrammatically):

> A hotel advertising itself as being in Braamfontein but was actually closer to Hillbrow seemed to fit the bill...

The hotel, unless I am reading this very wrongly, *was not in Hillbrow*. Having given no evidence of violence, illegal activity or threat to her person in either Hillbrow or the neighbouring Braamfontein where she was staying, Cassere ends her column with this question:

> Does anybody else remember the days when you could walk clear across Hillbrow, then a vibrant, cosmopolitan area, in complete safety?

South Africa had been fully free of its apartheid regime for two years and three and half months. Is Cassere asking her readers to recall with approval days when movement by the majority of the population—'our people' as she calls them—was restricted by pass laws, and when the ruling white regime, without recourse to scars or nose-rings, maintained its control over the country through the use of secret police, paramilitary forces, the death penalty, Saracens, automatic weapons, tear gas and all the other paraphernalia of officially sanctioned and barbarous violence?

6: Adult education for critical thinking

Critical thinking is underwritten by critical theory. The phrase 'critical theory' has been used increasingly in adult education literature in the past decade or more in a variety of ways: to denote a philosophical framework, a mode of analysis, and a strategy for action. Critical theory is identified with the Institute for Social Research which was established in Franfurt in 1924, moved to the United States in the nineteen thirties, and was re-established in Frankfurt after the Second World War. The institute and its work have become known as the Frankfurt School, a name denoting both a body of research and thinking, and an institution.

While critical theory is important, it is only part of the story. The thinking exemplified by Mandela, Turner and Qabula, for example, is influenced by socialist theory, and in the case of Turner, also by existentialism. To develop a pedagogy of critical thinking we need to use ideas from all three bodies of theory. In this chapter, therefore, as I go looking for 'an adult education for critical thinking', I will draw on the ideas of writers and thinkers like Jurgen Habermas, a leading figure in the Frankfurt School; Michael Welton and Michael Collins, both of whom interpret critical theory in adult educational terms; Paula Allman and John Wallis who interpret Marx; Paulo Freire, whose many sources include Marx and Sartre; and Jack Mezirow who illustrates a key point in one of his texts by quoting Albert Camus. I will also describe a play.

Collective understanding
In classical Greek drama dreadful and wonderful things happen to the central characters. Their names, echoing down two and half thousand years, still stir the imagination: Agamemnon, Clytaemnestra, Oedipus, Antigone, Jocasta, Orestes. These are the kings and queens, the great families, the people who speak to oracles, unknowingly commit incest and patricide, destroy and

create. While these characters play out their destinies before an audience which knows their stories already, the chorus comments. The chorus is a collective. It comprises the citizens of Thebes or Athens or wherever the play is set. From its position *within the play*, the chorus provides a commentary, placing the events in a fuller historical context, stating the problems and challenges, making judgements and, when it is all over, tying up the loose ends. It is the people of the chorus who do the reflecting, who do the learning, who survive and transcend.

Some kinds of logical thinking, reflection and meditation may be solitary activities but the kinds of critical thinking I have described in the chapters above derive from our social and political experiences and feed back into them. Adult educators helping to promote this kind of thinking, therefore, will be concerned with the collective, with people who are brought together by a common experience or history, a shared community or social class, a shared interest or common oppression. Adult education for critical thinking is a denial of the ideology of individualism that underpins so much educational practice. We may strive to be monarchs but the truth of our existence is to be found in our lives along with others. It is in the consciously examined company of others that we will most effectively reflect, learn, survive and transcend.

This vision of adult education for critical thinking, then, carries with it an idea of a group of people working in solidarity with one another and, by implication, in potential solidarity with everyone of a similar disposition, or living in similar circumstances. A group of Aboriginal people in the city of Sydney may start by examining their own individual experiences, but the educator among them will encourage them to compare, make distinctions and collate, so that a composite picture begins to develop. Once this picture takes on sufficient form the adult educator will encourage the group to make reference to Aboriginal and other histories, social and political theory, the law and any other fields of study or theory that may help them locate their own conditions and experiences within the broader Aboriginal struggle.

This emphasis on collective learning can be seen in the theory and practice of Freire. In the nineteen sixties in Brazil and then Chile, Freire worked with groups of people defined by their common history of oppression, helping them engage in an emancipatory form of learning. He constructs his theory on the learning done by the community group: the people of a village, the residents of a tenement block, the people of a dispossessed social class. He uses the collective term 'the oppressed' and the plurals 'the people' 'the leaders', 'the learners' and 'the participants'. In recounting actual learning events, he refers to 'the peasants' or 'the villagers' or 'the tenement dwellers' and when quoting verbatim a response from someone in the group, he often attributes it to the whole group as if it were a collective statement. So, when describing a study circle in which tenement dwellers in Santiago discuss a drawing of a number of men, one of whom is drunk, he says:

> ... they manifest the need to rate the drunkard highly. He is the 'only one useful to his country because he works while the others gab.' After praising the drunkard, the participants identify themselves with him, as workers who drink—'decent workers' (1972a: 90).

In his theoretical writing Freire argues that his collective education for conscientization is more authentic and so more genuinely educational than the traditional individualistic 'banking education', yet in the accounts he gives of the actual processes he and colleagues used, he often seems to take the collective element for granted. Allman, on the other hand, in her description of her application of Freiran theory to her practice in England, addresses the question of collective learning directly. Allman (1987) describes a learning group engaging in the kind of discussion often associated with the principles and practices of group dynamics. The discussion is controlled by a leader and each person is given an equal opportunity to speak. There may be debates, Allman says, but all these actually do is enable each member of the group to test, defend and clarify what she or he already thinks. The result is an exchange of 'pre-existing ideas, knowledge and questions arising' which Allman describes as 'a sharing of monologues'. She contrasts this with a group engaging in a form of 'dialogic learning' inspired by Freiran thinking. The members in this kind of discussion question the knowledge they already possess, examine why they think the way they do, and evaluate and reshape their ideas. This group develops 'trust, care, collaboration and commitment' in the place of 'competition and individualism'. Any artificial allocation of time to individuals would be out of place since all present are engaged as a group in understanding how they give meaning to the objects of their discussion. Indeed Allman describes how in such a group considerable time may apparently be given over to one person, allowing that person to explore in depth her or his values or assumptions or ideologies, with the others in the group helping by asking questions and identifying how that person has constructed her or his meanings.

A lot of adult education theory draws on the discipline of psychology, but the emphasis on learning as a collective activity means that two major families of psychological theory are of limited use in developing an adult education for critical thinking. For example, what Welton (1987a: 52) describes as 'inspirational humanistic psychology' has resulted in a form of experiential adult education which concentrates on the individual. The words 'self' (as in self-awareness or self-actualisation), 'own' (as in developing one's own potential) and 'personal' (as in personal growth) in the discourse of experiential adult education emphasise this concern; and although this form of education may make use of a range of group processes such as role play, simulation exercises, games, and structured and unstructured discussions, the aim is almost always to help each person in the group 'develop' as an individual. Indeed, the group has no reason for existence outside the specific learning activity, and once the activity is over the group disbands.

In its worst forms this kind of adult education seems to ignore all reference to existing bodies of knowledge, and to foster in the learner an almost solipsistic concentration on the self (Newman, 1993: 153-156). The learner's affective experience becomes the only valid source of information; and the learner is encouraged to delve deep into her or his own emotional past in search of some kind of inner human essence that predates her or his socialisation. There are in this kind of experiential education echoes of the Platonic idea that we spend our lives trying to remember the knowledge we forgot at birth. Welton describes it as being based on a 'decontextualised and abstract concept of self' that 'forgets that we are social individuals' (1987a: 52).

Behavioural psychology has resulted in forms of adult education that are of even less value for adult educators concerned with collective learning and critical thinking. Humanist adult education, for all its concentration on the decontextualised individual, does concern itself with the learner as a unique and sentient being. Adult education deriving from behavioural psychology has in some of its quite mainstream manifestations all but suppressed the idea of the learner as a human being at all. In the nineteen seventies and into the eighties, the emphasis in a lot of adult education, training and human resource development was on curriculum design, implementation and evaluation by objectives. In this kind of training, the objectives of the organisation are paramount and the learner is required to acquire the necessary skills, knowledge and values in order to help achieve those objectives. The learner is reduced to a means to the organisation's ends. In the nineteen eighties and into the nineties the emphasis shifted from objectives to competencies. In this form of curriculum design, jobs (such as nursing) and roles (such as supervisor) are described in terms of a limited number of competencies. Each competency is broken up into elements. And performance criteria are established for each of the elements. Training can then be organised so as to equip a learner or learners with the particular competencies needed to do a specific job or perform a specific role. In the worst forms of competency-based training, the concept of the person is lost, sacrificed as it were, to what Collins (1991: 6) describes as 'the cult of efficiency and technical rationality'; and the learner is effectively reduced to a locus for a cluster of functions.

Constructing knowledge

Adult education for critical thinking resists this reduction of people to means and functions. Equally, it resists the reduction of people to self-obsessed beings in pursuit of personal fulfilment. We are, in Welton's term, 'social individuals'. Each of us may be unique, but each of us is living within, contributing to, and an integral part of, a complex and constantly shifting collective culture. 'Culture' here is the concept writ large. It encompasses the economic, political, social, aesthetic and spiritual elements that go together to make up our lives. Adult education for critical thinking examines both culture, and the people who compose it. It examines the diversities and unities, the interactions and contradictions, between these two manifestations of collective human life.

In order to examine how we engage with the world and construct our culture a number of adult educators (Welton, 1991a, 1995; Collins, 1991; Mezirow, 1981, 1991; Briton, 1996) have drawn on Habermas's 'knowledge constitutive interests'.

Habermas (1972: 308) postulates three 'categories of processes of inquiry'. In each category knowledge is generated from human activities motivated by a different kind of interest. We create knowledge to meet our *technical* interests. This technical (or, as some interpreters of Habermas now call it, 'instrumental') knowledge grows out of our efforts to engage with and manage our material environment. It enables us to control aspects of nature, to work and to produce. It helps us to predict instrumental outcomes. It is the knowledge that underpins the formal, 'rational' logic we draw on when solving technical problems. This pursuit of our technical interests results in the generation of knowledge in every area of our lives, be it the personal, community, workplace, public, or the area of formal study. In the area of formal study it results in disciplines such as geology and physics.

We also create knowledge to meet our *practical* interests. This practical (now often called 'communicative' or 'interpretive') knowledge grows out of our study and interpretation of the human condition. It helps us understand how we make meaning through symbolic interaction, and how we give meaning to our social lives. It helps us communicate and reach consensus. We use it when we address human problems through rational discourse and the interpretation of texts. Knowledge generated out of this kind of human interest is formalised in the descriptive social sciences such as anthropology, sociology, history and theology.

And we create knowledge to meet our *emancipatory* interests. This emancipatory (or 'critical') knowledge grows out of our desire to be free from unjust constraints. We create it in our efforts to identify, evaluate and, where necessary, change the cultural forces that limit the way we live. In terms of ourselves, this knowledge helps us understand how we internalise myths, ideas and ideologies, all of which can work against us. In terms of our interaction with others, this kind of knowledge helps us understand the power relations that obtain in any society, and the belief and value systems upon which various forms of power are based. This kind of knowledge helps us to identify and resist both internalised and external domination. (Habermas, 1972; Mezirow, 1981, 1991; Welton, 1993b).

It is not as easy as it is in the cases of knowledge derived from our technical and practical interests to list the ways in which knowledge derived from our emancipatory interests is formalised in the world of academic study. Emancipatory knowledge is to be found in the disciplines of psychoanalysis and the critique of ideology, and in some kinds of philosophical, social and political studies. But in fact there is the potential for this kind of knowledge to be found in all disciplines and all contexts. Each of the three forms of knowledge is separate in its own way, meeting different interests and observing different 'logical-methodological' rules; but emancipatory knowledge can sublate the other two. Technical and practical knowledge can be challenged, shown to be limited and wanting, but nonetheless taken up and used in the pursuit of emancipatory interests and the creation of emancipatory knowledge. In terms of formal study, physics, geology, computer studies, geography, history, literary criticism, theology, theatre studies, communication studies and all the rest can be put to the service of creating emancipatory knowledge; that is, knowledge which will help us challenge domination. Central to critical theory is the struggle for social justice, and all three forms of knowledge can have their place in that struggle.

If adult educators promoting critical thinking are interested in how we generate our own culture, they are equally interested in the sometimes opposing, sometimes complementary question of how our cultures generate us. Here, we can look to Mezirow (1981, 1991, 1995, 1998) and his discussion of the frames of reference which influence and constrain the way we think, feel and act. Mezirow uses the terms 'meaning perspectives' and 'meaning schemes'. He argues that these 'are learned as generalised subtexts which we have assimilated from our narrative interaction with our culture and our parents'; and that they 'selectively shape and delimit expectation, perception and cognition by predisposing our intentions and purposes, that is, setting our line of action'. We tend to dismiss as aberrations ideas which do not fit in with these frames of reference (1995: 43, 44).

These meaning perspectives and meaning schemes, then, are cultural and psychological *constructs*—in earlier writing Mezirow uses the phrase 'structures of psycho-cultural assumptions' (1981); in more recent writing he talks of 'premises' (1995). And the educator's role will involve three interrelated activities. First, we will help ourselves and others engage in reflection, not just on the content and processes of our thoughts, feelings and actions, but on the premises, the presuppositions, that underpin these thoughts, feelings and actions. Second, we will help ourselves and others redefine those premises, and so replace culturally and psychologically assimilated givens with meaning schemes and meaning perspectives we have knowingly played a part in constructing. Third, we will help ourselves and others decide how to act on the new insights and understandings we have gained from this transformative kind of learning. In the course of his 1981 article, Mezirow quotes Camus' description of an intellectual as 'a mind that watches itself' as a way of capturing the state of mind we need to achieve for transformative learning.

Adult educators promoting critical thinking will also look to Freire (1972a and b, 1976, 1985, 1994) who analyses the way we can become trapped in oppressive cultures, and experience the world through an imposed, limited and therefore 'naive' form of consciousness. This kind of consciousness implies a form of fatalism: social history is something that happens to us, not something that we play an active part in constructing. Freire formulated these views in Brazil where the colonial past of the country meant that one culture had literally been imposed on others. The indigenous people, the descendants of slaves and other, minority, populations lived within a system that in many respects took a 'foreign' European culture as the norm. Only the privileged had access to the political and cultural institutions that held sway over the population, whilst the remainder of the population 'lived in silence'. For Freire, then, the educator's role is to help people trapped in this kind of silence, this kind of naive consciousness, to become aware of the world around them as something they can change. By looking at the world through their own eyes, by naming the world in their own words and not those imposed on them by an oppressor or an invading culture, learners can shift from a naive consciousness to a critical consciousness. Learners can cease being 'objects of social history' and become 'subjects of their own destiny'.

Creating consciousness

As the references to Mezirow and Freire indicate, if we are to engage in an adult education for critical thinking we will need to examine and form an understanding of consciousness. In Sophocles' play *Oedipus Rex*, Oedipus learns that despite a life spent trying avoid the Delphic oracle's predictions, he has indeed been the murderer of his father and has indeed slept with his mother. Tradition in classical Greek drama has it that violent action takes place off-stage. Devastated, Oedipus leaves the stage, to return minutes later having blinded himself by spearing his eyes with needles. In classical Greek drama the actors wear masks. On the night I saw the play at the National Theatre in London the actor playing Oedipus re-entered wearing a mask whose eyeholes streamed with blood. It was an extraordinary moment. Oedipus presented a horrific figure, once glorious king, now blinded and pathetic wretch. Strangely, although we knew he had done everything in his power to prevent the prediction coming true, there was no sense of injustice. The Oracle's prediction had been inevitable. But there was a welling up of feeling. A huge sorrow. For Oedipus, for ourselves, for all humanity. All was there in the collective sigh that met Oedipus as he turned his bloodied mask to face us.

Consciousness is to do with knowledge, awareness, and feeling. At that performance of *Oedipus Rex*, we in the audience already had a certain amount of knowledge. We knew the story (and its modern analogies in psychoanalytical theory). It came as no surprise to learn that the man whom Oedipus had killed at the crossroads had been his real father, nor that the woman whom he had married to become king was his mother. And we learnt more as the play took place, coming to understand the characters and the events as they were interpreted in this particular production by these particular actors.

We were aware. The play was presented to us, a huge picture, a performance, changing and unfolding in front of our eyes. We were kept aware of ourselves as an audience by the chorus moving, sometimes rushing, forward to address us directly. And we were aware of others around us. The seating in the theatre was curved and sloped in the form of an amphitheatre, so that others in the audience were always in the periphery of our vision. Using some of the categories phenomenologists use to examine experience (Schutz, 1967; Willis, 1998), our awareness was a physical one, defined by our bodies as we sat within chairs in the theatre, seeing, listening and reacting; a spatial one defined by the interior of the theatre itself, our position in the theatre and our distance from the stage; one of time defined by the duration of the play and the sense of the passage of time as we were caught up in the play; and one of social relations defined by the people we were with, the rest of the audience, the performers in the play and, above all, the chorus.

And we experienced emotions. Thrill at the noise and spectacle at the outset of the production. Perplexity at the ordinariness of these great people. Pleasure, and an underlying sympathy, as we identified with them. Dread as the story unfolded and the moment when Oedipus would learn the truth approached. Bated breath as the seer Tiresias told him. A kind of despairing tension while Oedipus was off stage, prolonged by the commentary of the chorus. Then that sigh. And in the end relief, subdued talk as the lights came up and, released, we could rise from our seats, climb the steps of the aisle, and leave the auditorium.

Adult educators concerned with critical thinking are interested in how consciousness is generated. Those, like Allman and Wallis (1990), following Marx, are likely to see consciousness being created in our dialectical relationships with the objects, people and events that make up our worlds; and developing and changing as a result of the actions we take to deal with those relationships. In this view of the construction of consciousness, these adult educators are at odds with those theories that propose that consciousness is something we are born with; that it is within us from the outset. Adult educators concerned with critical thinking, therefore, are more likely to be in accord with Sartrean existentialism which maintains that there is no such thing as 'human nature' if by that we mean some force, or set of characteristics, that determines our actions. They are likely to agree with the argument that we are free to make choices—to have ice cream or jelly, to live or to kill ourselves—and that it is in the very process of experiencing this 'vertigo of possibility', of confronting and being confronted by this world of choice, of sensing this 'vacancy' in ourselves which we are free to fill in any way we can imagine, that we develop consciousness (Turner, 1980; Sartre, 1976).

When I see a bad movie or listen to loud music, it is to lose myself, to experience the film or the music without reflecting on myself and my reactions to that experience. I am conscious, but it is more like an extreme form of Sartre's 'non-thetic' or 'unreflective' consciousness:

> My attitude has no "outside";... it is a pure mode of losing myself in the world, of causing myself to be drunk in by things as ink is by a blotter... (Sartre, 1976: 259).

But at that production of *Oedipus Rex*, it was impossible to lose myself. While the audience sat apparently passively, the chorus reminded us of our existence, commenting on the action and calling on us to reflect, pass judgements, and examine our own reactions. They reminded us of the knowledge we possessed, they called on us to account for our reactions and emotions, and they constantly reminded us of who we were. More than that, because a Greek chorus portrays the citizens in the city-state where the play is set, and because the plays were written to be performed before the citizens of a city-state (in those not so golden days, this meant the free men of the state), there is a close, almost symbiotic relationship between chorus and audience. The chorus is an audience itself to the events in the play. At the same time it is a representation of the audience in the theatre. In this manifestation the chorus not only speaks to us but for us, and from time to time enters the action in the play on our behalf. The heightened consciousness I experienced was constructed through surrogate action carried out by the chorus on my behalf. I was both absorbed in the play and made crucially aware of my absorption in the play, a state of mind close to what Sartre describes as 'reflective consciousness'. This form of consciousness, Sartre tells us (1976: 260) 'has the self directly for an object'.

I have chosen to describe a piece of classical Greek theatre as a way of examining consciousness, particularly because the chorus provides a useful metaphor. But there are some who would find the catharsis induced by the play inappropriate. Catharsis, after all, involves an emotional release, perhaps even a sadness. And there is in the concept an implication of passivity. The audience sits in the theatre, moved, but physically inactive.

Theatre activists like the South African Astrid von Kotze (1988) and the Brazilian Augusto Boal (1979) do not want catharsis, but praxis. They do not want sympathy from the audience, but a Brechtian empathy. Through performance they want to create a fusion of reflection with action, a tension that will impel their audience to examine ways to engage in and influence their social and political histories.

In my attempt to describe consciousness, then, I need to add agency. And if I am to stay with the image of theatre and performance, then I need to move from the National Theatre in London to the factory in South Africa where von Kotze and her companions performed a twenty-minute play within a union meeting. After the play, von Kotze observed:

> But something has changed—the general mood has been transformed. The issues of the day have been brought closer. People have made connections between their individual experiences and the collective struggle. Some questions have been answered, some asked so that people start thinking about issues. The audience is pleased that their struggle has been given an importance by being made into a play. The general union meeting resumes with greater energy and spirit (1988: 12).

The play had become part of the worker-spectators' industrial and political struggle.

Or I need to look to Boal's work in Brazil. Boal used performance as a way of helping people examine oppression and formulate ways of combating it. After extensive research into the life of a community Boal would produce a play that presented some aspect of that community's life in the form of a problem. By involving the audience in discussion and encouraging them to intervene in the performance itself Boal sought to change them from spectators to actors.

Or I need to turn to the brief but vivid account by McGivney and Murray (1991: 32-33) of the use of puppetry in Rajasthan, India. They describe how puppeteer-educators used puppetry followed by discussion to alert villagers to the dangers of alcohol abuse, and to mobilise people to take action. Often the performances produced vigorous discussion, and sometimes resulted in direct and radical action. In one village the women decided to smash any bottles they came across. In another, the villagers decided to stop drinking, impose fines on drinkers and place the revenue from the fines in a village fund for seed and fertiliser.

The consciousness conjured up by these latter examples is made up of knowledge, awareness, feelings *and* intentionality. To be fully conscious involves an engagement of the will. Consciousness is not so much a state of mind as a repeated manifestation of intention. There is no sadness or passivity in this vision of consciousness. There is the exhilaration that comes with thinking, judging, making decisions and acting. Oedipus gives way to Maeler.

Communicative action
The sigh in the theatre was a shared one. The mood in the union meeting was of a heightened solidarity. The villagers' decision to stop drinking was a communal one. Adult educators promoting critical thinking are interested in understanding the phenomena of sharing, solidarity and communality. They are interested in consensus, not of the deadening, lowest-common-denominator kind to be found in some kinds of managed encounters, but consensus of the kind Allman (1987) was seeking in her radical dialogic discussion group. Some will look, as Allman does, to Freire's concept of dialogue based on love, humility, faith, trust and hope which enables people to develop and share in a heightened form of social and political consciousness (Freire, 1972a: 62-64). And some will look again to Habermas (1984, 1987), this time to his associated concepts of the ideal speech act and communicative action.

Most activities we engage in will involve communicating with others. Even when an activity is apparently solitary, as in the case of someone sailing solo round the world, it will usually be premised on extensive communication with others. The medium in some forms of human communication may be sophisticated, but whether we publish or broadcast, whether we communicate across the world on the internet, or across a table in a cafe, in effect we are still simply speaking to each other. In developing his concept of communicative action, Habermas proposes a number of conditions that go together to create 'an ideal speech situation'. He argues that whenever one person speaks to another with the intention of reaching an understanding, whether the speaker knows it or not, he or she makes a number of 'validity claims'. These claims are to truth, rightness and truthfulness: that is, that what the speaker says is true; that the speaker has a right—an authority or legitimate reason—to say it; and that the speaker is sincere in saying it (Habermas, 1984: 99, 307).

Each of these validity claims is a 'criticizable validity claim' in that it can be tested and met with a yes/no answer. When someone speaks we can ask whether he or she is meeting these claims. For truth, we can ask: Has the speaker included all relevant information? Has the speaker done everything possible to represent all data fully and correctly? Has the speaker revealed and accurately represented all sources? Do we as hearers accept and share the knowledge of the speaker? For legitimacy: Is the speaker observing the required norms? Is the speaker in the appropriate role and context? Does the speaker have the genuine accord of those on whose behalf she or he is speaking? And for sincerity: Can we trust the speaker? Has the speaker disclosed all vested interests, and all responsibilities to other parties? Has the speaker been open and frank about her or his motives for speaking, about her or his beliefs, intentions, feelings and desires?

Each of these criticisable validity claims, Habermas argues, can be judged against one of the three 'worlds' the speakers and hearers inhabit (1984: 99-100). In asking if the utterance is true, we are in fact asking if there is there a 'fit' or a 'misfit' between the speech act on the one hand, and the objective world on the other. In asking if the speaker has a right to make the utterance, we are asking if there is a fit with the social world. And in asking if the utterance is sincere we are asking if there is a fit with our subjective world.

In a discussion of argumentation elsewhere in the same text (1984: 23) Habermas offers two other validity claims, but these would appear to differ in that they depend not on meeting a yes/no test, but on the reactions and judgement of the hearers. These additional validity claims are related to the comprehensibility of what is said, and the aesthetic qualities of what is said. So for comprehensibility we might ask: Is the speaker clear? Do we understand? Is she or he employing the language, the structures of argument and the genre of speech necessary to make what she or he is saying accessible? And for the aesthetics of what is said, we might ask: Does the utterance conform with or represent the kinds of value that please us as hearers?

Communicative action, then, occurs when the communication is intelligible, and when everyone involved tries to meet all three criticisable validity claims and so achieve the conditions of the ideal speech situation in everything she or he says (Habermas, 1984: 99). In communicative action we do not seek to achieve a lowest common denominator consensus, nor the kind of consensus that, however humanely or courteously, brings the dissenter into line for the sake of some 'common good'. We seek another kind of consensus altogether in which the agreement established is related to the mode and conditions of the communication itself. This consensus allows for difference of viewpoint, but enables real communication. In communicative action, then, each of us can speak frankly and openly, examine, test and revise our own and others' views of the world, and act on and change both ourselves and the social world of which we are a part. In terms of Habermas's domains of human interest, this encounter is emancipatory. All present will do everything they can to identify the internalised and external forms of coercion, the blocks and impediments, the behaviours and conditions, that prevent open communication and constructive action.

Dialectical analysis

Habermas's communicative action has affinities with Allman's depiction of dialogue, but Allman (1987) emphasises another interest of adult educators promoting critical thinking. She seeks to construct dialogue on a form of dialectical analysis, and in doing so she is drawing more on the ideas of Hegel and Marx than the critical theorists.

Dialectical analysis differs in significant ways from formal logic. For a start it envisages movement and continual change in all the components of an argument, rather than the stability that is assumed in the premises and conclusion of the formal syllogism. Allman makes this point in the following way:

> Formal logic or rational thought... places the objects of our thought in isolation from its movement. For example, we tend to think about men or women, not their interactions, and therefore we conceive of them as separate and fixed categories (1987: 223).

She argues that this tendency leads to mystification and reification, and that:

> As a consequence, much of what we think and communicate is stale and partial knowledge by virtue of the fact that it is knowl-

edge which is removed from the historical movement of material conditions and relations (1987: 223).

As these quotations suggest, dialectical analysis focuses on the relationships and interactions between 'objects of our thought'. We seek to understand objects or ideas in dynamic relationship to one another, and examine what mediates that relationship. So we might analyse men and women in terms of the economy, or the law, or work, or the advent and development of the women's movement in the second half of this century, all of which mediate the relationship between them in different but nonetheless interconnected and material ways. Mandela in his address at the Rivonia trial depicted the relationship between white people and black people in the South Africa of that time as being mediated by unjust laws and 'the politics of the division of colour'.

Dialectical analysis focuses on contradictions, finding them in almost any aspect of our lives. The meaning of contradiction here is not the narrow one of outright opposition, but is widened to include concepts such as difference or lack of connection, reflection, and internal inconsistency. Using dialectical analysis we can examine certain objects and ideas that may appear to have no connection at all, such as colour and size, or justice and time, and deduce relationships. We can examine pairs of opposed objects or ideas which 'reflect' each other, such as white people and black people, or the First World and the Third World, or small and large. In these pairs, each object or idea implies the existence of the other, and neither can exist in that form without the other. The First World depends on there being a Third World, and vice versa. Remove either one and the other concept becomes meaningless. And we can examine an object or idea by identifying the inconsistencies within it that nonetheless go to make it up as a whole. So the experience of pleasure may include within it both self-denial and gratification, acts for oneself and acts in the interests of others, the physical and the intellectual, and activity and inactivity. And to give a classic example, to be an individual in a group we need to be both sufficiently similar to the rest of the people in the group to be identified with the group, and uniquely different. Within individuality, then, there is both universality and particularity.

As these last two examples indicate, dialectical analysis does not necessarily opt for one side of a contradiction against the other. It does not lead us to decide that in a pair of contradictory ideas or objects one is true while the other is false and must therefore be dismissed from our analysis. Instead, in the process of examining the relationships between objects and ideas, we may well absorb both sides of a contradiction into a new object or idea. So the contradictions identified in the experience of pleasure contribute to a more complete idea of pleasure. Or we may negate or diminish one part of the contradiction but at the same time preserve it in a new and more complete idea or object. This is the Hegelian idea of sublation, of both overcoming an object or idea *and* preserving it. Mandela, as he played his part in ushering out apartheid and so diminishing the power and influence of the white minority in South Africa, nonetheless argued that the existence of that minority be preserved within a new and fuller concept—described by Archbishop Tutu at the time as 'the rainbow nation'.

White people and black people, men and women, the First World and the Third World—the objects or ideas within these contradictory pairs often exist in an unequal power relation to each other. Dialectical analysis enables us to form an understanding of these power relations by identifying the parties in the relationship, establishing the nature of the relationship, and examining what mediates that relationship. So we can examine the countries of the First World and the countries of the Third World, establish the nature of the unequal power relationships between them, and then locate and focus on what mediates those relationships. In this case we may focus on international trade, or transnational corporations, or agencies such as the International Monetary Fund and the World Bank, or the kind of racism that allows people in a First World country to connive at the exploitation of labour in a Third World country of a kind they would never tolerate within the borders of their own.

If we keep in mind that Allman associates her idea of dialogue closely with dialectical analysis, then we can begin to see just how different her radical dialogic discussion group could be to the conventional one.

[Dialogue] centres on a theme, object or issue of significance in the life experience of the participants. The object, theme or issue mediates the communication within the dialogue, as participants first explore the ways in which they think about it or make sense of it and then look critically at that sense-making (Allman, 1987: 222).

Conflict of interests

Adult education for critical thinking, then, through its focus on knowledge created to meet emancipatory interests and its use of dialectical analysis, will recognise the existence of conflict in human affairs. In a sense adult educators promoting critical thinking continue to apply a Marxist analysis of the conflict of class interests, but their interpretation of the social classes involved in the conflict will in all likelihood extend beyond the parameters of the factory and the production of wealth. One of the classes will remain essentially unchanged. This class is made up of the owners of wealth, the possessors of property, the people who control (or represent those who control) the means of production, those whom my time in the unions taught me to call quite simply 'the bosses'. Of course this class will appear in modern dress. The men in top hats may still exist (at the odd ceremonial occasion) but representatives of this class will normally be seen in lounge suits and power dressing over lunch in a corporate boardroom and in the corridors of some government bureaucracies, or decked out in lurid colours on the floors of stock and commodities exchanges, or in shirtsleeves on phones in front of computer screens.

The class in conflict or potential conflict with these modern capitalists, on the other hand, has undergone a sea change. Ernesto Laclau, for example, argues that the working class in the industrialised west has undergone a 'numerical decline and economic fragmentation' and can no longer be portrayed as 'the universal class' of the Marxist tradition (1987: 30). A working class with only its labour power to sell clearly still exists but, as Herbert Marcuse (1964: 25) already recognised some thirty five years ago, there has been a 'transformation of physical energy into technical and mental skills' in many forms of work, resulting in the creation of a new and substantial class of people who may have been released from physical labour but who are subjected to new forms of boredom, fatigue and tension in the modern information technology and service industries. To these old and new kinds of working class we can add people whose actual or potential opposition to modern capitalism derives not from their work but their association with one or more of that plethora of community groups and social movements that go together to make up civil, as opposed to state or corporate, society. And to these we can add the people living at or below subsistence level in both the industrialised and non-industrialised parts of our world—the literal and metaphorical fringe dwellers of our societies—whose 'class' is defined by their exclusion from the mainstream economies and the world of work.

Adult education for critical thinking is concerned with the positions we adopt, the sides we take, the alliances we form and the solidarities we enter into. This kind of adult education is not detached and dispassionate. It helps us explain how knowledge, consciousness and power are generated and controlled; and then examines how knowledge, consciousness and power can be generated and controlled in ways that will enable of us to live in equitable, peaceful and sustainable ways on a habitable planet. Adult education for critical thinking is constructed on an ethical stance. It is a form of education by and for those wanting to understand the world in order to change it. It is education for social justice.

The critical, socialist and existentialist theories that underpin critical thinking are of central importance to adult education. Together they provide an intellectual base and a method for adult educators and their learners to engage in critical thinking. Together they provide a theory and practice of learning. Together they allow us to identify the central issue over which adult educators and their learners will have to struggle. Should capitalist, militarist and anti-environmental forces set the parameters in which we develop consciousness, create knowledge and describe power, so as to meet the interests of a few; or should we be able, unfettered and without parameters, to develop consciousness, knowledge and power in the interests of everyone? In short, who should have control?

Section 3: Control

7: Physical force and institutional control

Sometimes we write to deal with our dismay. I spent a morning in a squatters' camp in Durban. I gained entry through another Australian who was also visiting South Africa. She had been at a bus stop in central Durban some weeks before and had struck up a conversation with Sithando Ntshingila, a resident of Cato Crest camp. He had invited her to visit the camp, and I accompanied her on her second visit.

The camp covered two sides of a small valley, a mass of closely packed dwellings inhabited by anything up to ten thousand people. Most of the dwellings were made from iron, tin, mud and wood, but there were also some houses set on concrete bases and made of bricks which you could see the occupiers had developed from an original hut. Ntshingila met us at the edge of the camp and led us in along paths winding between the dwellings to a hut, where we sat and talked.

Ntshingila was out of work, and told us he had no official position within the social structure of the camp. However he had been greeted by people we passed in a way that suggested he was much respected. He talked of life in the camp, of the struggle to get even basic facilities, and of the projects he was setting up. These included a car washing cooperative and a market gardens cooperative, and a plan to help the homeless on the streets of central Durban. He talked about a job-training program for unemployed people in the camp, established, he said, with little or no community consultation. And he talked with a kind of wry disillusion about the post-apartheid South African government, remarking that the new bureaucrats from whom he tried to get funding for his community projects were not markedly different from the old ones. 'They speak Zulu instead of English or Afrikaans now,' he said with a smile, 'but they still speak the same language.'

Ntshingila had limped badly as he led us through the camp. And now that we sat facing each other and talking I could see that his right arm was all but useless, and that he had to lift it with his left hand to place it across his lap or on the arm of the chair. He told us that in the nineteen seventies he had been active in the Young Christian Workers and outspoken about workers' rights in his workplace. He had been picked up and taken in by the police, and warned to stop his activism. He had maintained his membership of the YCW and continued advocating its ideas; and had been picked up and warned again. Since none of what he was doing was unlawful, he had continued as before, and in 1984 he was picked up yet again. This third time, he said, he was beaten up. The beating was so brutal that he almost died, his right leg was permanently damaged, and his right arm paralysed. He has not been in formal employment since.

Sitting opposite Ntshingila, listening to him, looking into his eyes, watching him smile, I had the clear impression of being in the presence of a good person. It is difficult to imagine the narrow-mindedness of those authorities who saw Ntshingila as a threat to the state. It is difficult to imagine that they could so dislike someone so good. It is difficult to imagine the kind of moral vacuum a person must live in to beat someone into permanent physical disability. And it is amazing to think that, because the change in government in South Africa occurred through transition rather than revolution, some of the people that beat Ntshingila up may still have been in full-time employment in the South African police force.

Those police officers sought to control Ntshingila with force. Physical force is one of the ways in which people exert control over the world of objects and people around them. There are both benign and malign uses of physical force. We break the ground with a plough in order to sow a crop. We break the ground with an earth mover in order to build a damn to provide water for a town. We forge steel. We crush grapes. In even these examples there are likely to be people who interpret the actions as unnecessary, or inimical to the environment, or of danger to our personal health, but many would see these uses of physical force as benign. We also use force on other people. Here the distinction between malign and benign uses becomes more problematical. We lock people up who are ostensibly mentally unbalanced and a

60

danger to themselves and others around them. We round up boat people who have landed illegally on our shores, put them in a detention centre, and then perhaps deport them against their will back to their own country. Here, perhaps by appealing to some limited utilitarian concept of the greatest happiness for the greatest number of people (within the 'host' country), we can interpret these uses of physical force as benign, but the argument becomes more difficult once we appeal to any absolute set of moral values that might apply beyond the borders of a single community or country.

There are fewer problems in identifying the malign uses of physical force. Developers destroy the environment for short term gain, endangering the livelihoods and diminishing the quality of life for future generations. A government uses police or paramilitary forces to suppress peaceful protest. A dictator or oligarchy employs imprisonment, torture, and murder by roving hit squads in order to stay in power.

The control of people through physical force will only rarely happen spontaneously. Behind many manifestations of physical force is an organisation or institution: a ministry of health, a political party, a corporation, a street gang, a family, the tactical response group of the police, the armed services, a government... Indeed, physical force is often an expression of an institutional form of control.

There will be times when our response to the institution that uses physical force will be ambivalent. The citizens of Sydney may read newspaper reports of armed police conducting a dawn raid on several houses occupied by Aboriginal people in an inner city suburb, and many may condemn the action, judging it an act of intimidation rather than policing. But when our house is burgled or our children are threatened by a stranger in the street, we will contact that same police service, seeking its protection and help.

All of us submit ourselves to forms of institutional control. We give over a range of our freedoms in exchange for the membership, services and protection those institutions provide. We agree to the rules of a local sports club in order to have use of the club's facilities. We run with a gang in return for a sense of belonging. We abide by the requirements of our employment in return for a wage or salary. We follow the educational paths set by schools, colleges and universities in return for recognised qualifications. We submit to the laws and regulations imposed by a government in return for the services and security that government provides us.

Institutional control is everywhere in our lives. Some forms will be benign. We are required by law to pay taxes, but some of those taxes go towards a system of health care available to everyone. (Of course there may those of a different political persuasion who would call this patronising or molly-coddling rather than benign.) Some forms of institutional control may be gratuitous, doctrinaire, and without any real countervailing benefits. An education department closes down a successful school for narrowly interpreted budgetary reasons, disadvantaging the communities that use it. Some forms may move beyond the gratuitous and become oppressive. A bureaucracy seeks too much information about us and trades the information with other bureaucracies without consulting us. And some forms of institutional control will be obviously malign. A powerful and profitable corporation 'downsizes' its workforce at a particular plant, throwing numbers of people into unemployment and seriously affecting the economy of the surrounding locality, all in order to depress wage demands and secure even higher profits.

The intimate relationship between institutional control and physical force can be seen in the way some institutions resort to force to impose their concepts of stability and order. Those people who beat Ntshingila were expressing the will of the South African government of the time which was committed to the oppression of black activists who opposed the policy of apartheid. Many governments around the world still impose the death penalty. Many institutions, be they health, penal, educational, or military, use physical forms of coercion such as restriction of movement, incarceration, corporal punishment and gratuitous physical labour to bring individual members in line with an institutionally expected norm.

The relationship between institutional control and physical force can also be seen in the way some institutions seem to change their principles and practices only in response to physical force, or to the show of physical force. The French education system, and many other French institutions, adapted to the mood of the times only after French students and workers took to the streets in 1968 for several weeks of extraordinary civil disruption. People power altered a longstanding political regime in the Philippines in 1986. And in 1989 across Eastern Europe people took to the streets, bringing about (with widely varying results) the end of a number of rigid governmental systems.

It is possible, however, that the relationship between institutional control and physical force may be even closer than the examples above suggest. Many institutions do not need to resort to the use of physical force. We submit to their control because of the *threat* of physical force implicit in their existence. We keep up the payments on our house, not because we have a profound moral belief in the bank's right to receive the money, but because of the fear somewhere in the back of our mind that if we fall behind in our payments we might be forcibly evicted.

Those images of eviction are powerful ones. Institutions such as banks carry with them a history from which they cannot escape. Banks use the electronic media in particular to try and construct an image of geniality, service, and a concern for the ordinary person. Their modern advertising presents them as benign. But such advertising does not remove from our minds those other, darker images of foreclosure and forcible eviction. The eighteenth century English debtors' prison, and the summary violence of raw nineteenth-century north American capitalism make pictures in the mind that die hard. Nor perhaps do the bankers really want those images to disappear from our minds, since the banks' control over us, their imposition of financial discipline on us, depends on the fear those images represent. In our hearts we know that banks, by the nature of the commodity they trade in, are concerned with money first, and with people a long way behind. This knowledge is reinforced every now and again when a bank, given a clear choice, opts for a policy or a form of action that conforms with its darker image. Despite marking up profits in many millions of dollars, a bank still evicts people. A bank increases fees in order to dissuade small account holders. And a bank in a small community, trading on its image of the trusted adviser, vigorously recommends (aggressively markets, as they say nowadays) a form of loan based on Swiss francs. When local people, who in other circumstances would not have considered buying houses or funding businesses based on foreign currencies, take up the loans and then lose enormously, the bank not only denies its own responsibility in the affair, but goes ahead and tries to call in the debts.

Physical force in fact or as a threat underpins many social relationships. Since social relationships are formalised in all kinds of institution, from the family to school to work to banks to governments, we could argue that these institutions are actually structured embodiments of physical force. In such cases, institutional control and physical force are not just closely related. They are one and the same.

8: Control by ideas

To physical force and institutional control we need to add control by ideas. This is by far and away the most interesting and pervasive form of social control, and by far and away the most difficult to describe. Control by ideas is, in its turn, closely bound up with institutional control and physical force. Institutions may be made up of people, procedures that include the threat of physical force, budgets, and often buildings, but they are also constructed on ideas. The people within many of these institutions will be required to abide by these ideas, and many of these institutions will promote their ideas in the world at large.

There are several interconnected ways of looking at social control by ideas. We can look at what Turner describes as 'hidden social forces'. We can talk of reification. We can look at the use of symbol, illusion and image. We can examine the way given wisdoms become embedded in language. We can examine the use of ideas that divert. And we can relate these various interpretations of control by ideas to the concept of hegemony.

Hidden social forces

Turner, in his description of market forces quoted in an earlier chapter, gives an example of hidden social forces. Market forces are actually people producing, selling, buying and consuming. These people make choices that produce gluts and bring prices down or cause shortages and send prices up. However much we dress all this activity up, Turner says, it is actually other people telling us what to do.

The market, then, is people engaged in physical activities and in making choices about physical activities. But the market becomes institutionalised. Patterns of behaviour are established and these are formalised in actual institutions, such as markets in a town centre or on the edge of a city, then markets in the form of stock markets and commodities markets, then markets in terms of such things as futures and currencies. These markets are often institutions in a very recognisable form, with buildings, defined memberships, rules and regulations, and ideas in the form of generally accepted principles, theories, values and assumptions. But a further manifestation of the market occurs. We come to think of the market as an entity in itself, a source of power with its own existence, a kind of force in the Star Wars genre ('May the Force be with you!') with a will of its own. Market forces become something beyond our control to which, if we want to survive and prosper, we must carefully and respectfully respond.

Of course, if we pause for a moment, we can see that even at this international level, and not just at the level of apples and oranges, market forces are the result of human actions and human choices. Thus on 28 March, 1996 three traders working for an international financial conglomerate, two of them based in London, one in Hong Kong, set about dumping a portfolio of shares worth about $600 million on the Australian stock exchange in the closing minutes of trading. In a complex trading play the conglomerate stood to make at least $500 million and the three main players stood to make millions of dollars' worth of bonuses. The 'sting' failed (and the matter ended up in the the Federal Court of Australia) due to the conglomerate's own ineptitude and its brokers' refusal to dump the shares at bargain basement prices. However, had the three traders succeeded, their actions stood to 'wipe $15 billion off the value of Australia's major public companies' and would have had 'devastating consequences to pension funds and hundreds of thousands of individual shareholders' (Hills, 1998).

Despite this kind of example, the idea of market forces being something beyond our control persists, and is reinforced by a range of 'experts', bureaucrats and politicians. We are told that our economies are subject to market forces, that we must respond to market forces and, most disturbing of all because of the naive and fatalistic nature of the idea, we must let market forces decide. But of course these experts, bureaucrats and politicians have made choices. They have chosen the particular political and economic ideology of economic rationalism, which is based on deregulation and competition, over other equally possible policies based on ideas such as cooperation, consultation and vigorous state intervention to prevent inequity. Yet they do everything in their power to convince the population that they had no choice and that their actions are the necessary response to market forces. Through the widespread promotion of the idea of the independent power of the market, they and the class they represent set out to exercise their desired kind of social control.

It is ironic to note that at a time of threatening world recession some of these experts, bureaucrats and politicians could rapidly abandon the idea that market forces should be let run free and begin arguing for controls. In doing this they underlined just how thoroughly the concept of the market as some independent, almost magical force is a construct of people's making, a device created for the purpose of telling others what to do.

Reification

Sophisticated markets like the futures and currency markets are distanced from real, tangible *things*, yet the idea of the market as captured in the phrase 'market forces' is not. We need to be careful here. We deal with our world by classifying elements in it, grouping those elements, searching for commonalities, and labelling those commonalities so as to develop abstractions, such as 'circular' or 'poverty' or 'happiness' or 'beauty'. But sometimes, while apparently engaging in the same intellectual process, we do the opposite. We classify, group, search for commonalities and label; and then ascribe to the grouping a reality that the collection of elements does not actually have. Instead of developing an abstract concept of the market, we reify it.

Reification is a forceful tool for social control. Those in power promote the idea of monolithic entities capable of remarkable singlemindedness in such words and phrases as 'the Government', 'the Ministry', 'the Corporation', 'the Executive Committee' and 'the Union Movement'. But these so-called entities are really collections of individuals, groupings and factions with differing ideas, opinions, beliefs and doubts. In fact a phrase like 'the Government has decided... ' is nonsensical, since in reality it is an identifiable person, or a group of identifiable people, who has decided. A judge can appeal to the apparently ultimate authority of society when sentencing a convicted criminal to gaol. Yet when we look again at the situation the decision is not society's, but his or hers. In the mouths of many politicians and members of the business community concepts such as production, profit and progress take on the character of universal objectives, objects even, with existences of their own. These concepts were formerly associated with ways of describing what people did in those clearly delimited parts of their lives to do with earning a living, and so were means to ends. Now we increase production as an end in itself. We manage a business for profit, rather than for what that profit might make possible for investors and employees in other parts of their lives. Progress, any progress in any domain, we come to believe, is good.

One of the most powerful examples of reification is to be found in the concept of the nation. Our nation, for example, can call us to arms. Of course when we examine this phenomenon a little more closely, it may be the overweening pride of a dictator that leads a country into war, or a politician fearful of losing the next election, or an alliance of industrial interests, or a group of zealots in control of the political machine and the mass media, or a part of a population driven to violent reaction against oppression. The idea of the nation can have great force, but in fact a nation is a conglomeration of widely varying objects, people, interests, environments, systems, and practices and does not exist as a single entity, as a single *thing*, at all.

Symbol, illusion and image

To give a nation an apparent unity, to assist in the reification of the idea, we often resort to symbol, illusion and image. These, too, are forceful tools for social control. Symbols can have extraordinary power over people. We represent our nation with a flag and, cleverly used, this symbol can make people buy products, unite or divide people, motivate people to strive for high performance in the sports and the arts, and, as we have already noted, lead people to their deaths.

Illusions can comfort, mislead, motivate and control. The federal democratic system in Australia is supposedly based on one person, one vote, and each person's vote is meant to be of roughly equal value. But in the Australian democratic system this is not the case, as we can see if we compare the value of the vote of an elector voting against the incumbent in a very safe seat with the value of the vote of an elector in a seat that could go either way. One elector, in effect, does not have a vote of any value at all, while the other has a vote that may affect the outcome of the ballot in her or his electorate, and in a close-run election could conceivably decide the political colour of the next government. One person, one vote is an assumption that will not stand up to scrutiny. In this particular respect, the idea of a democratically elected federal government in Australia is an illusion (although perhaps we could argue that voters in Australia accept these kinds of anomaly as part of an imperfect electoral system that we nonetheless subscribe to in the absence of anything better).

And as only a cursory glance at the techniques of propaganda and advertising will tell us, images are used to influence, control, and effect forms of social engineering. From the mid-nineteen eighties onwards, for example, the promoters of the Liberal Party in Australia have appealed to the image of the family and called for a return to traditional family values. The family referred to has been the nuclear family of mother, father and children and just such a family, depicted standing in front of a picket-fenced bungalow, appeared on the cover of a party policy document.

This image can have a number of distinct purposes. It can be used to make us conform. The family is presented as an important institution within society and perhaps the most important one. A very particular kind of family is then depicted, establishing a norm towards which we should all aspire. Once we have a norm we can use it to exclude. The depiction and promotion of this 'ordinary' middle-class nuclear family as the basic social unit leaves little place for single people, gay or lesbian couples, or people who share a house or a flat, or live in other types of community. It throws doubt on the appropriateness of larger, extended families, and may imply that a single-parent family is abnormal. And the image is used to denote a particular moral life and political philosophy. Implicit in the image are the ideas of a suburban self-sufficiency, orderliness and self-discipline. The image is of people who will aspire to the usual objects—house, car, etc.—promoted by a consumer society, but not strive for the eccentric or exceptional. They are people who will do everything in their power to avoid 'falling back' on the state for support in terms of welfare payments and the like. And they are a family in which the parents will exercise discipline and control over their children, while the presence of the children and the responsibilities that go with having children will in turn exercise control over the parents.

Given wisdoms

Institutional control and control by ideas can go hand in hand, as is the case in most of the examples given directly above, but control by ideas can transcend institutions. Certain ideas take on lives of their own, become predominant in a culture, and exist without any clear relation to particular parties, people, or locations of power. Again we need to be careful here, since this independence may be illusory. After all, ideas must come from someone, and once in existence an idea can serve a defined interest. Nonetheless, certain ideas do take on this apparent independence, and enter our language as given wisdoms, commonsense sayings, and truisms attributable to no-one in particular, and to everyone. These sayings can exercise control. They state the norm, the accepted, the universal commonsense, against which most of us will not argue. Thus we may say: 'You cannot stand in the way of progress', making it easier for a developer to move us out of our house to make way for a freeway (or more likely a tollway). Or we may say: 'Competition improves the quality of service', opening the way for the downgrading of a publicly owned utility and the subsequent loss of equity in the service provided. Or 'Talent will always out', taking some of the pressure off education authorities to upgrade a school in a disadvantaged area.

Women have been victimised and controlled by ideas lodged in the phrasing and structure of the language. They have been excluded by the use of the masculine pronoun, or relegated to second class roles in phrases such as 'women's work' or reviled by the large range of commonplace but insulting epithets the language provides for men, and some women as well, to use against women. Minorities, be they ethnic, cultural, religious, racial or defined by a physical or intellectual disability, have been victimised and controlled in similar or analogous ways. In Australia, for example, the word 'spastic' has been used as an insult implying stupidity.

Ideas that divert

Ideas can delight or ensnare us, and divert us from pursuing a humane and just life. As we have seen, these ideas can be lodged in platitudes, but they can also come in the form of sophisticated theories, philosophies and discourses, whole 'languages' in themselves. For example, in the past fifteen or twenty years many in

70

the academic world and beyond have been delighted and ensnared by post-structuralist and postmodern discourses. Post-structuralists have focussed on literature and culture, developing ways of deconstructing texts to examine multiplicities of meaning. They have thrown into question the author's purpose, disassociated the author from the text, and suggested that the reader (or listener, viewer and observer, because 'text' here means any act of communication) can 'position' her or himself in relation to the text in a multiplicity of ways. The reader is encouraged to retain a sceptical, even playful, relationship to the text, and so can now go in search of a whole variety of sometimes conflicting meanings (Best and Kellner, 1991).

These ideas can be liberating. They open up a text and give the reader the choice of a number of new roles. But they can divert both the author and the reader from the business of communicating for a clear and decided purpose. Searching for the author's meaning, if the author is trying to clarify complex concepts, can be hard work. It can be all too easy to abandon the effort and opt for a number of diverse meanings, leaving the problems the author might have posed unresolved. Or to use the language of Dreyfus and Rabinow (1982: 113, 124), it can be all too easy to adopt 'a hermeneutics of suspicion' and to forget that there will be times when 'serious speakers know exactly what they mean'.

In the introduction to *Defining the Enemy* (1994) I said this:

> [I] offer the text to the reader, hoping that you will position yourself in relation to the text in several ways—as serious student of adult education, as critic in constant and challenging dialogue, as political comrade, as someone ready to be amused and entertained, as co-writer improving on the text, as the enemy of my enemies and therefore, as the saying goes and if ever we meet, my friend.

Reading this now, I worry. I allowed myself to indulge in, and be diverted by, a form of rhetoric. Some of the statement is hyperbole. I did not really expect the reader to be co-writer. Some of it is incorrect. I did not want anyone to read the book simply for entertainment. And although I may have said it, I did not really want the reader to make whatever she or he wanted of the text. On the contrary, I wrote the book to attack certain ideas, and to persuade the reader to adopt mine. I accepted full responsibility

71

for what I had written, and I wanted the reader to read from the beginning to the end making every effort to understand what I was trying to say. In no way did I want to let either myself or the reader off the hook.

Writers on postmodernity extend post-structuralist ideas beyond the text and into discussions of society, culture, economics and politics. 'Text' in this case becomes 'life'. As one would expect from the nature of the discourse itself, they express a wide range of sometimes highly divergent views. Nonetheless they deal with a number of themes which, when collected together, are recognised as constituting a body of literature on postmodernity.

Writers on postmodernity, then, suggest that we are emerging from a period of several hundred years in which people in those many parts of the world under the influence of European thought struggled to find rational explanations for both substantial and insubstantial phenomena (Kumar, 1997: 96-97). During this epoch the ideal of the enlightened, autonomous person was central to our concepts of society, morality and intellectual endeavour. And the project of humankind was to establish order and bring the world under control. Some writers talk of this epoch in terms of 'grand narratives'. These grand narratives are the themes or flows of ideas and activities that have marked this epoch, such as 'Enlightenment', 'Emancipation', 'Industrialisation' or 'Capitalism/ Socialism'. (In the larger world view of these writers, both capitalism and socialism would be considered part of the same broad 'project'.) These writers suggest that these grand narratives are drawing to a close, and that old ways of thinking and old forms of social organisation are breaking down. In such a context, power may be seen more correctly as dispersed and decentred rather than hierarchical and centralised. History may be seen as fragmented or stratified rather than chronological. Identity may be seen as multi-faceted and variable, rather than singular and whole. Images may exist in their own right without reference to any substance. Rational argument and logical exposition may be replaced by flights of fancy. Disconnections may be as important as connections:

> Postmodernity is marked by a view of the human world as irreducibly and irrevocably pluralistic, split into a multitude of sov-

ereign units and sites of authority, with no horizontal or vertical order, either in actuality or in potency (Bauman, 1992: 35).

These kinds of idea provide alternative ways of describing and analysing. If commonsense logic or more formal or critical ways of reasoning fail to produce useful ideas or solutions, then the alternative forms of viewing the world proposed by writers on postmodernity may. We can try deconstructing rather than interpreting a text. We can look at an organisation as a scattering of locations of power and not as a hierarchy. We can examine identity as a decentred collection of others and not as a single autonomous self.

The ideas that recur in a postmodernity discourse can be exhilarating, but they are also diverting, in the sense of a *divertissement* that can lull us into an agreeable kind of inactivity, that can seduce and even corrupt us. Two associated ideas recur in the literature on postmodernity. These are ending (expressed in the use of the prefix 'post' in a number of terms and the declaration of the death of, variously, society, man and history) and fragmentation (expressed in the use of the word itself and the associated ideas of pluralism, decentredness and individualism) (Kumar, 1997). Ending and fragmentation carry an evocative sense of the epochal and apocalyptic. But both are negative concepts. If we draw our view of the world from these ideas it becomes easy to sit on the sideline adopting the detached and passive role of observer. We can watch the end without suggesting a new beginning. We can listen to the closing words of a grand narrative, thrilling at the silence that follows, but making no effort to construct a new story in its place. We can exclaim at the spectacle of fragmentation, gaining futile insights into ideas, institutions and cultures at the moment of their supposed demise. If we adopt a view of history that is marked out in epochs, then the people within any epoch become minuscule and their successes and suffering of minimal importance. A ten year drought in the region of the Southern Sahara is just a moment in time; the wars that dot the planet interesting examples of the end of the grand Imperial/Super Power narrative. We can note and comment but if we are at the end, and amidst disintegration, there is nothing we can actually do.

Of course the postmodernity discourse is just a discourse. Some grand narratives may be coming to an end but others continue being vigorously told. Patriarchy continues undiminished across much of the globe, its sorry day-to-day story of the oppression of women being occasionally gruesomely embellished with the burning of a widow or the public execution of an alleged adulteress. Capitalism does not seem to have fragmented and come to an end, but rather consolidated into more powerful transnational forms. Power as expressed in some kinds of social movement may be decentred, but centralised states, backed up by hierarchical public services, sophisticated surveillance systems, police, courts and prisons still exercise extraordinary control over many of us.

Terry Eagleton (1991, x-xi) looks back at the decade of the nineteen eighties and identifies these kinds of disparity between ideas and evidence in the post modern discourse on ideology. He writes of 'a remarkable resurgence of ideological movements throughout the world'. He points to Islamic fundamentalism, 'a still tenacious neo-Stalinism' in some Eastern European countries, the struggle of revolutionary nationalism with imperialist power in many countries including northern Ireland, 'a peculiarly noxious brand of Christian Evangelicalism' in the USA, and to the period of Thatcherism which he describes as 'the most ideologically aggressive and explicit regime in living political memory' in Britain. He goes on:

> Meanwhile, somewhere on the left bank, it is announced that the concept of ideology is now obsolete. How are we to account for this absurdity? Why is it in a world racked by ideological conflict, the very notion of ideology has evaporated without trace from the writings of post modernism and post structuralism?

But perhaps the most telling weakness of the postmodernity discourse lies in an inherent misrepresentation in the term itself. 'Postmodern' carries a chronological implication of the ultrarecent. Yet most of the literature is not really about time so much as forms, positions, language and image. And once we ignore the chronological implications in the term, we can see that the postmodern has been around for a very long time. There have been many societies that have been decentred and disparate, whether they were in Ancient Greece, Aboriginal Australia or the highlands of Papua New Guinea. The Hindu cosmology in all its extraordinary multiplicity, its openness to many interpretations, its mixture of seriousness and playfulness, is intriguingly 'postmodern'. And if the invitation to the reader to do what she or he will with a text is a mark of the postmodern, then in English literature we have that wonderfully 'postmodern' eighteenth century masterpiece *The Life and Opinions of Tristram Shandy, Gentleman*, which Laurence Sterne wrote slap bang in the middle of the Age of Enlightenment.

Hegemony

Hidden social forces, reification, the use of symbol, illusion and image, given wisdoms, and ideas that divert can all be seen as contributing to, or evidence of, the phenomenon of hegemony. Hegemony is control by consent. It describes that form of control in which people connive in their own oppression, in which one group of people accept as normal, or natural, conditions that are in the interests of another group altogether. In Brazil, after the military coup in 1964, many tenant farmers working the land to produce food were dispossessed and their land cleared to make way for the export crop of coffee. Even though food shortages resulted, this process was promoted and accepted by many as 'good economics' (California Newsreel, 1978). Some women in the workplace still accept lower pay and lower status than men because they see themselves as having other domestic and child rearing responsibilities (Cockburn, 1991: 169). When men accept the lower status of women and do nothing to redress this inequity, we have a straightforward example of oppression. But when some women accept their lower status as natural and normal, and see no reason to struggle against this inequity, we have an example of hegemony.

Hegemonic control is achieved by making particular ideas so mainstream and 'common sense' that those in opposition are marginalised. A dissenter becomes an outsider expressing nonsensical points of view which can be summarily dismissed by ignoring the arguments and holding the person of the dissenter up to ridicule. Phrases such as: 'You must be joking' or 'Surely you cannot believe that' are used to intimidate and silence opposition. In Australia in the early nineteen nineties, competency-based curricula became the accepted form for industrial training. This approach to training was taken up by government, the corporate sector and the education service with extraordinary rapidity. This alone suggested that in the interests of everyone the principles behind competency-based training should have been subjected to critical scrutiny; yet in response to a detailed critique, a supporter of competency-based training felt that all he needed to say was: 'It is nice to see people from the far right and the far left in bed together on this one'.

Sometimes hegemonic ideas are reinforced by ruling opposition out altogether. This can be seen in the commonplace statement by people who support capital's continuing and devastating exploitation of the environment. 'Growth', they say, 'is the only way to go.'

Section 4: Learning

9: Learning as social individuals

We can learn, and help others learn, to use benign forms of social control; and we can learn, and help others learn, to resist malign forms. If we use learning in this way, then learning becomes a tool in the struggle for social justice.

Once we decide to pit learning against control, the temptation is to look for different kinds of learning and argue as, I have done elsewhere (1995a), that these different kinds of learning can be used in the struggle for or against different kinds of control. But I grow uneasy with this straightforward matching. As we have seen, one kind of control can exploit, subsume or sublate other kinds of control, making any kind of matching difficult. And I am no longer sure that there are different *kinds* of learning. The word 'learning' has been about for some time, so it is probably more reasonable to assume that there is a single phenomenon to which the one word refers; and that the different styles and kinds of learning identified in the literature on adult education, be they drawn from the behaviourists, cognitivists, humanists, critical theorists or whomsoever, actually refer to different *aspects* of learning.

I live and write within a culture that likes dividing in order to understand, so I shall describe eight aspects of learning: instrumental, communicative, interpretive, transformative, critical, political, essential and moral. The meanings I ascribe to these terms will sometimes coincide with the meanings ascribed to them by other writers on adult education, but not always. The first four aspects are more to do with learning to be social individuals. The second four are more to do with learning to be moral human beings. When all these aspects are manifest we have a complete kind of learning which will serve in the struggle against unwanted and unjust forms of social control.

An instrumental aspect
To make a start, then, learning will have an instrumental aspect.

This is the aspect of learning to do with ploughing the fields, buildings dams, forging steel and crushing grapes. It is closely associated with Habermas's ideas about the generation of knowledge for *technical* interests, in that we learn in order to control or manipulate our environment. This aspect of learning will include task learning, competency-based learning and learning designed to achieve behavioural objectives, but we must not make the assumption that it is therefore necessarily straightforward or of a lower order. The environments we try to control and manipulate with this aspect of learning will include the complex physical environment that modern science has identified and described for us, the complex industrial, technological and electronic environments we have created, and our modern social, economic, legal, and political environments.

What helps us mark the instrumental off from other aspects of learning is that, for the purposes of this particular aspect of learning, the environment is perceived as inanimate: a surrounding that can indeed be manipulated in a reasonably mechanistic way if we do our learning well. The law and the courts that administer the law are to be understood and used. Financial markets are to be studied and exploited. Soil is to be analysed in order to sow and harvest crops. Even some of the more obviously 'human relations' parts of our world are regarded as environments that can be worked to suit our purposes. Some management training, for example, is instrumental (even though it may parade as something else) since the people to be managed are perceived as components of an organisational environment that will respond in standard ways to standardised stimuli. Managers are taught patterns of behaviour in order to resolve conflicts, standardised forms of consultation in order to win employees' compliance, and controlled forms of discussion in order to arrive at decisions.

The instrumental aspect of learning can sometimes involve sophisticated processes. Michael Kaye, for example, describes how 'story-telling' and 'story-listening' can contribute to a corporate culture 'which fosters productivity and a good quality of work life' (1996: 133). We might normally associate story-telling with more mysterious aspects of learning. After all, stories can reveal the soul. They can talk of gods and demons. They can contain the wisdom of a people. They can inspire and delight. They can cause reverie and flights of imagination. They can be a momentary, irrational diversion, and they are the stuff of great literature. Kaye takes storytelling, this old and most accessible of art forms, and puts it to the instrumental service of managers in the modern corporate world.

A communicative aspect

Learning will have a communicative aspect. There are problems of definition here since a lot of what is called 'communicative learning' or 'communication skills learning' is actually instrumental, in that it is engaged in for pragmatic (and sometimes self-serving) reasons such as managing organisations, fostering productivity, promoting the 'communicator's' product or viewpoint, or asserting the 'communicator's' person and personality. For the most part, the instrumental nature of this so-called communicative learning is obvious, since it is based on the teaching and learning of formula responses such as the much touted 'I' statements, and it promotes the use of obviously hypocritical and manipulative euphemisms such as 'let me share with you' (meaning, of course, 'I am going to tell you').

In contrast, we engage in genuinely communicative learning in order to establish a better understanding between people as an end in itself. This aspect of learning has some associations with Habermas's conditions for the ideal speech act. People engaging in communicative learning try to use language as a vehicle for conveying considered ideas rather than platitude, prejudice or cliché. They try to understand their own positions, and to express those positions clearly. They learn to listen, and to respond frankly, with integrity, to what they hear. Both Carl Rogers and John Heron provide ideas on the processes of listening and responding. Both provide ideas on the management of this kind of communicative learning. Rogers (1983) promotes a subtle, receptive, and at times apparently non-directive form of facilitation, while Heron (1993) promotes more proactive forms of intervention for the group leader to use.

The communicative aspect of learning is to do with understanding how people relate, how we cooperate and collaborate, form alliances and factions, vie with each other, and conceivably reach consensus. It is also to do with how we react in these relationships and encounters, and so is concerned with the affective as well as the rational parts of our lives. Again both Rogers (1970) and Heron (1989) write about group dynamics, and identify the sometimes difficult emotional stages through which a group of people may have to pass, or through which a facilitator may have to take a group, in order to achieve communication.

In this respect there are also associations between this communicative aspect of learning and Habermas's ideas about the generation of knowledge to meet our *practical* interests, in that this is the aspect of learning that helps us understand how we make meaning through symbolic interaction, and how we construct and give meaning to our social lives. But since there is an emphasis on how we communicate, that is, how we manage ourselves and other human beings in the process of communicating, this aspect of learning is not as far as we might first suspect from the instrumental aspect of learning and is therefore also closely associated with Habermas's generation of *technical* knowledge.

An interpretive aspect
Learning will have an interpretive aspect. This is that aspect to do with understanding and interpreting the human condition, with coming to understand what being human might mean. It is to do with how people interpret themselves and the world of which they are a part, and is more squarely associated with Habermas's ideas about the generation of knowledge to meet our *practical* interests. Where the instrumental aspect of learning helps us understand and manipulate our environment, and the communicative aspect helps us understand and engage openly with others, the interpretive aspect of learning helps us understand ourselves.

A lot of experiential education contributes to this interpretive aspect of learning; and there seem to be two main and associated forms of experiential education. In one form, a facilitator uses various methods including visualisation, writing, pair work, group work and dialogue to help people recall and then reflect on certain life experiences. These experiences are normally to do with significant events or significant phases in the learners' lives. In the other form the facilitator uses structured exercises such as games or role play or simulation exercises in order to construct an experience, and then uses further exercises including pair work, group work and dialogue to help the learners reflect on that constructed experience. The two forms can elide, since a structured exercise might well trigger in some of the learners memories of other significant events in their lives, and both kinds of experience might become the object of reflection during the debriefing.

Mark Tennant and Philip Pogson (1995) suggest two other ways in which experience is acknowledged in education. These are when teachers link their teaching to the prior experience of the learners, or when they link their teaching to the current work or home experiences of the learners. In these two cases, however, the learners' experience is a yardstick against which the teacher's instruction and illustrations are tested, a means of elaboration, validation and evaluation rather than a substantive part of the teaching and learning.

The source material for the two main forms of experiential learning, then, is the learner her or himself. Critics, amongst whom I count myself, will argue that this kind of learning has a tendency to become decontextualised and self-indulgent, but advocates argue that experiential education is not as inward-looking as it can seem since we all share a common humanity and therefore a common human experience and that, in coming to understand ourselves, we come to understand the human condition a little better; that by learning about ourselves we learn about others.

Learning from experience has been represented by a number of educators in diagrammatic form. David Kolb (1984: 41) depicts learning as a cycle in which the learner moves from concrete experience to reflective observation to abstract conceptualisation to active experimentation; then to concrete experience again, and so on round the cycle. He argues that the learning process can start at any point in this cycle. Peter Jarvis (1987a) presents a more complex diagram than Kolb, but acknowledges elements of the cycle within it. Jarvis's diagram traces a number of alternative paths a learner can follow from the starting point of her or his person, situation and experience. David Boud, Rosemary Keogh and David Walker (1985) abandon the cyclical model and present a diagram which shows the process of reflection on experience projecting the learner forward into new behaviours, perspectives and commitments to action.

These kinds of diagram produce an uneasy tension. The writers are using symbols of the flow chart and production line to denote the complexities of human experience and the mysteries of thinking, reflection, understanding and learning. Indeed when I return to the Kolb cycle, I find it too ordered, too regular, too predictable. It seems to imply an imperative: that we must move through the cycle, that we must move on to the next stage, rather than letting the experiences enter into our souls to rest there, develop, change and influence us in some more disordered, unexpected and 'natural' way.

In *The Action Research Planner* (1982), Stephen Kemmis and Robin McTaggart expand Kolb's cycle into a spiral. Others such as Laurie Field (1990) and Hank Schaafsma (1995) apply this action-research spiral to training and learning in the workplace. The imperative in the diagram of the spiral becomes even more obvious. The researchers and workers go through the processes of planning, acting, observing, reflecting, drawing conclusions, revising the plans, acting on the revised plans and so on over and over again, working their way up (or down) the spiral. The spiral looks like an uncoiling spring topped by an arrowhead pointing towards ever more efficient practices that will produce increased productivity, higher profits and, as then tends to happen, smaller workforces.

When I read the literature on experiential learning I am struck by the oddly mechanistic overtones alluded to above, and by the ordinariness of the experience. Often there seems to be a concentration on personal experience, and the self-serving emotional aspects of that personal experience. Rarely do the writers referred to above talk of grand experience—of prolonged struggle, of great art, of sporting triumphs, of talking till dawn, of grinding, patient application, of war, of moments of intellectual breakthrough, of unswerving loyalty and affection, of spiritual enlightenment, of languorous or passionate physical love, of excess. A lot of experiential education scrabbles around in the foothills of everyday experience where the learning to be done will be numbingly ordinary, rather than scaling the heights, where the learning is likely to involve new challenges, provide new panoramas, and bring about change.

Learning with a truly interpretive aspect will enable us to take our own and others' experiences, turn them into stories, and then examine them for their meanings, in much same the way we interpret films or plays or books, seeing what they mean for us, seeing what messages they carry, seeing what insights they provide into the human condition. And just as we do with a book or a film, we will apply our own judgement, putting aside those experiences that are banal or self-serving, and concentrating on those that hold our attention, that reveal, surprise, excite or inspire, that are extraordinary in themselves or that make the ordinary extraordinary, that hold the promise of insight and an extension of our understanding of what it is to be human.

A transformative aspect

Learning will have a transformative aspect. This is the aspect of learning to do with understanding the values, the conditioning, the 'subconscious', the ideas, the unwittingly absorbed pressure of peers, the assumptions, preconceptions and prejudices that constrain the way we think, feel and act. This aspect of learning requires us to look into ourselves, not for some universal human essence, but for the particular intellectual and emotional baggage that we have accumulated from our family and friends, our peers, our colleagues and our compatriots. It helps us understand how our personal psychological histories and our acculturation lead us to form particular kinds of expectation and, having formed those expectations, how we distort the evidence of our senses to conform with our expectations. While the interpretive aspect of learning helps us consciously interpret experience, the transformative aspect enables us to understand the forces that colour and guide our interpretations.

This aspect of learning is transformative since once we have become aware of the ways in which our personal psychological histories and our culture distort the way we experience the world, we can take action to influence or alter their effects. We can examine our prejudices, our preconceptions, our ideas, our values and our expectations, and change them so that we interpret new evidence and new experience in more open and comprehensive ways. And if we transform the way we experience the world, we transform ourselves. We will think and act, we will conduct our lives, differently.

This aspect of learning has very close associations with Mezirow's learning for perspective transformation (1981, 1991) and his discussion of frameworks, states of mind and premises (1994, 1995). Indeed it is Mezirow who, in a body of scholarly and reflective writing spanning more than twenty five years, has been largely responsible for introducing the discussion of this kind of learning into the English language literature of adult education, and for making the term 'transformative learning' current.

It is less easy to locate the transformative aspect of learning in relation to Habermas's ideas on the generation of knowledge. Transformative learning involves self-examination but that self-examination involves coming to understand the effects of our culture upon us, so is more overtly contextualised than the interpretive aspect of learning. This transformative aspect of learning is to do with understanding our interaction with others and in this respect there are affinities with Habermas's generation of knowledge for *practical* interests. But equally, this transformative aspect of learning is concerned with how we come to change our frameworks and so liberate ourselves, to some degree at least, from the psychological and cultural influences that constrain the way we live. In this respect, this transformative aspect of learning has strong associations with Habermas's ideas on the generation of knowledge to meet our *emancipatory* interests.

I see the transformative aspect of learning still concentrating on the individual learner. We recognise that the individual can change but we do not mount a concerted challenge on the society in which the learner lives and does the changing. And in the literature on transformative learning I also see a connection with the instrumental aspect of learning, in the implication that the learner's life has been, as it were, pre-determined by events in her or his cultural and psychological history. This transformative aspect of learning, then, may be a kind of breaking free from both behaviouralist and Freudian paradigms, an act of personal assertion in which we defy various twentieth century oracles who would otherwise tell our story for us.

10: Learning as moral beings

The shift between the first group and the second is not clearly marked, but these next four aspects of learning help us move beyond our quest to be effective in our social lives, and are concerned with ideas of responsibility and change.

A critical aspect

Learning, then, has a critical aspect. In this aspect we take responsibility for our knowledge. We come to understand how each of us has discovered, gathered, created and taken on facts, skills, ideas, and values, and so constructed a knowledge, a view, a way of relating to the world, that is unique.

In this aspect of learning there is a dialectic. We exist in contradictory relationship to the world around us: self to others, individual to collective, here as opposed to there. In this critical aspect of learning we examine the knowledge which we generate in order to explain, manage and mediate that relationship. This knowledge will be more than a construction of facts, skills, ideas and values. It will include the awareness and the feelings which we develop in order to deal with our self in relation to the world. This aspect of learning, then, helps us understand how we construct and develop our consciousness.

For most of us our world is a social world, so this critical aspect of learning is to do with each of us coming to understand our self in relation to other people. Again there is a dialectic, in that the focus is on the contradictory nature of that relationship and what mediates it. For Maeler, his illness must have been an utterly individual experience, yet it brought him energetically into the company of others. This critical aspect of learning helps us understand how we construct a consciousness that can entertain both a sense of utter isolation from all other people, and a sense of commonality. It helps us recognise how, in the same encounter with others, we can experience loneliness and anxiety, and comradliness and joy. It helps us understand how we are subjects (potentially at least) in our own eyes but objects in the eyes of others. It is about understanding how we impose on others, and how others impose upon us. It is about examining the extent to which we are limited in our actions and the extent to which we are free. This aspect of learning, then, is about understanding conflicts of interest, and identifying what causes, maintains and might change the nature of those conflicts.

This aspect of learning has associations with the forms of heightened consciousness or 'meta-awareness' that thinkers and educators like Sartre and Mezirow and Freire identify, and which is implicit in Habermas's ideas on generating knowledge for *emancipatory* interests. This heightened form of consciousness enables us to come to know ourselves and the world with which we interact, and to appraise the knowledge, ideas and values we generate in that interaction.

A political aspect

Closely associated with the critical aspect of learning is a political aspect. In this aspect of learning we examine conflicts of interest in order to make judgements. In making judgements we take sides. And in taking sides we join with others to take action. This aspect of learning is about defining the parties to relationships, identifying the kinds of control—physical, institutional and hegemonic—that are used to maintain and mediate those relationships, and then joining with others to combat and alter the forms of control we do not want. It is about understanding the uses and misuses of power. It is learning for emancipation in the practical and social, as well as the intellectual, domains.

Or to put it a slightly different way, this political aspect of learning is to do with ideas, people and action. It is to do with critically analysing faiths, beliefs, ideologies and arguments in both intellectual and pragmatic terms. It is to do with judging the people who promote these faiths, beliefs, ideologies and arguments, and entering into forms of complicity, alliance or solidarity with those with whom we have common interests. And it is to do with taking action to advance those common interests. Turner (1980: 85) talks of three elements in the process of 'seeing the world in a new way':

> I must come to see the world as able to be changed. I must come to see myself as having the capacity to play a part in changing it.

And I must see that my capacity to do this can be realised only in cooperation with other people. To grasp these three facts involves a fundamental shift in psychological attitude towards the world, rather than a simple change of intellectual awareness. Such a shift only occurs once I find myself involved in action.

Welton, a Canadian adult educator, has produced a body of writing over the past fifteen years which can help us understand both the critical and political aspects of learning. His writing comprises papers, journal articles and edited books, and I see it having four interconnected but distinct strands.

In the first strand (1987b, 1991b) Welton examines, and revises, some of the history of Canadian adult education, looking at people's struggles for a fair and democratic life in the nineteenth and twentieth centuries. As part of this project, he writes with Jim Lotz (1987, 1997) about the Antigonish movement in Nova Scotia, providing us with a case study of adult education in the service of small farming and fishing communities in the poorest part of Canada during the first half of the twentieth century.

In the second strand of his writing (1991c, 1993a) Welton examines current social and community action in Canada. He looks at the struggle for decent living and working conditions, and for equity and social justice, both in the modern workplace and in local urban community contexts. In the previous strand of his writing he examined social movements in Canada's history. Now he examines modern society, as it manifests itself in industry and modern social movements such as the women's movement and the environmental movement; and he looks at the ways these different congregations of people can be used as sites for learning that will bring about beneficial social change.

In a third strand in his writing (1991a, 1993b, 1995) Welton looks for a theoretical construct to help him explain the way learning is integral to social and community action. It is in this strand that he most clearly relates critical learning to political learning, writing articles and chapters that examine Habermas's ideas on the generation of knowledge and on the conditions for the ideal speech act. In writing about critical theory, Welton is seeking to counteract the emphases on the instrumental or the entirely personal in much of the writing on adult education in the nineteen seventies, eighties and nineties. This strand in his writing, then, is both an attempt to interpret adult education theory in political terms, and is a political act in itself.

And in a fourth strand (1993a, 1995) Welton examines the concepts of the system, civil society and the lifeworld. In this writing he goes beyond an examination of local action or particular social movements to a more comprehensive social analysis. His concept of civil society subsumes local action and individual social movements into an idea of representation, resistance and action that incorporates a vast array of 'ordinary' communal activities. Here is writing that looks at questions of how we give meaning to our lives through various forms of representation and organisation, and how we engage in and conduct learning within these different but intersecting spheres of daily existence.

Welton is a historian and in all his writing there is a sense of the present, vividly informed by history, and made crucially important by the alternative futures open to us. This is particularly marked in this fourth strand of his writing, with the concepts of the state, civil society and the lifeworld being offered to us not just as features in an analysis of contemporary society but as the vehicles through which we exercise crucial choices about alternative futures.

An essential aspect
Learning has an essential aspect. This has to do with coming to sense, to feel, to appreciate and perhaps to know the essence within events, within experiences, within our human existence. It is to be found in the appreciation of the arts, in the appreciation of the environment, in the appreciation of others, and in the appreciation of one's self. It involves reverie, and something more than reverie. It is a release from the constraints of some of the other aspects of learning I have tried to describe. It is not analysis in the rationalist sense, nor self-examination in the psychoanalytical sense, nor appraisal in the critical sense. This aspect of learning involves both being conscious of experience as it happens, and transcending it. It is concerned with coming to appreciate meaning.

I really looked at a painting for the first time in 1960 when I went to a Sydney exhibition of a painter called Ian Fairweather. I was twenty and rarely went to galleries, but I had read a review claiming that Fairweather was the best Australian painter alive. I went alone and walked around the several rooms looking at painting after painting. All were colourful, scruffy disarrays of shapes and lines. Often Fairweather would create a background of splashes of colour over which he would superimpose untidy outlines in darker tones. Shades of mauve and yellow predominated, with the outlines in brush-strokes of darkish brown. There were variations, and sometimes the background would be in splashes of darker colours with the outlines in white.

One painting, however, was predominantly in blue, with the background blue-white or the white of the paper, and the shapes outlined in a darker blue. I had noticed a man standing in front of the painting, apparently entranced, and for a time I watched him rather than the painting. When he moved away I assumed his place. The painting was reasonably large and I was standing back from it. At first it seemed completely without form, a striking mass of lines and hues. Then I began to see the lines as shapes arranged in rows, one row above the other. Now these shapes assumed the outlines of people, and the whole painting began to give off the impression of a medieval frieze. For a while the impression held firm, then other lines, which had been without clear significance, began assuming shapes and I had the impression not just of rows of figures in tiers, but of more rows of figures behind as well. The painting had been two dimensional but now took on an indeterminate depth. After a while the sense of a medieval frieze began to slip away. The painting as a whole suggested the untidiness of Australian bush, and I began to sense another kind of movement. The rows of figures seemed to come forward out of the painting, out of the bush...

I, in my turn, stood entranced, knowing for the first time how a painting can grow before the eyes, occupy its own time, create its own space, continually renew itself and, in a mysterious way, develop an essence of its own.

In the nineteen nineties I occasionally go walking along the Sydney coastline from Bondi to Coogee. There are two points on the walk—at the south end of Bondi and again at the south end of Tamarama—where you can lean against the railing on the top of a cliff and look down at the surfers lying or sitting on their boards, floating on the swell, and waiting. When a set of waves rolls in, you can watch them paddle to position themselves, judge the moment, and then dig their arms into the water in powerful strokes. Those that catch a wave nose their boards down and across the face and scramble to their feet. Depending on the wave and the temperament of the individual, some will guide their boards in a hectic zig-zag up and down the face of the wave; while others will crouch low and speed down and along the front of the wave and, on those rare and extraordinary days when the waves are curling over, into the tube.

But sometimes there are several who make no effort to catch a wave. They may, of course, be low in the various pecking orders that obtain in the surfers' world. They may be observing the sometimes rudely imposed codes and courtesies that exist between visitors and the locals. But some are simply not trying to catch waves. They sit or lie on their boards, motionless except for the occasional paddle of their hands in the water to steady or correct the position of their board.

As the cartoon character of the surfing world has it: 'Take out a six-pack of goodvibes, call up Mister Infinity, and tell him to cancel tomorrow.'

Some surfers achieve a form of meditation. They float on the arhythmic swell, between the cool of the water and the heat of the sun, surrounded by colours and glare: the white of the distant sand, the reds of the roofs of the houses stretching away up the hills and out onto the headlands, the blue of the ocean, the greens and greys and browns of the water around them. They are cut off from the land by the line of breakers, behind the waves, the crash of the surf muffled by massive bodies of water. They become part of the environment, and can release themselves from their sense of self. This is a kind of focussed reverie, a concentration on the phenomena that make up the experience of being. It is not a trance. The sea is potentially treacherous and surfers know this. Part of their being is engaged in sensing the currents, noting their distance from the rocks, maintaining their balance on a narrow piece of fibre-glass, watching the water for unwelcome shadows. They are both aware, and beyond awareness. They are intensely in the moment, and they have transcended it.

The surfing example might give the impression that the essential aspect of learning is complete in itself, but this form of focussed reverie can result in profound personal and political change. Some surfers come to treasure their experience beyond the waves, and reflect, talk, read and write about it in order to understand it better. The experience leads them into forms of personal, intellectual and mystical inquiry. An adult educator friend, Alex Nelson, who has researched and written about learning and belief, talks of a long-time surfer friend who works the night shift at a coal mine in order to be free to surf every morning. His friend 'reads' the rocks and the sand and the waves and the winds, and knows the plantlife and wildlife. To walk along the beach and converse with him, Alex says, is to be in the presence of someone who is wise.

This kind of contemplation can lead to action. Some surfers develop such an appreciation of their environment that they become environmental activists, and join in the struggle to convince everyone to relate responsibly to all kinds of environment.

The art gallery example might give the impression that this essential aspect of learning occurs accidentally, but of course it has been formalised into various kinds of study such as literary and dramatic criticism, film and media studies, and the study of the fine arts. In sensitive forms of cultural studies, a learner's initial sense of discovery is expanded. Further ways of understanding works of art are developed, intellectual tools to assist in analysis are offered, and the act of appreciation is placed within larger aesthetic, social and philosophical contexts. So, in his writings in the period after the Second World War, Raymond Williams (McIlroy and Westwood, 1993), for example, depicts literary criticism as a way to the meaning of things and therefore an important mode of social and political clarification. There was, in his mind, every good reason to link literary and socio-political criticism in the same journal he helped establish.

I have described this essential aspect of learning as focussed reverie and likened it in the surfing example to a form of meditation. John McIntyre (1996) discusses meditation as adult learning, using as his case study a retreat at which participants are helped to learn meditation as practised by Theravadan Buddhism. In this thoughtful, reflective piece of writing, McIntyre theorises on the process of learning meditation in terms of Schutz's (1967) social phenomenology, using the concepts of identity, perspective, situation and context to frame his analysis. The important learning for the meditator occurs, McIntyre argues, when our 'conceptualising, typifying mind' is replaced by a powerful 'noting' consciousness. This apparently individual experience of learning meditation in the closed environment of a retreat may help the meditator develop frames of reference for her or his life beyond the retreat. Learning meditation, McIntyre argues, can have a social as well as personal dimension.

McIntyre's view of meditation involves noting mental and physical phenomena 'as they really are'; but there are other forms of meditation that eschew this heightened kind of attention and seek to establish a stillness by blocking out external stimuli. Bernard Neville discusses a number of different forms of meditation, including 'gentle speculation on an idea, the deeply felt contemplation of an image, autogenic training, focus on a phrase or mantra, repose in a state of deep quiet without thoughts or images, [and] guided and spontaneous fantasies' (1989: 235). Some of these forms of meditation are associated with physical stillness, others with gentle movement, as in the case of T'ai Chi, Zen walking meditation, and some kinds of dancing. Neville argues, however, that all forms of meditation have in common 'a turning from the outer world to the inner, a stilling of the mind's activity and a receptive rather than assertive engagement with reality' (p. 231). They have similarities with, but are not the same as, the states of sleep or trance. While McIntyre seeks to understand the process of learning meditation, Neville examines the uses of meditation in education, arguing that both simple and more profound forms of meditation can be used by teachers and learners to aid or enhance the learning process. However, Neville goes way beyond an examination of meditation as a teaching or learning aid. His discussion of meditation occurs within a book called *Educating Psyche* (1989) and is part of a detailed discussion of 'emotion, imagination and the unconscious in learning'. Understanding meditation, therefore, is one way of understanding how we engage with reality in order to sense, apprehend and perhaps comprehend its essence.

A moral aspect
Learning has a moral aspect. But I feel unhappy with this statement so I am going to shift from the descriptive to the prescriptive, abandon the word 'aspect' for the moment, and say that *all* learning *should* be moral, and that moral learning is best understood in stories about people and practice.

Section 5: People and Practice

11: People

One of my small but important pleasures is stopping off at Moor's Espresso Bar in Sussex Street, Sydney most mornings. The coffee is good. Nat, Tony and Robert Ianni, the three brothers who run the place, are always friendly and seem to know all their customers by name. The style is low key: you give your order and pay at the back of the shop before sitting on one of the stools set along counters. There are copies of the Sydney Morning Herald, the Financial Review and other papers available. And the shop is opposite the Labour Council building and near the offices of a number of unions. This means that as well as drinking good coffee and reading the papers I sometimes encounter union friends and acquaintances and can catch up on news and hear versions of industrial and political events that may not always surface in the papers.

I treasure my contact with the unions. Unions come in different shapes and sizes and, like all other kinds of organisation, can go off the rails; but for the most part I would maintain that they are moral organisations. Unions were formed by working people coming together to protect themselves against oppression and exploitation by unrestrained managements. They are based on the ideas of community, mutual support, and caring. The caring may be of a rough and ready kind on occasions but it is built into the structure, since unions can only offer protection for the individual member if that individual member joins with other members and struggles for their protection as well.

Some of the most moral people I have met have been union officials. These are people who devote their lives to protecting their members' health and safety and improving their members' pay and conditions. This often means making sacrifices, and officials can work long hours and spend many days away from home as they travel around the state or country from workplace to workplace, from meeting to meeting, from one point of conflict to another. Because these officials deal with conflicts they are often depicted as trouble makers; but in fact their role is to resolve problems, to find solutions, to represent and guard the interests of others.

Tas Bull worked for years for the Waterside Workers Federation (now amalgamated with the Seafarers and others into the Maritime Union of Australia) as an organiser, then Assistant General Secretary, and then General Secretary until his retirement in 1993. He told me there had been times when non-union figures simply could not understand that he did not have a price nor that he was prepared to go through extended periods of hardship, stress and sometimes considerable personal risk for no other reason than to represent and protect the members of his union. One such person, sent by certain foreign interests to test him out, was a 'a nice clean Aussie, a convicted murderer'. Tas has a way of looking at you as he tells a story. 'They felt he would be the appropriate person to have a chat,' he said.

I had arranged to meet Tas in Moor's one Friday morning. We had a coffee, then went to the MUA headquarters where we found an empty office, sat down and, after turning a tape recorder on, I asked Tas how he had learnt his morality.

Tas talked about his life and times. He had gone to sea in 1946, leaving his home in Tasmania, and heading out on a British tanker chartered to an American oil company. He had his fifteenth birthday in the Persian Gulf, and for the next four years worked as a seafarer on international shipping. The poverty he saw in and around the ports of Abadan in the Gulf, Bombay, Andalusia in Franco's Spain, South America and 'even in the rich countries' of Northern Europe and North America 'came as a bit of a shock to me after Hobart'. His mother had told him stories of the hardships and injustices that working people had experienced during the depression, and the poverty Tas was now seeing as a young seafarer 'fed into her stories of just how inhuman man could be to man'.

A formative event occurred on that first voyage. A dispute developed over the quality of the food and the crew went on strike. Tas continues the story in these words:

> An American field officer from Standard Oil Company with his lace-up oil man's boots and all the rest of it came on board and

straight down to the crew's quarters which made an enormous impression on the British working class seamen. He wasn't accompanied by these white uniformed British officers but was in his working man's gear. He sat his arse on the table and said: 'Look here you guys, this is disgusting. These limey bastards, we have to stay after them all the time. We're paying for the ship on charter, you know, to provide good food and there'll be something done about this. Unfortunately there's nothing to be done up here in the Persian Gulf where things have got to be brought in, but as soon as the ship gets back to Australia it'll have more vegetables and food and fruit and so on on board than it'll have oil.' God what a guy. 'And there'll be no problem about this dispute. You have a right to bring it to our attention'. Pretty impressive stuff. So of course the people who influenced events amongst the crew said: 'Well, we'll accept that. This is wonderful.' We came out of the Persian gulf and someone says: 'Here, something's gone wrong. We don't seem to heading for Australia at all.' We weren't. We were heading for Bombay. In Bombay the whole crew was sacked and replaced with an Indian crew.

It was, Tas said, 'a little industrial lesson very early on in the piece'.

In 1950 Tas returned to Australia to work on coastal shipping and this meant joining the Seaman's Union of Australia. Conditions were much better and seeing what could be achieved by a union that was properly organised 'had a profound effect on me'. Nine out of the eleven full time officials in the Seamen's Union were Communists. These were dedicated people and they and other 'great orators who were around at the time' provided Tas with the beginnings of a political education. In 1951 he joined the Communist Party of Australia and took an active part in the campaign against Government moves to outlaw the Party. He left the Party in 1959 but has never abandoned his basic belief in 'the importance of people working together'.

During his nine years in the Party, Tas attended a class or 'school' of some kind almost every week, as well as occasional longer residential schools. These educational programs introduced him to political theories, and gave him the tools to examine problems and to look for solutions. These were the years following the miners' strike in 1949, and members of the Communist Party, concerned about the Party's survival, went through a period of intense analysis. Tas describes himself as a 'cautious official' and suggests that he developed this self-analytical aspect of his person and practice during this period. Two books had a major influence on him. These were *The Grapes of Wrath* 'which seemed to bring alive some of the things my mother had told me' and *The Great Conspiracy*. Later he married an Argentinian who has continued to provide him with a critique from another cultural perspective. 'What seems to us a very radical position, in South America is basically a working class position.'

Tas learnt by doing. As a young member of the Communist Party, he found himself placed alongside some prominent political speakers in the Town Hall in Hobart and asked to be the curtain-raiser. Afterwards, he was given some hints by older members on what to do and not to do the next time. Good speakers, he learnt, were people 'who felt something' and who approached a meeting 'with reasonably tidy minds'.

In the nineteen fifties Tas joined the Waterside Workers Federation in Hobart. In 1967, having transferred to Sydney, he was elected as an official in the Sydney branch. There, in something of the same way he had learnt to speak in public, he learnt to write. Tom Nelson, the Secretary of the Branch, expected his officials to contribute regularly for the weekly bulletin.

> Tom was famous for his so-called blue pencil and you'd get back your material with about three quarters of it knocked out and what he would say is: 'I think if you have a good look at it probably what's there is what you really wanted to say'.

Tas was elected to the position of Assistant General Secretary of the Waterside Workers Federation in 1983 and then to the position of General Secretary in 1984. Within a period of fifteen months Tas had moved from the role of a union organiser concerned with localised workplace issues to a post in which the decisions and actions he took could have a significant impact on the economic life of the whole country.

In July 1984 the Federal Government announced a major push to restructure the ports, and during this period of waterfront reform, which lasted until the end of 1992, Tas had to help his union and its members adapt to changes in work practices and the reduction of manning levels, protect as many of his members' jobs as possible in an increasingly complex industrial context, and secure the survival of the union in a sometimes delicate, sometimes hostile political climate. The Australian Council of Trade Unions had embraced the Government's plans so the support it gave the Waterside Workers Federation was subject to the union's willingness to accept reform of the industry. A minder of a Federal Government Minister was less accommodating and told Tas to his face during a break in a meeting: 'We're going to fuckin' get you!' Tas talks of waking in the early hours of the morning wondering whether the union would 'last another day', and then going to work and acting and speaking in a way that would lift the morale of everyone around him.

But my original question had been about learning morality, and Tas told the following story:

Towards the end of the reform period the union was in dispute with a major stevedoring company and under attack from a range of other organisations. The union was receiving a very bad press, and the executive committee decided to run a properly funded, professionally managed public campaign in response. This was going to be costly and in order to raise the funds it was decided to levy $20 in four lots of $5 from every member. At the same time another issue arose and the union called national stop work meetings. Notice was so short that they were unable to stop the midnight shift leading up to the meeting, and in Sydney could only find Harold Park raceway as a venue.

> I had to leave on the twelve o'clock plane to go to Melbourne or Adelaide to conduct a second meeting that day so I stand up at this meeting talking to about a quarter of the people who had just worked a midnight shift, tell them we're going to propose a national twenty-four hour stoppage so they're going to lose a day's wages, propose a levy of $20, and tell them I'm going to get a plane at twelve o'clock so I really haven't got time to stay here and have a much of a debate. Pretty cheeky stuff. And the reason we called the meeting was over some bad news, one further thing that had been ripped off us as a consequence of the reform. There was no difficulty getting out to the airport because the only debate was: why is it only twenty dollars? Why don't we have an ongoing five dollars a week levy until this whole thing is over? And every single port in Australia—forty six ports—voted unanimously. It's that kind of experience which really restores your confidence, restores your faith.

In a series of lectures entitled *A Truly Civil Society* (1995) Eva Cox discusses the concept of social capital. Social capital is made up of the trust, the sense of community, the goodwill and reciprocity generated by people engaging in such everyday activities as helping out neighbours, sharing in a car pool, staying in touch by telephone, and playing their part in civic groups. Social capital, Cox argues, is increased rather than depleted the more we use it (p. 19). Tas tried to be 'on the level' at all times so that, whatever else the members of his union thought of him, they believed what he said. In the nature of social capital, this openness helped develop the solidarity Tas experienced in that Harold Park hall (and in ports all around the country). Tas expressed the phenomenon in the terms of our conversation. The unanimous demonstration by his union's members that they were ready to play their part in the struggle, he said, 'in its turn maintains this thing called morality'.

12: Practice

A large company in Australia recently announced that one of its manufacturing plants would be closed in two years' time. Thousands of workers were to be made redundant. I felt betrayed (although not nearly so badly as the workers must have done) since nine years earlier I had played a part in training a consultative council in another plant owned by the same company. As we understood it then, workers would accept greater flexibility in work practices but in return would have a say in the way those work practices were organised; career paths would be made available to all; and any loss of jobs would be through natural attrition. It now becomes clear that while I and others were helping establish this cooperative mode of industrial relations in one plant in one city, the same company was letting another plant in another city run down, and was ready to throw a large number of the workforce into unemployment.

A trade union course
Strong unions are necessary to help people stand up to this kind of disregard for the welfare of working people and the welfare of the communities from which they come. Industrial relations is an arena in which forces are continually pitted against each other, and where choices have to be made. There are rights and wrongs, and in the final analysis the unions are for the rights and against the wrongs. It was because I subscribe to this belief that I found myself sitting on the floor to the side of a large training room one Monday morning, listening to Tas Bull address a group of some sixty five trade unionists. They were the first intake of a new project called 'Organising Works' which had been set up by the Australian Council of Trade Unions and which was aimed at developing a new cohort of union officials with specialist skills in recruitment. The project employed young people with a union or

political background, located them in a variety of unions, appointed an experienced union organiser as a mentor to each, and provided them with training in union organising. The training program consisted of one day per week and two four-day residential courses over a year. I had been asked to design and conduct the second of the four-day residential courses, and was waiting for Tas to hand the group over.

Clearly my four days had to deal with issues and skills relating to recruiting new members. However, sitting to the side and looking at the sixty-five young people, I was struck by the thought that even if only a third of them committed themselves to the union movement and stayed the distance, then in ten or fifteen years' time there would be this core of activists across the unions, all of whom had been trained together and knew each other well. As I waited I made a decision to shift the focus of the four days, as much as I could within the program already planned, to the business of encouraging effective friendships between individuals and a sense of solidarity in the group as a whole. If I put this idea into Cox's language, then I made a decision to try and create some social capital that might contribute to the construction of a truly civil society.

The moment Tas handed the group over, therefore, I suggested that the participants break up the formal layout of the large training room; and for the rest of the four days they worked in a whole variety of groups. The theme for the Monday was their practice, and I asked them each to devise a metaphor or image to describe themselves in their jobs, and then to work in threes and, by sharing and discussing the metaphors, to examine themselves, their practice and the practice of their unions. In the afternoon and the evening I asked them to work in groups of seven, recount stories about their recruiting successes, and then begin building up theories and rules to underwrite those success stories.

Tuesday's theme was politics and power, and in the morning we ran a series of exercises that required them to work in groups of five and examine different forms of social control. In the afternoon they met in groups of twenty or so to discuss international and national socio-political issues of the moment. And in the late afternoon and the evening each group mounted and then presented an exhibition outlining their deliberations.

104

Wednesday's theme was recruiting groups of workers. The morning and the first session of the afternoon were given over to an exercise requiring each participant to make a short presentation to five or six others. And in the last session of the afternoon, from 4.00 to 6.00, I asked the participants to form four choirs.

This was the make-or-break session. I had prepared a program sheet each evening outlining the next day, and had titled the last session of the Wednesday afternoon 'Forming an Organising Works Choir', but had added no further details. During the day a number of participants reacted to the entry on the program. One participant approached me over lunch. 'You won't get me to sing, you know!' she said. Another commented within my hearing that singing was not what a union training course should be about. I was told that a group gathered in one of the corridors and contemplated boycotting the session.

There was no boycott and everyone entered the training room at 4.00. I announced that in keeping with the theme of the day I wanted to examine the processes by which groups formed and how we could use a knowledge of those processes. I talked of a scene in the film *A Fish Called Wanda* where Kevin Kline opens a safe in which he expects to see a stash of money. The safe is empty, and Kline breaks all the conventional film acting rules by stating his emotions in words. With a very particular rising inflection, he says: 'I'm disappointed. I'm very DISAPPOINTED!' I explained that I was going to ask the participants to form groups, that we would do this in stages, and that at each stage they were to express their emotions in words, just as Kline had done in the film. We practised expressing different emotions, with the group of sixty-five participants shouting out, with the rising inflection, 'I'm disapPOINTED!' and 'I'm very DIS-TRESSED!' and 'I'm feeling HAPPY!'. I divided the participants into four groups and announced that each group was going to form a choir, compose a song about the union movement to the tune of 'Three Blind Mice', rehearse it and then perform it. As we did this, we would work through Tuckman's (1965) stages of group formation: forming, storming, norming and performing.

I sent the groups to different corners of the room, telling them that each group was in the *forming* stage and that this stage was often marked by anxiety, dependence on directions, and a testing out of what kinds of behaviour would be acceptable. I asked them to verbalise these emotions and reactions in the Kevin Kline fashion. As the groups formed in each corner of the room there was lots of shouting and emoting (and lots of laughter). I then explained that they were moving into the *storming* stage, and that in this stage there was conflict between sub-groups; that there was emotional resistance to the task in hand; and that this often translated into rebellion against the leader. I suggested that in each choir three factions—the dags, the dingbats and the silly galahs—were emerging, and I asked them to go through this storming stage, verbalising their emotions. Again there was a lot of noise with the factions shouting at each other and then a considerable number of people shouting in mock (I hope) anger at me. I just managed to get the whole crowd back under control, and explained that in the *norming* stage of the group process people began to adopt roles, there was a development of an open exchange of views, and the group began to function. I suggested that they needed to move into this stage and get on with composing and rehearsing their songs; and that they would probably need a conductor, an administrator or two, perhaps a sub-group of composers, a director of rehearsals and, of course, sopranos, contraltos, tenors and basses. There followed about half an hour of increasing rowdiness, as each of the choirs sorted themselves out, composed their songs and began rehearsing. The noise grew so loud that another course in a training room nearby abandoned their session and came into our room to watch. I managed somehow to get a few moments' silence and announced that we would move to the *performing* stage. I explained that according to Tuckman's stages, this was where interpersonal problems were resolved or put to one side and constructive attempts were made to complete the task. We then had a concert in which, one after the other, the choirs performed their songs to the rest of us. Without exception the songs were extremely irreverent and very funny. At the end of the concert, over some considerable noise I will admit, I explained that according to Brown (1979) there was another and final *mourning* stage in which members of a group recognised that the group would disband and often expressed sorrow mixed with a further kind of anxiety as the now established ties were abandoned and an uncertain future had to be faced. I suggested that each of the choirs verbalise these emotions in the

Kevin Kline manner as they disbanded, and that we make our way to the bar.

I am pleased to say that the session in the bar was rowdy, as was the meal that followed, as was the rest of the evening. I am also pleased to say that the session marked the moment in the four days when the group as a whole appeared to abandon political and factional differences (whether they were left wing, centre or right wing, dag, ratbag or dingbat), and temporarily at least to coalesce in the way Tuckman would have expected. It is, as they say, nice when the theory actually works.

A women's refuge

Despite the apparent light-heartedness of the session spent organising choirs, the Organising Works project was a training program with a strong moral purpose. It was part of a push to strengthen the union movement in order to promote the interests of working people and help working people protect themselves. Another example of moral learning can be found in the story of the establishment of Elsie Women's Refuge in Sydney in the mid-nineteen seventies. Here the forces pitted against one another were social forces. Individual women sought refuge from the abusive and violent behaviour of individual partners, but the forces they were struggling against were the customs and practice, the rituals and regulations, the ideologies and prejudices entrenched in a patriarchal society.

The story of Elsie Women's Refuge, as told by Sallie Saunders, Maire Sheehan, Mez Egg, Bobbie Townsend and Joey Bassan (1994), is exciting and complex. The establishment of the refuge marked the beginning of the Women's Refuge Movement in Australia. For the mainly middle-class women who squatted in the property and publicised its existence, the refuge marked a move away from reformist modes of feminist action to radical action. For the mainly working class women who sought refuge there, it provided a secure physical and social environment where, in the company of others, they could begin constructing new lives for themselves. For everyone involved, Elsie Women's Refuge provided a stimulus for sometimes exhilarating, sometimes uncomfortable learning.

This learning occurred in a number of ways. For example, the publicised fact of the refuge's existence helped women make that final decision to leave a violent and oppressive relationship. For many the decision was momentous, an act of empowerment, a transformation in itself, an extraordinary experience in learning in action.

The house itself became a learning centre. Simply by arriving there, women learnt that they were not alone, that their experience of domestic violence was shared by others. They could listen to others' stories, and begin telling their own. They could join in the conversations, many of which would go on late into the night, sharing in the excitement of exchanging information, discovering new ideas, and beginning to place their own experience in a wider social and political context. In this way they would begin rebuilding their own self-confidence. And they could take part in discussions which brought together women who had experienced domestic violence and women who had already developed their feminist thinking, and which enabled people from both groups to deepen their understanding about patriarchal forms of social control.

The organisation and management of the refuge provided opportunities for learning. The women who established it made an early decision that there would be no hierarchy. Everyone was to be involved in decision making, meaning that everyone had the opportunity to learn about the organisation and the kinds of process a group of people must go through to make it work. As the centre expanded and the administrative and financial challenges became greater, the opportunities for this kind of learning increased. Other properties had to be found, set up and managed, systems of child care put in place, methods of budgeting and distributing financial resources devised, and a food-buying cooperative established.

The opportunities for learning extended beyond the refuge itself. A number of the women saw Elsie Women's Refuge as an exercise in the political education of the public. By publicising the refuge, they were not only letting victims of domestic violence know of it existence, they were making public the issue of women's oppression. The refuge became a focus for education and learning in relation to the women's movement.

And the women's refuge movement, of which Elsie Women's Refuge was an important part, served not just as a site for the kinds of learning listed above but as a site for the generation of new knowledge and new forms of action: a process John Holford (1995) describes as 'cognitive praxis'. As the movement progressed, the women involved developed new forms of expertise in cooperative organisation and consensual management, more information about domestic violence, new understandings of the workings of a patriarchal society, new forms of social and political action, and new understandings of the effects of social class.

The new understandings about class were liberating for some and painful for others. Saunders *et al* recount how a year down the track the middle class women seemed to be adopting roles that mirrored male roles in a patriarchal society. They occupied the 'public domain', dealing with the media, seeking funding and liaising with other agencies; while the working class women occupied the 'private domain', looking after the children and doing the cleaning and shopping. In decision-making meetings, the procedural knowledge of the middle class women tended to dominate over the lived experience of the working class women. And when Elsie Women's Refuge attracted Federal Government funding in 1975 and could pay workers, middle class women took on the paid roles.

Resentment increased and what followed was a very simple and straightforward coup. The working class women asked the middle class women to leave; and then set about devising new understandings and strategies—engaging in a cognitive praxis—aimed at preventing similar divisions happening again.

Forum theatre

My third example of moral learning is a project set up in 1997 and aimed at changing the conditions, and therefore some of the possible futures, for young people living in an inner city suburb of Sydney. Here the forces against which the learning was pitted are not so clear. The young people were disadvantaged, without prospects, discriminated against because of race or social class or accommodation, held in check because of political inaction, marked out by others because of prejudice, or disinterest, or a lack of compassion. The enemies were others, us, them, the powers that be, virtually everyone.

Glebe, the suburb in question, has a multi-cultural population. There are Housing Commission estates of renovated Victorian houses and high rise towers where people of Anglo-Celtic,

Vietnamese, Lebanese and Aboriginal background live. In another part of the suburb Tranby Aboriginal Co-operative College caters for locals but also brings Aboriginal people into the suburb from other parts of the state and the country. The suburb is close to the University of Sydney and so has a permanent population of academics living in family houses, and a transient population of Australian and international students living in rooms, flats, shared houses and squats. The suburb is close to the Rozelle container terminal, the Sydney fish markets, an area of small businesses, workshops and warehouses off Broadway, and the central business district of Sydney, and so houses people from all social classes and a wide range of jobs and professions. Glebe Point Road, which runs through the suburb to the harbour, has numerous cafes, restaurants offering cuisine from many parts of the world, a major Sydney bookshop, a youth hostel, and a backpackers' hostel. A long time institution called Johnny McColl's Community Gym trains boxers and remains unchanged in character and atmosphere from the nineteen fifties. On the western boundary of Glebe is Harold Park Raceway, Sydney's major venue for horse trotting, and on the eastern boundary is the Wentworth Park Raceway, Sydney's major venue for greyhound racing. And there are a some celebrated and less celebrated pubs.

Glebe has always had an association with crime. It has a history of gangland families and organised crime going back to the 1850s. More recently it has had a high incidence of car theft and petty theft, including bag-snatching and shop-lifting on Glebe Point Road. According to a local youth worker nearly every business owner has been affected by crime, including theft, vandalism, and even standover tactics by kids as young as twelve. Indeed, most of the people committing these crimes are young people. Some of the theft is done to sustain drug taking habits, but it is also part of a culture that has developed in an area of Sydney where young people perceive that there is no real future for them.

The project I want to describe was initiated by Glebe Youth Centre, was funded by a grant of $56,000 from the NSW Attorney General's Department, and was aimed at addressing some of the issues and problems affecting young people in the suburb. It was planned in detail over six months before being launched and was

110

constructed around 'community meetings', a small grants program for young people, outreach work, and forum theatre.

The monthly community meetings were for representatives of agencies and organisations that controlled, influenced or impinged on the lives of young people in the area. These representatives included councillors, police officers, the Aboriginal liaison officer from the local high school, schoolteachers, people from the housing, community services and juvenile justice departments, Johnny McColl or someone else from the gym, shopkeepers, and people from the local council precinct committees. Working parties were established out of these meetings to examine particular issues and make proposals. Each working party was seen as having a limited life related to its particular task. A policy of encouraging alliances between different people was established. These alliances were to exist only so long as they served some purpose.

$10,000 from the main project grant was put into a small grants fund, to which young people and others could apply to fund their own projects and enterprises. Other funds were put aside to help establish training programs.

The outreach part of the project targeted business owners. A small group of workers and volunteers, mostly in their early or mid-twenties, contacted one hundred and seventy businesses, meeting shopkeepers and others business people face to face. The aim was to hear their stories, get them involved in offering positive alternatives to young people, and to invite them to participate in a piece of forum theatre.

Forum theatre draws on the ideas and practice of Boal (1979) and is a form of interactive theatre which sets out to canvass a matter that has crucial relevance to the people gathered, to recast that matter as a problem, and to involve everyone—the 'director', 'actors' and 'audience'—in a search for solutions. Central to forum theatre are an examination of the ways in which we are controlled, whether by force, institutions or ideas, and a search for ways in which we can throw off that control. Boal's thinking has close associations with the thinking of his Brazilian compatriot Freire (1972a, 1972b) and his kind of theatre helps people engage in an intense kind of learning.

The forum theatre evening was held at the hall at the Glebe Youth Centre. About twenty shopkeepers and another twenty five people associated in different ways with the centre, the suburb and the project attended.

The evening opened with welcomes from the Youth Club coordinator and the local member of parliament, and a briefing on the program as a whole. The director of the forum theatre was introduced and without an absolutely clear line of demarcation the evening shifted from meeting to theatre. While the director was on stage speaking about the program for the evening a young man entered from the street and walked through the hall to the stage, asking what was going on. The director, in reality a part-time worker in the youth centre, tried to explain but the young man became abusive, jumped up on stage and pushed past the director saying: 'Is this the light switch?' The lights went off, and a police officer came in at the back of the hall with a torch. The officer moved around the hall, then on to the stage at the front where, with gun drawn, he caught the director in the beam of his torch, began challenging him, and then recognised him. The director greeted the 'police officer' and as the officer withdrew off-stage a shopkeeper jumped up from her seat in the audience, declared 'I'm late', and ran up on stage. The director greeted the 'shopkeeper'. She took her place behind a counter and the director interviewed her as he or others in the outreach project had interviewed the shopkeepers in the audience. With the players now introduced, the director withdrew, the young man came back on stage, and a piece of theatre commenced. It was a story of misunderstandings, faults on all sides, fear, anger, and an escalation towards violence:

The young man is outside the shop. He shouts to mates on the other side of the street, then turns into the shop. He moves around the shop, picking up objects, disturbing the display, harassing the shopkeeper. The shopkeeper grows increasingly intimidated, and when the young man steps behind the counter, she cracks, shouting at him to get out. The young man leaves.

The police officer passes by and the shopkeeper calls him in, but their encounter is unsatisfactory. No damage has been caused, nothing has been stolen. The officer responds to a call on his radio and leaves, suggesting that the shopkeeper file a report.

The director crossed the stage on a skateboard holding up a sign saying 'two days later':

The young man is in the street. The shopkeeper sees him and phones the police. The young man calls to a friend and in response to a question says he is going to buy a CD. He enters, and the shopkeeper tells him to get out. The young man says he wants to buy a CD. 'Do you have the money?' the shopkeeper asks. 'Money! Money! All you people ever think about is money,' the young man shouts back. The police officer arrives and tells the young man to leave. When the young man asks why, the police officer says; 'The shopkeeper has already reported you once.' The young man becomes abusive and the officer grabs him. As the young man is being dragged away he shouts: 'I'm coming back! And I'm going to blow your fucking shop up!'

The lights came up and the director walked on stage. Into the shocked silence, he asked: 'Well, was that a true story?' After a moment's pause, a number of people in the audience said: 'Yes.'

There are problems in talking of forum theatre in some generic way since Boal's ideas have been adapted and used in different kinds of community theatre, in forms of 'playback' theatre and 'agitprop' and political theatre. In the particular adaptation of forum theatre used at the Glebe Youth Centre extensive research is carried out from which the actors construct a piece of theatre around an aspect of the lives of the audience, presenting it as a problem. The piece is played through once, discussed, and then started again. The second time round people in the audience can stop the performance at any point, and propose changes. The director invites the person who has stopped the action to explain why she or he did so, calls for other comments and discussion, and then invites the person on stage to replace the actor she or he has stopped. The play is restarted or taken up from a particular point and the newcomer on stage takes over the role and attempts to alter the course of events in order to find a better solution. If the play takes a turn that is unrealistic or unsatisfactory, other members of the audience can stop the play, explain why, and propose other lines of action. With the director facilitating the process, the piece of theatre is reworked again and again, with different members of the audience coming on to stage, taking over the different roles, and trying to act out the scene in order to achieve a satisfactory outcome.

As can happen in forum theatre, the play in the Glebe Youth Centre was not completed a second time. The play was restarted or taken up again at different points in the story several times. Four shopkeepers came up from the audience at different times to try different strategies to avoid or minimise the confrontation. Others from the audience intervened. One shopkeeper stopped the play, commented that young people rarely came into his shop alone, and then joined the young man on stage playing his mate. The audience became engrossed, and as the evening progressed the discussion widened to other issues relating to young people in the suburb: their lack of future, the policy of the housing commission, questions of racism, possible job creation schemes, training opportunities...

At a point when the discussion had clearly taken over from the performance, the director asked the audience to divide up into four separate groups. Each group had a facilitator who encouraged the group members to list and discuss ideas that might address any of the issues raised during the evening; and to decide on the kinds of action they could take. Since the evening was part of a continuing project there was no formal conclusion. The director and the actors stepped out of their roles and joined in the discussions. One by one the groups completed their discussions and began dispersing. For a while the hall was abuzz with conversation as the larger groups broke up and people lingered on, talking through the issues or just chatting. Gradually the noise abated as people left, and the workers most centrally concerned with the project settled down to look through the proposals developed by the groups, debrief the whole evening, and begin discussing ways of taking the project into the next phase.

Section 6: Civil society

13: Social movements

The Organising Works program took place within the Australian union movement. The learning at Elsie women's refuge was done within the women's movement. We could argue that the piece of forum theatre at Glebe Youth Centre was an educational event within a community development movement. Each in its different way is an example of learning located within a social movement.

In social movements, people join together on a local, national or international basis and take collective action to oppose, or bring about, some kind of change. To do this they may need to learn new skills and new information. They may need to examine their own values and assumptions, and the values and assumptions of others. They may need to form new understandings of different kinds of social control, and develop new forms of action to exert or oppose that control. In all these activities they may generate ideas not previously known. Social movements can be sites for personal and collective learning, and for the creation of new kinds of knowledge (Welton, 1993a; Holford, 1995). And if adult educators are going to contribute to this kind of intense and generative learning, then we need to form an understanding of what social movements are, and how they work.

Finding a definition for social movements can be difficult, as a number of commentators over the years have attested (Wilkinson, 1971; Diani and Eyerman, 1992; Johnston and Klandermans, 1995). For my own part I have tried to form an understanding of social movements by examining them in three different ways: by grouping them into general categories, identifying the kinds of role people can take on in a social movement, and identifying the phases some social movements appear to pass through.

Categories
Categorising social movements is none too easy in itself. Matthias Finger (1989) and Welton (1993a), for example, both

divide social movements into 'old' and 'new', but Finger lists feminism as an 'old' social movement, while Welton includes it in a list of 'new' ones.

Then there are problems about what qualifies as a social movement, and what does not. Finger sees new social movements in the widespread interest in personal growth and self-transformation. He argues they exist in a context of 'modernity in crisis' and goes on:

> ... [T]he new movements are not political.... They take as their starting point the idea that politics, like modernity, has failed and that effective social change can only stem from fundamental personal transformation (1989, p. 18).

But I believe that in making this point he has stopped talking about social movements and is discussing another phenomenon altogether. For there to be a social movement there must be group activity and shared interests that extend beyond the personal transformation of the individuals. Social movements are surely 'political' in that people engage in action together, even if they share a disillusion in 'politics'. Individuals may undergo forms of personal transformation in the course of being involved in a social movement, but the social action and the personal change are more likely to go hand in hand, rather than social change stemming from personal transformation.

And Holford (1995) reminds us that social movements are not all necessarily democratic nor directed towards some general good. Fascism can be described as a social movement and, depending on where we stand ideologically, social movements may be judged rational, irrational, socially constructive or pathological.

With these caveats in mind, I will group together some social movements that I believe *are* social movements, and are socially constructive; and I will suggest characteristics that are common to each group:

Social movements, then, can be categorised as structured, semi-structured and unstructured. In the category of structured social movements I would place trade unions, some of the churches, and some political parties; in the category of semi-structured social movements I would place the activities of environmentalists, feminists, peace activists, people struggling for the recognition of indigenous peoples' rights, and human rights activists; and in the category of unstructured social movements I would place those engaged in the campaign to prevent the spread of HIV/AIDS and to support people with HIV/AIDS, some of the groupings and lists of social activists on the world wide web, and people engaged in recent forms of cultural and community action.

In a seminar paper (1995b) I categorised social movements as old, new and postmodern, taking the names 'old' and 'new' as established labels from the literature on social movements and adding 'postmodern'. But these labels have proved unsatisfactory. An Aboriginal participant in a workshop commented that 'new' was hardly an appropriate label for the struggle for the recognition of indigenous peoples' rights, pointing up the problem of using labels that suggest age when the categories they indicate are most clearly distinguished by structure. Hence my use of 'structured' and 'semi-structured'. And as I have already indicated, while there are insights to be found in the postmodern discourse, there are also confusions. As a result I have abandoned the label 'postmodern', and replaced it with the prosaic term 'unstructured', which both avoids the false association with chronology and, rather more directly than the term 'postmodern' does, denotes absence or denial of formal structures.

Divisions between the categories of structured, semi-structured and unstructured social movements are not hard and fast. People associated with different kinds of social movement will cooperate and join in common campaigns. For example, trade unions will join with human rights activists in struggling for workers' rights, and human rights activists will help combat institutionalised prejudice against AIDS sufferers. Nonetheless, the movements in each of the three categories do tend to share certain reasonably clear characteristics which in turn mark them off from the other categories.

Structured social movements such as trade unions, churches and political parties, as the label would suggest, have an infrastructure of activists and organisers. They have headquarters. They have leaders and officers who carry authority. They tend to have clear visions of a desired future, often expressed in recognised texts, or policy documents, or manifestos. They have traditions and past prophets and heroes. And they have a reasonably defined membership, with individual members sometimes actually holding proof of membership in the form of a membership ticket or by virtue of having been ritually recognised in some way.

The trade union movement in Australia is an example of a structured social movement. Within it are different unions, and variations in political stance, but there is a peak body, the Australian Council of Trade Unions, which gives the movement a coherence. It is not simply an organisation, since an organisation normally has clear boundaries. In the Australian trade union movement, there are some organisations on the periphery, such as workers' health centres or university research centres, and some people, such as political figures or academics, whose membership of the movement is not always clear. But as one moves towards the 'centre', the people involved will be paid-up members of unions which are affiliated to the ACTU. The movement has a vision of the future, formalised in the ACTU's constitution and policy documents. There are present leaders with recognised authority who have the right to speak on behalf of the whole movement. There are traditions and rituals, most in evidence at the biennial ACTU conference. The movement has a history, going back to the Stonemasons' campaign for an eight-hour day in 1848 and beyond, peopled with revered heroes and past prophets.

The sixty-five people I worked with on the Organising Works program came from a range of different unions. Some of these unions represented very different kinds of worker in very different kinds of industry. Some of the unions were industrial rivals of others. Some unions had considerable political differences. Yet it was clear that everyone present was a member of the same movement; and I was able to make assumptions about certain common understandings, cultures and language, and could appeal to and build on a sense of solidarity.

Semi-structured social movements such as the environmental, women's and human rights movements are more likely to be networks of people, without a central body or point of reference, although there may be a number of congregations of influence and power at different points in the network. There will be a less easily defined or permanent cadre of organisers. Activists will take on the roles of organisers as the need arises. There will be recognised visionaries and prophets but few overall leaders. Present leaders will tend to emerge in relation to particular episodes in the struggles the movement is concerned with, but will not necessarily carry their authority or influence into another episode. Semi-structured social movements have a sense of working towards some end, but their vision of the future may not be so clearly defined. As a result they rarely have manifestos, or single policy documents, but they will often have a considerable body of literature to draw upon. And although semi-structured social movements are unlikely to have initiation rituals or membership tickets, there is a very strong sense of membership. People *know* they are members.

The environmental movement is an example of a semi-structured social movement. It is made up of a web of formal and informal organisations, groupings, and individuals. It has no headquarters or generally accepted peak body, although some structured organisations within the movement such as the Australian Conservation Foundation or the Wilderness Society or Greenpeace have influence and power in particular aspects of environmental activism and have the ear of powerbrokers in the wider society. There are many foci—recycling glass bottles, protecting whales, preserving wetlands, urban planning, using non-destructive forms of agriculture, opposing the use of nuclear power, and so on—yet a person knows if she or he is a member of the movement and shares with others a desire for some kind of environmentally sustainable future. This desire may not be expressed in a clearly articulated vision. Some environmentalists may desire a socialist future or a responsibly conducted free enterprise future or a zero growth future or a future constructed on small communities; but all will see themselves as working for a future that involves a use of resources so as to permit *further* futures.

The women's movement is another example of a semi-structured social movement. It, too, is a vast network with no headquarters. There are considerable differences of opinion between radical, socialist, liberal and postmodern feminists as to what a feminist or post-feminist future might look like. There is a large and eclectic body of literature. There are influential figures who come and go, but no-one in formal authority. There are revered figures but their actions and ideas are continually subject to review and revision. (Witness the way Simone de Beauvoir's life and work have been criticised.) Nonetheless, for all the variety of viewpoints, for all the differences in the way members of the movement express their feminism, everyone in the movement *knows* she is a member, and everyone in the movement can recognise other members. There may be no formal organisational structure to the movement but there is a coherence that makes it one of the most powerful social forces in our lives.

Three commentators on social movements, Russell Dalton, Manfred Kuechler and Wilhelm Burklin (1990), distinguish between what they call 'old' and 'new' (and I call 'structured' and 'semi-structured') social movements on the basis of a number of features. These include structure, ideology and political style, and their views on these features tie in with what I have said above. But they also argue that old and new social movements differ in terms of their bases of support, and the motivations of the people who participate. They cite a body of research and opinion that suggests that old social movements were class-based; that they derived from 'a combination of economic interests and distinct social networks' (p. 12). This view, I believe, is difficult to sustain. It may have been true at one stage that the trade union movement was class-based (in its particular case, working-class-based) but, with the unionisation of the public sector, and of professions such as teaching in many of the countries where unions are active, this is no longer the case. Nor do I believe that such a view was ever sustainable in the case of certain churches or even certain political parties which appealed to people of all classes.

Dalton, Kuechler and Burklin also maintain that while old social movements garner their support from distinct classes, new social movements are value, or issue-based. This distinction, again, is difficult to sustain since social movements such as unions, churches and political parties all construct their internal solidarity on sets of values and can take action over issues, often in much the same way that new movements do.

This leads me also to take issue with the discussion by Dalton, Kuechler and Burklin in the same text on motivation. The body of research and opinion they cite suggests that people join old social movements out of self-interest: that workers, for example, join a union to improve their economic position. This view holds that the goals of old social movements are instrumental and aimed at benefiting the members of the collective 'even if society or other social groups must pay the cost'; while the participants in new social movements 'are motivated by ideological goals and pursuit of collective goods' (p. 12). But this particular distinction between old and new social movements does not stand up to scrutiny. People participate in both kinds of movement for both instrumental and ideological reasons. Many members of left-wing unions, for example, are motivated by a political vision of a more equitably managed economy and society which, if achieved, they would see as constituting a collective good. Some members of the women's movement seek changes that would gain them a higher level of personal participation in the economic life of the country—that is, access to better job prospects and better pay. When peace activists struggle to ensure a future for themselves and their children in a world free of nuclear weapons, who can say whether they are acting in their own interests or for a collective good?

My third category of social movement falls outside the discussion of some commentators on social movements, since they see social movements by definition as having a structure, even if decentralised and fluid, and their members being united by a common ideology or set of beliefs (Foss and Larkin, 1986: 2; Kuechler and Dalton, 1990: 277-8). However, I do believe that there is another way in which an accumulation of people act in a kind of concert, and through the weight of their actions bring about social change. These accumulations of people I call 'unstructured' social movements, and two of the examples I gave above were the sum of people and activities associated with the campaigns to prevent the spread of HIV/AIDS and to support people with HIV/AIDS; and the sum of people and activities associated with recent forms of cultural and community action.

If I compare unstructured social movements to structured and semi-structured ones, then they have much less coherence and little or no discernible infrastructure. There may be networks but these are loose, impermanent, and not always inclusive of everyone involved. There may be a number of networks of different kinds and sizes, with little connection between them. As a result unstructured social movements have no headquarters, and few congregations of influence and power. Membership is unclear. Some people move in and out of the movement, depending on their contacts, alliances and concerns of the moment. Perhaps the most significant feature that marks unstructured movements off from other movements is that there is unlikely to be a desired future. People will be united in different ways for different lengths of time by a shared interest or dismay. They will have a cause, but it will be found more in a shared reaction against current events, in a shared emotion, than in a common support for some particular end. There may be times when members of an unstructured movement may not be aware that they are members.

In the case of the movement associated with HIV/AIDS, it may appear at first sight to conform in a number of ways to the set of characteristics I suggested for semi-structured social movements. But I suggest it falls more within the category of unstructured social movement because it is dispersed, its membership is unclear, and because there seems to be no clearly desired future beyond a world free from the virus and the illnesses that go with it. But it is a social movement nonetheless, with many people engaged in action, and 'united' in their actions by a powerful compassion or resistance to prejudice. It is a movement that permeates other movements and other organisations. Parts of it are to be found in government departments, parts in trade unions and churches, parts in professions such as the medical and welfare professions, parts in sectors of society such as the gay and lesbian communities, and parts in community groups. In some of these locations and amongst some of these groups there are networks and congregations of influence and power, but they are not clearly part of an overall network. Indeed 'network' can be an inappropriate image to apply to the whole movement as parts of the movement have little or no links with any others. But while the movement may be difficult to describe and define, it has been a powerful and recognisable force in our society and the results of its actions are there to be seen in the extraordinary changes over the last fifteen years in the way many Australians think and behave.

The social movement associated with recent forms of cultural and community action is more difficult to describe. It is interesting to note the kinds of people who gathered around the project at the Glebe Youth Centre and who contributed to the forum theatre. The director was only a part-time worker at the centre. Other parts of his life were dedicated to environmental activism, to a fringe theatre group, and to surfing. The 'policeman' was a founding member of the fringe theatre group. Another person who helped with the staging and the decoration and layout of the hall was an artist engaged at the time in an iconoclastic exercise which involved perching beautifully sculpted clay pigeons on prominent statues around the Central Business District of Sydney. Another worker on the project was a young Scotswoman in the midst of a backpacking trip who had made contact with the youth centre while in Sydney. She had worked in similar projects addressing issues of crime and unemployment in Argyle and had experience in outreach, workshops, and performance as a form of political action.

There are, I believe, people in Australia and elsewhere today who see themselves, as a number associated with the piece of forum theatre did, as activists in some kind of generic sense, rather than activists for a particular cause. These are people who find themselves unattracted by structures and the prescribed ideologies of the structured social movements, and who do not want to devote their energies to single-issue causes, in the way some semi-structured social movements do. Generic activists are not new but these ones tend to eschew the more conventional political and community action methods such as lobbying, marching, demonstrating, picketing, pamphleteering and so on, and are more likely to use the techniques of performance, drawing on role play, socio-drama and political theatre. These activists will run workshops, perform street theatre, and organise events like festivals, carnivals and community celebrations. Some of these activities may occur in their own right, but others will be incorporated into the activities of other movements. So these kinds of activist will provide 'invisible theatre' during an environmental demonstration, will perform as part of the organised events at a rally against the use of nuclear power, will conduct a series of workshops within a community as part of that community's own efforts to address an issue dividing it, and will animate events motivated by their own interest in bringing people together to celebrate that togetherness. In this movement, small groups come together, disband and reform in different configurations. There is no clear membership and few stable organisations. There is no agreed vision of the future, but people in this movement share a disquiet about the present. They share a pleasure in per-

formance. They enjoy making people think through their perfor-
mance-action. And they dislike injustice.

We need to recognise that some social movements display the
characteristics of more than one category. In 1995 the French
Government rejigged its laws relating to immigration and as a
result of some of the changes a considerable number people from
former French colonies who had lived in France for years found
themselves abruptly without a legal right to be there. A movement quickly developed called *Les Sans Papiers* (People Without
Papers). Some members were ready to come forward, openly
admitting that they were now illegally in the country. These people quickly set up an organisation with a headquarters, 'office
bearers' and a support system for people thrown into unemployment and off any welfare system. They campaigned, spoke to the
media, and even made a film putting their case. In many respects
this part of the movement had the characteristics of a structured
social movement. Under pressure some people without papers
took direct action. In 1996 a number who were being threatened
with deportation sought refuge in a church in Paris. Some went
on a hunger strike. Around this action a range of groups associated with churches, political organisations and community groups
gathered offering support in the form of financial assistance,
demonstrations, and vigils and picketing outside the church. The
gathering of people around the occupation of the church had
many of the characteristics of a semi-structured social movement. And in the background were the people without papers
who had not come forward publicly. Some surfaced briefly to
make use of the support systems including a hostel and child care
centre that had been established in Paris. Leaders of the movement made links through immigrant communities. Others made
contact as individuals and still others were simply known to be
there. People without papers were united by a fear and a sense of
injustice. Their supporters in the mainstream French community
were drawn into solidarity with them through a sense of outrage.
A shifting and widespread association of people had developed
with some of the characteristics of an unstructured social movement.

We might be tempted for a moment to think that the forms I
have described are simply stages; that an unstructured movement
is a semi-structured movement in embryo and that it will even-

tually develop through a semi-structured stage into a structured movement. But those performance activists show no sign of abandoning their thoroughly anarchic organisational patterns, nor of developing any coherent and generally accepted visions of the future. Their real satisfaction appears to remain in the moment of performance. And while parts of the environmental movement may take on structured forms, many other parts remain vigorously resistant to anything but the most local of organisational structures. Indeed, we could argue that environmentalists have succeeded in bringing environmental issues to the fore precisely because they have remained a dispersed, semi-structured social movement: a large number of activists and activist organisations, some in touch with others, some not, constantly demonstrating and taking action at thousands of sites in relation to thousands of issues around the world.

This division of social movements into three categories is offered as a working analysis for adult educators trying to understand how we might offer our help to groups of people engaged in struggle. A movement that has the characteristics of a structured social movement will have officers we can talk to. There will be reasonably clear goals we can help people work towards. It will have a structure within which we may be able to locate reasonably formal education and training programs. It will have a history, rituals and traditions we can relate our learning to and upon which we may be able to build. And we will be able to establish the movement's educational requirements, negotiate the form of the educational program, and draw the actual learners from a defined and accessible membership.

A semi-structured social movement will present different challenges. There will be a membership with which to work but establishing meaningful or representative contact may be more difficult. We may have to spend more time getting a feel for the ways the network operates, locating the effective congregations of influence and power, and understanding the struggle or struggles people are involved in. There will be literature, various histories and reasonably recognised authorities we can refer to, but the goals may not be clear. There may be occasions when we can help conduct formal education and training programs but we will also be able to help by offering educational activities much closer to the action in the form of workshops, discussion groups, and structured exercises directly related to events in the struggle.

For an unstructured social movement the challenges will be different again. There will be a much less stable constituency with whom to relate, and no clear goals around which to construct any comprehensive program of learning. Our role is more likely to be that of adviser, facilitator of moments of reflection, provider of ad hoc learning events to groups of people who gather at various and disparate events, and in moments of shared feeling. Or we may simply create learning programs on our own initiative, offering these as yet another facet of the many other disconnected facets we believe provide evidence that the movement is there.

Roles

My second way of examining and understanding social movements is to identify the different kinds of role people perform in them. Lotz and Welton (1987) talk of the three typical leaders of a social movement: the prophet (the visionary), the messiah (the charismatic leader) and the organiser (the administrator). I will add some more, and suggest that most social movements will have some from among the following: visionaries, charismatic figures, administrators, activists, artists, communicators, educators, as well, of course, as a constituency of people. These roles will be most obvious in structured social movements, but some will be recognisable in semi-structured social movements, and a number may be there in the unstructured forms, although perhaps they will not be so immediately recognisable and may not actually be located in a single person or even a group of people.

One of the clearest examples of a movement comprising people in a number of these different roles is to be found in the accounts which I alluded to earlier by Lotz and Welton (1987, 1997) of the Antigonish movement in the 1930s in Nova Scotia, Canada. Two remarkable men, both Catholic priests, were responsible for the initiation of the movement. One, Father Jimmy Tompkins, was a small wiry man, by all accounts forever given to challenging, needling and questioning. He fell into disfavour with the church authorities and in 1922 was sent away to an impoverished fishing community at Canso. People were poor, undernourished and dispirited. The fishing folk had some control over production but no control over the distribution of their produce and so were slaves to government authorities and the middlemen. Tompkins was moved by the injustice and poverty and angered by the ignorance that often went with it, and over the next few years he 'talked to individuals, badgered and upset them, [and] prodded them towards action' (Lotz and Welton, 1997: 91-92). He met with groups of fisherfolk in country stores and on the docks, organised public meetings, set up a reading room in his own house, brought experts into the area to offer advice, wrote to authorities, published articles, distributed leaflets, pamphlets and books, and organised literacy classes and study groups. He would, in a description quoted by Lotz and Welton, 'scurry around all day, minding everyone's business at the top of his voice' (1997: 68). He won the support of the communities he worked with and his tireless activism played a major part in getting a government commission into the plight of the area set up, and in establishing an educational movement aimed at providing people with the knowledge and skills to take control of their own economic lives.

Tompkins was the visionary of the Antigonish movement and he groomed his cousin, Father Moses Coady, to be the leader. With Tompkins' encouragement Coady involved himself in adult education, and in 1929 was appointed Director of the Extension Studies Department of St Frances Xavier College in Antigonish. From there Coady and others would go out to fishing communities and farming communities, call a public meeting and urge people to engage in collective learning and action. Coady was a large man, and slow to start when he spoke. He would stumble over his words, search for phrases, and punch the air with his large hands, but gradually he would find a fluency, the ideas would come and the words would flow, until he held the audience in his thrall (Crane, 1987). Coady was the charismatic figure. Once a community was inspired, a range of educational activities was put in place. These included kitchen discussion groups, study circles, radio discussion groups, and leadership schools and workshops at St Francis Xavier College. Along with the learning went action, and these communities would be encouraged to establish cooperatives and credit unions and so take control of the distribution of production and the income from those cooperatives. Tompkins and Coady approached a public servant with experience in rural matters called Angus MacDonald, persuaded him to give up a secure public sector post and join them at St Francis Xavier. MacDonald became the administrator. These three men could not have maintained the momentum without the help of many others who organised events at a local level and kept projects ticking over. Many of these were nuns, clerics and lay people of the Catholic and other churches. These formed the cadre of activists. And of course the movement could not have happened without the fishing and farming communities who took up the challenge and set about taking control of their own lives. They were the constituency.

Three other roles are commonly played out in social movements. There are people who celebrate the activities of a social movement through poetry, storytelling, song, drama and dance, the crafting of banners, drawing and painting, photography, video, and images, stories and discussion on the net. Or by painting a mural. These are the artists. Social movements have people who take on the role of promoting the message of the movement to the larger public. These are the communicators. And social movements can have people who help members of the movement develop their knowledge and skills, clarify and develop their ideas, and reflect on and learn from their experience. These are the educators. Of course two or more roles might be performed by one person, and we could argue that in the Antigonish movement Coady played the role of charismatic leader within the movement and communicator to the world outside it. It is a little strange to talk about a single educator within a social movement which itself was devoted to education, but if we look for the person who performed the role of helping others within the Antigonish movement develop their skills and clarify their thinking, then in the early days this would have been Tompkins. And many of the people within the movement who told their stories at meetings and discussions and study groups, and who shared their hopes and disappointments and joys in newspaper articles, letters and leaflets, were the artists.

Once we have identified the roles people play in social movements, adult educators can offer programs of education and training that are analogous to human resource development programs in a corporation. Just as the training officer in a corporation helps people learn their roles in order to make an organisation function more efficiently, so an adult educator can help people within a social movement refine and extend their roles in ways that will make the movement more likely to pursue its interests or achieve its goals effectively. The goal of the corporation may be profit, while the goals of the social movement may be social change and social justice, but some of the actual training—in organisation, communication with the public, and ways of arriving at decisions, for example—may have similarities.

If the analogy with human resource development has a coldly pragmatic feel to it, then we should also remember that a social movement has a constituency, and that adult educators can offer programs of formal and informal educational activities aimed at motivating members and potential members of a social movement to take up the cause. This kind of education for participation and mobilisation will include organising debates, seminars and workshops, holding meetings, discussions and conversations, and broadcasting information and ideas through the print and electronic media. In the way Jimmy Tomkins did, it will involve continually challenging ourselves and others to think, and to act.

Phases

A third way of analysing social movements is to look at the phases through which they pass. Lotz and Welton suggest that social movements often follow 'a well-defined course, from initial agitation to eventual institutionalisation, eradication or transformation' (1987, p. 78). I believe we can take these ideas and expand them into the following phases: initial agitation, consolidation, institutionalisation, bureaucratisation, and then either eradication or transformation.

I have presented these phases to groups of unionists in a number of training sessions. I ask them what they know about the beginnings of the movement in Australia, and what they imagine the first steps towards forming their union might have been. We talk about the period of initial agitation: the growth of resentment at injustice in the workplace, spontaneous outbreaks of action, the resistance by the bosses, struggle, excitement, uncertainty, mistakes, suffering and violence. We talk of the period of consolidation: how people need to build on victories and to regroup after defeats, and how in this process a sense of solidarity develops and a union is formed. We look at the processes of institutionalisation: how a union becomes established as both a legal and organisational entity with a constitution and formal membership rules; how people are elected and appointed; and how policies are formulated. We discuss the ways in which customs and traditions come about and a particular union culture is generated.

Donald Schon (1971) argues that once an organisation is established the people within it can spend more and more of their energies maintaining the infrastructure and plant of the organisation and less and less time on the original purposes of the organisation. They become particularly inventive and energetic in resisting change (or staying the same). He calls this 'dynamic conservatism'. I ask the group whether their own unions are displaying signs of this phenomenon. This normally leads into a discussion of the dangers of bureaucratisation. We look at the options for movements that have reached this stage: eradication or transformation. This point in the session usually involves a detailed discussion of the forces—employer groups, lobby groups, sections of the government, sections of the mass media—at work against unions, and I end by asking the group to consider the kinds of action their unions could take, both to oppose these forces bent on their eradication, and to enter into a phase of renewal. With the Organising Works group I have presented the phases and argued that their project is part of a concerted effort by the peak union body at encouraging renewal and transformation.

Social movements are sites of struggle and the learning done and the knowledge generated will be put to the test by people engaged in struggle. The challenge for the adult educator is to provide learning that is really relevant and facilitate the generation of knowledge that is really useful. But, as both Horton and Mandela knew, social movements can also be sites of violence, and the adult educator may be helping people make crucial choices. In this case the learning must not only be really relevant and the generation of knowledge really useful. Both will have to be really *good*.

14: Complicity, alliances and solidarity

There can be cooperation between social movements. I was at a 'hoe-down' in a wild west theme bar in Eugene, Oregon, USA on a Sunday evening. A number of organisations had banded together to eat, sing and line-dance together in order to raise money for Project Care, which trained volunteers in crisis and personal advocacy work. The friends who had taken me along described the organisations as 'social justice groups' and as far as I could make out they were an eclectic mob. There were people from neighbourhood groups, community activist groups, trade unions and churches. Some of the churches, as I understood it, had radically different dogma. It was a gathering of groups, an organised manifestation of civil society, that we would find much less common in Australia, and it marked out a feature of the USA political scene that, until then, I had not really understood.

As Noam Chomsky (1992) points out, the two major political parties in the USA are both parties of big business. To get involved at any kind of senior level obviously involves being wealthy or having extremely wealthy interests behind you. Voting in the USA is not compulsory, so even the President can be elected by a minority of the voting-age population. These factors led me to think that relatively few people in the USA actively involved themselves in politics, even at the most basic level of casting their votes. However, on my visits to the USA I have come to understand that there is another, local level of political and community action, made up of an extraordinarily diverse number of groups dynamically engaged in organising, fundraising, campaigning, protesting, and providing services aimed at creating a more humane and equitable society. Perhaps having despaired of affecting national politics, these groups are ready to liaise with each other across sometimes considerable ideological divides in energetic pursuit of local social justice.

There can be cross-membership between social movements. My hosts in Eugene who took me to the hoe-down were Beth and Steven Deutsch. Beth is active in local economic and racial justice projects and in the Quakers. Steven is a recently retired university lecturer ('professor' as they call them there), active in the Quakers, and a committed trade unionist with widespread contacts with unions in other countries. Both are active campaigners for peace. 'Peacemaking,' Steven told me, 'not passive-ism.'

And members of one movement can provide services for, or help out, other movements. Back in Australia that artist who placed sculpted pigeons on statues around Sydney, and the director of the forum theatre at Glebe Youth Centre were contacted by a group organising a political demonstration and asked to construct giant wire-and-papier-maché heads of certain politicians, and to provide stilt walkers to wear them. They were contacted because the artist was known for his ability as a caricaturist, and the director was known for his performance and circus skills. Since they were sympathetic to the issues, they agreed to help. Although they received no money, in effect they 'contracted' their services out, rather in the manner of consultants in the corporate world.

Adult educators can help these kinds of encounter between social movements happen, and help ourselves and the members of social movements we work with learn from these encounters. To do this we need not only to understand the different kinds of social movement that can exist, the phases they move through, and the roles people play within them, but the different kinds of liaison that can occur or be brokered between them. As a way of doing this I want to look at moments of complicity, at formally negotiated alliances, and at the development of solidarities.

Complicity

Perhaps, in that factory canteen in Johannesburg in the middle of a clothing trades strike, when that shop steward and I exchanged amused glances, we were partners in complicity. Perhaps for just an instant we were close to being subjects together in an identical experience. If it is not a contradiction in terms, complicity is a *moment* of solidarity. The closeness is brief, perhaps transitory. The communion may be unplanned, unspoken perhaps, and even covert, but it can nonetheless be intense.

A number of years ago in Kent in the UK, through a series of misunderstandings, some misinformation, and my own naivety I found myself, a male, chairing an address to some sixty adult education tutors entitled 'Women in Adult Education'. The speaker, a woman, quickly raised the issue of my position and I spent a moment or two trying to step down, being urged to stay in the chair, and then having to chair a discussion on why I was still there. It was one of those moments. Somehow we agreed to proceed, and the afternoon passed reasonably well until towards the end when a woman in the audience raised an issue which was off the point yet on which I knew the speaker had very strong and opposing views. The speaker glanced at me and the message was clear. She acknowledged the comment, spoke for just a moment and then I chipped in. The speaker and I shared thoughts on the issue for another moment or two and then I brought the meeting to a close.

Complicity clearly requires some kind of affinity and commonality. The shop steward in Johannesburg and I were very different in many respects yet we were both unionists. The speaker at that address on 'Women in Adult Education' had chosen to highlight the inappropriateness of my presence in the chair, yet we shared a commitment to the profession of adult education that saw us working together to prevent a meeting of adult educators ending on a counter-productive and acrimonious note. We can see acts of complicity between people in political or industrial contexts where the ideological differences may be huge but where both sides are interested in maintaining the structure which enables them to express their differences. People who dislike this kind of complicity between union and employer advocates in the Australian Industrial Relations Commission, for example, refer disparagingly to 'the industrial relations club'.

Complicity is difficult to plan for or promote. My hope in putting those Organising Works participants into a variety of different groups was to provide the shared experience upon which, even years later and across all sorts of political and industrial divides, such kinds of unspoken momentary agreements might be constructed.

But those participants in the Organising Works program were unionists together. Preparing people for moments of complicity across the boundaries of different social movements will be more

135

difficult. Here in all likelihood we will be working with members of only one of the potential parties to the complicity, and all we can hope is to make them aware of the phenomenon and help them learn how to be vigilant for such moments. Here we will help people learn to listen, not in the formula fashion often described as 'active listening', but in a full and complete sense by giving over all their attention to the other person, to what the other person is saying and not saying, to the other person's gestures, to the other person's choice of words and mode of speaking, to the other person's mood, feelings, views, assumptions, values and ideologies. We will encourage people to be alert for the moment when the other person has met the validity claims Habermas describes as necessary for communicative action. We will encourage people to be alert for the moment when by a glance or a smile or a gesture or a word, others invite us, or we invite them, to be subjects together in a moment of social action. It is a glance or a smile that says, with all the force a moment of complicity can have: 'You and I are in this together.'

Alliance

Alliances are very different from acts of complicity. Alliances are formal agreements between two or more parties to cooperate or, at the very least, not to work against each other. They are pragmatic affairs. They are deals. They are struck to promote the self-interests of both parties and for this reason they are impermanent. As soon as an alliance does not meet the interests of one of the parties, that party will withdraw and the alliance is broken.

Successful alliances are formed when the potential parties to an alliance examine their conflicting and common interests. Where common interests in general outweigh conflicting ones, the members of the two organisations or movements may be able to enter into a reasonably open-ended and wide ranging alliance. Where there is a single but strong point of common interest, then an alliance may be formed but it will be for a limited time in order to achieve a clearly defined objective. Of course where the conflicting interests completely outweigh any common ones, then no alliance is possible. We can see this play of common and conflicting interests behind the fairly permanent alliances of certain churches over social justice issues and their separate stances over matters of doctrine. We can see it behind the very close

136

alliance over a considerable number of months in the nineteen seventies of a middle class group of residents and the very left wing Builders Labourers Federation in order to save an area of bushland called Kelly's bush from development in the Sydney suburb of Hunters Hill. And we can see it behind the very focussed and limited alliances of a number of groups—small left wing political groups, human rights groups, peace activists, environmentalists, some members of the French community in Australia, some members of the Pacific Islander communities in Australia, some mainstream political parties—in the protests against France's nuclear testing in the Pacific in 1995.

Alliances can be formed between people with very different causes. Paddington market in Sydney operates around a church and in an adjoining schoolyard on Saturdays. The stalls sell a mixture of clothing, artwork and craftwork. There are street entertainers, tarot card readers, and palm readers. Massages and vegetarian food are for sale in the church hall. On the opposite side of Oxford Street from the market are fashionable clothing boutiques. Nearby are the Sydney Sports Stadium and the Sydney Cricket ground where major, often international, sporting events take place. Amidst those trendy boutiques and directly opposite the church is a pub with a long association with the Irish working class past of the suburb. And a kilometre or so back down Oxford Street is the centre of Sydney's gay community. All these features mean that a diversity of people is drawn to the market.

An environmental activist was standing on Oxford Street next to the market handing out leaflets putting the anti-woodchipping case. He expected the genial approval from the people who looked a little like throwbacks to the nineteen sixties, and disinterest from the boutique goers, but had not anticipated the hostility from three timberworkers from the South Coast who were up in Sydney for a football match. One of the timberworkers wanted to hit the environmentalist, and his two mates had to restrain him. There followed an abusive, then a tense, then a more measured discussion between the four of them. All three timberworkers were self-employed contractors and the one who had wanted to hit the environmentalist had mortgaged himself to the hilt in order to buy one of those massive trucks that haul old growth logs out of the forests. He did not think much of the environmentalists' efforts to kill off the timber industry, destroy his livelihood

137

and ruin him financially. The environmentalist stood his ground, putting his case and asking questions. Gradually it transpired that there were areas of common interest. Both sides wanted to create jobs. 'Not all greenies,' the environmentalist said, 'are against employment.' Both sides loved forests. 'We live in the bloody things,' one of the timberworkers said. 'We don't want to destroy them. We want to use them.' And both sides were against the large, impersonal, transnational companies that controlled the major part of the timber industry: the environmentalist for what he saw as a rapacious disregard for the environment, the timberworkers for what they saw as the restriction and exploitation of small operators like themselves. The discussion ended in a gruff exchange of handshakes.

While no alliances were formed during the discussion, it demonstrated that common interests can be established across considerable divides. Perhaps the breakthrough came when both sides realised the other did not come from a structured movement with a single viewpoint, but from a semi-structured movement comprising a variety of sub groupings and a variety of viewpoints. And perhaps the handshake was made possible when both sides realised that in the multinationals they had a common enemy.

There is a role for adult educators in brokering alliances between groupings of activists. We can set up teaching and learning events to bring the members of different social movements together in order to identify and analyse their particular interests, and to develop strategies for working together to achieve those interests they hold in common. As I have written elsewhere (1994), this learning will be intense since it will almost inevitably involve helping ourselves and others identify and define our common enemies.

Solidarity

In its turn solidarity is very different from an alliance. Earlier I described complicity as 'a moment of solidarity'. I worried about the phrase being a contradiction in terms, because a major feature of solidarity is its permanence. When we enter into solidarity with others, we enter into a relationship based on a commitment to a common cause. This commitment puts us in a very special relationship with the others and results, even if we do not know them well, in a bond akin to loyalty. So, when we talk of a group of people being 'solid', we mean that they will not give up on the cause they espouse and they will not give up on each other. Like partners to a complicity, they are in it together, but this time they are in it for the duration.

Solidarity has some similarities to an alliance in that people who have entered into solidarity with one another have common interests and common enemies. But their agreement to work with one another has extended beyond the pragmatic or the self-interested. It has become a commitment and cannot be easily broken. Indeed, such is the personal and emotional investment in the common pursuit of a cause that the weakening or withdrawal of anyone is simply not envisaged. Even if events conspire to work against the interests of those involved, or put some people at risk, people in true solidarity remain loyal to one another. It is this loyalty in the face of adversity that explains the attitude of strikers to strike-breakers. They will be certainly very angry at the betrayal, but the major emotion is one of contempt, since for them a strike-breaker is morally deficient.

When I was in South Africa I was told of an extraordinary, and moving, demonstration of solidarity across class and race. It involved people from the black townships and white women from a movement called 'the Black Sash'. Again the events occurred during the apartheid era.

The Black Sash was formed at a tea party in a private suburban house in the nineteen-fifties. (It was clearly not of the kind of tea party Turner scathingly referred to in *The Eye of the Needle*.) The white women present expressed dismay at how the newly established policy of apartheid undermined their country's constitution and denied basic human rights to black people. To indicate their dismay, these women decided to protest, wearing black sashes slung over one shoulder and across their bodies. Their numbers grew and the Black Sash remained active throughout the period of apartheid. The main form of protest used by the Black Sash women was to stand in line in silence, heads bowed, outside parliament house, outside courts, at airports and other points where government leaders might be coming and going. The women were often partners of men in high government and corporate positions, and their silent vigils, wearing the black sash, caused these men severe embarrassment. Sometimes they would join in a vigil with black women. Sometimes, invited to official functions as the spouses of senior government and corporate figures, they would stow their sashes in their handbags, and on arrival, don the sashes and stand vigil. When the government banned all outdoor meetings, the Black Sash women demonstrated singly, silent figures standing at street corners or in a lobby or outside a government building. The movement used silent witness as its main form of public action, but also developed advice and advocacy services and a lobbying function. The Black Sash had been formed as a protest organisation and at an annual general meeting after the end of the apartheid government it was argued that the reason for the organisation's existence had ceased and a decision was taken to disband. The advice offices, now run by a trust, continue in eight different regions of South Africa.

In the nineteen seventies and eighties most forms of political action by black people were proscribed, and funerals in the black townships became occasions not just to mourn the dead or the murdered, but to engage in political protest. At large funerals the security forces would be present and, on request from the United Democratic Front or other organisations in the black townships, members of the Black Sash would attend, a handful of white women amongst thousands of black mourners.

Jillian Nicholson had been a member of the Black Sash and talked to me about these events in that matter of fact way that activists from the apartheid days in South Africa seem to have:

> We were invited because we were white and we were less likely to be shot at... They were political gatherings and the police would try to break them up—often brutally. The media were not always around. We did not always stop the violence but we were witnesses to it... The frightening part was the number of police—who were the instigators of the violence... so there was a sense all the time that something was going to happen... Quite often the magistrate banned the funerals. They would go on anyway and then it was really scary... It was a very tense and very emotional situation... In KwaMarshu, in the stadium the police could just surround you round the top, and it made people very militant and very angry... We did not play a part in the funeral itself. It was often all in Zulu... We were just there. We had black sashes on...
>
> Another time a particular township called Lamontville appeared to be terrorised by gangs who people thought were police-led

140

gangs. People were being shot up in the night and they asked us to go in there and hold vigils through the night, which we also did... It somehow connected us more with the women than the funerals did. It was often the women who were there. A lot of the men were actually living in the bush and were coming into their homes to have food in the day and then leaving again.

Jillian fell silent, but nodded when I said of the gangs:

So they were just assassination squads.

15: Lifeworld, civil society and the system

Solidarity cannot be constructed in the reasonably straightforward way an alliance can. Certainly those involved will need to have similar philosophies and ideologies, and these can be examined and discussed, and differences clarified and perhaps removed. Almost certainly, those in solidarity with one another will have common enemies. But solidarity is based on trust and in the normal course of events people need to spend time together for trust to develop. In this respect, alliances do not automatically lead to solidarities, but they may contribute by providing the time and occasion for potential solidarities to grow. And in this respect too, the adult educator may have an opportunity to provide some of those times and occasions for potential solidarities to grow.

When I can, I run a straightforward exercise. I used it to close an address at a conference of community workers, youth workers and adult educators in Sydney. I had talked about alliances and solidarities. These are the instructions I read out. The period I allowed for people to sit in silence alongside each other was somewhere between four and five minutes.

> Turn to the person next to you. If you are here, you are interested in social justice. Can you confirm this in a brief conversation?...
> Now can I ask you to be silent? Be completely silent, thoroughly present, and in the company of the person you have just spoken to.

If nothing else, the exercise broke the pattern of the formal plenary address by having an auditorium full of people sit motionless and silent for several minutes. But of course I wanted it to achieve more than that. The conference was about breaking down the barriers between people engaged in youth work, community work and adult education. I wanted people to articulate a conviction they shared and through a brief but intense experience establish a relationship. My hope was that some at least would take the experience on into the rest of the conference, and perhaps back into their activist lives; that they would continue to explore their shared values with these other people and consolidate the relationships into potential complicities, alliances and even solidarities.

This kind of exercise can have the *appearance* of great effect. The silence can become complete, so that in a space occupied by a large number of people you can hear the proverbial pin drop. With the silence comes a motionlessness. The moment, five minutes at the most, becomes a lacuna in the constant activity of our daily lives. And when released from the silence, people do turn to the person they were with, and they talk. Despite the apparent isolation the exercise puts upon them, they were together. Or if they were not, they are now, sharing their reactions to what can be an intense, and uncommon, experience.

If I go looking beyond the appearance of this exercise for some theoretical underpinnings, then I find some help in the concepts of 'the lifeworld', 'civil society' and 'the system'.

The lifeworld
The lifeworld is a concept that has been developed within the literature on critical theory. Habermas (1984, 1987, 1990) makes use of it and adult educators drawing on critical theory (Collins, 1991, 1995; Welton, 1995) have taken it into their thinking about the purpose of education. The lifeworld denotes those myriad shared understandings upon which we construct our lives and upon which we base our interactions with others. It is made up of those convictions, assumptions and presuppositions which we take for granted and which, for the most part, we do not even consciously consider in the course of our daily lives. Habermas uses a number of images to help in his explanation of the lifeworld. Here he uses the images of horizon and background:

> Subjects acting communicatively always come to an understanding in the horizon of a lifeworld. Their lifeworld is formed from more or less diffuse, always unproblematic background convictions. This lifeworld serves as a source of situation definitions that are presupposed by participants as unproblematic (1984: 70).

In a sense the lifeworld is made up of all those definitions that we do *not* need to clarify at the outset of any communication, since they are there and accepted without question by everyone involved.

Habermas also makes use of the image of a web:

> The lifeworld is the intuitively present, in this sense familiar and transparent, and at the same time vast and incalculable web of presuppositions that have to be satisfied if an actual utterance is to be meaningful, that is valid or invalid (1987: 131).

We make meaning of events, we judge people's actions and utterances, according to an incalculable number of givens. It is the lifeworld that provides the basis upon which we can establish understanding, and upon which we will assess the validity claims that underwrite ours and others' utterances.

When we act on our world, we take a segment of our lifeworld, bring it into the foreground, and consciously examine it. This segment ceases to be taken for granted, and is now a problem to be addressed. The rest of the lifeworld, however, remains unquestioned, continuing to provide the frameworks within which we think and the background against which we act. In this moment, therefore, we are both an *initiator*, in that we are taking action on some tiny segment of our lifeworld, and a *product* of the traditions and socialisation that constitute the vast remainder of that lifeworld.

The actor, Habermas says:

> ...is carried or supported from behind, as it were, by a lifeworld that not only forms the *context* for the process of reaching understanding but also furnishes *resources* for it (1990: 135).

These resources furnished by the lifeworld are of two kinds: the traditions and 'ingrained cultural background assumptions' upon which we can build communication; and the 'solidarity of groups integrated through values and the competences of socialised individuals' which we can make use of in order to take action. In making meaning and managing our lives, therefore, we draw upon countless givens, and the connections, relationships and capacities that come with those givens.

So my exercise could be seen as an attempt briefly to foreground the assumptions surrounding social justice that formed part of the lifeworld context of everyone present at the conference, and to help contribute to their lifeworld resources by encouraging or reinforcing solidarities.

As Habermas depicts it, even when we do make the critical effort to foreground segments of the lifeworld, the vast remainder goes unchallenged. This emphasis on the pervasiveness, the vastness and the incalculable nature of the lifeworld can be discouraging. It can have the effect of implying that we can do little; that we are unable in any but the most limited way to change how we and others think, feel and act. But such pessimism is at variance with the theories of educators such as Mezirow, who envisages changes in learners so complete that he uses the word 'transformation', or Freire, who envisages shifts in consciousness of whole groups of people and even of entire populations.

Such pessimism is also at variance with practice. When two major building sites were established close to each other in western Sydney, managements and unions established a jointly sponsored training centre nearby. The centre provided industrial and occupational health and safety training for workers already on site, and an introductory course on basic construction site skills for people who were long-term unemployed. Chris Harvey, the program coordinator, took a particular interest in the course for the long-term unemployed, and would use his influence with employers on the two sites to find work for anyone who had successfully completed it.

One particular intake of this course proved troublesome. The trainers reported to Chris that the fifteen participants would not settle down. A number appeared not to take the training seriously and some were openly uncooperative and even hostile. The trainers were losing patience. Chris suggested that the trainers give him some time alone with the group.

Chris opened the encounter by asking the group: 'How much do you think they earn on site?'

'Between four hundred and five hundred a week.'

'No. Anything up to fifteen hundred.'

Chris paused, then went on: 'Of course you don't stay on site for too long if you do drugs or drink alcohol. What do you reckon happens if you get caught stealing something?'

'You get thrown off the site?'

'No. You get your fingers broken.'

Chris paused again, and then said: 'I'll give you five minutes to think about all this. When I come back I want us to enter into a contract and the contract is that we are all going to take care of the trainers.' He looked around the training room and added: 'If you do not want to stay, I've got my car outside and I'll run you over to the train station now.'

The contract was duly agreed, the course continued with all present and learning hard, and at its completion Chris managed to place everyone who wanted work on the sites. Through a combination of promise and menace, by outlining a moral code, by handing responsibility to each individual and to the group as a whole, by imposing a duty of care, by applying pressure yet offering escape, Chris helped people in that group review and radically alter some of the assumptions upon which they constructed their lives and upon which they managed their relationships with others. It may only have been a segment of their lifeworld that changed, but it was a significant segment.

Civil Society

The lifeworld as background can be a difficult, abstract concept. 'Civil society', on the other hand, denotes a whole host of actual agencies, organisations and groups with which the adult educator can engage. The concept of civil society is not new but the term has resurfaced and been redefined in the past ten years or so and is now used to describe that pattern of relationships and groupings we enter into as we seek to manage and fulfil our lives. Jodi Dean argues that in its current meaning 'civil society... refers to the institutionalized components of the lifeworld' which 'preserve and renew cultural traditions, group solidarities, and individual and social identities' (1996: 220- 221). Cox, writing in an Australian context, describes civil society in terms of 'the familiar community groups' and lists these as 'non profit organisations such as P&Cs, local environment groups, Rotary, craft groups, neighbourhood centres, local sporting groups, some ethnic and religious groups, reading groups, fund raising organisations, playgroups and others which have an egalitarian voluntary structure' (1995: 18).

Civil society is constructed on trust. People join community and activist organisations—be they a car pool, a local choir, or the Parents and Citizens Association—because they want to and

146

because they are ready to cooperate with others on projects and activities that will protect or improve the quality of theirs and others everyday lives. Cox (1995: 15-17) describes four kinds of capital: financial capital, physical capital (in the form of the environment), human capital (in the form of people's skills and knowledge), and social capital (in the form of trust). She argues that with the first three forms of capital, there are times when spending it leads to a depletion of its stocks, but that in the case of social capital, the more we use it—that is the more we engage in encounters and groupings based on trust—the more we amass it. By accumulating social capital in this way we construct what she calls 'a *truly* civil society'.

Drawing on these ideas, then, I could argue that by asking a lecture-theatre full of people to share in a period of silence, I was asking them to engage in a moment of trust, and that by doing this we would together add to the social capital of the conference and the civil society of which the conference participants were a part.

While I was in South Africa I witnessed a wonderful instance of people going about constructing a civil society out of what for forty years had been a truly *uncivil* society. I had spent a day in Sharpeville with Shele Papane, Education Secretary for COSATU. He had introduced me to a number of people active in the unions or local politics during the day and there were five of us in the car when we drove back into Johannesburg that evening. We stopped off at a jazz club for a drink and to hear the first bracket of the evening by the South African Jazz Pioneers. I had a bad cold and had made noises about wanting to get a reasonably early night. As it was, we stayed the full evening (although Papane tells me I fell asleep on at least one occasion) and my companions delivered me back to my hotel in the early hours of the morning.

When we arrived at the club there were only a few people there. We occupied a table and talked and drank beer. Gradually people arrived, mostly in couples or small groups. There seemed, apart from my table, to be very few racially mixed couples or groups, but by the time the band assembled on the small stage a reasonable crowd, made up of marginally more black people than white, had assembled.

The South African Jazz Pioneers were a band of seven or eight pieces, made up of guitar, piano, drums and brass. The influences were eclectic: swing, traditional jazz, pop, modern chamber jazz, and black South African. The lead singer was a rake-like man, dressed in a dark, conventional suit. He looked so fragile that I wondered whether he would last the first song, let alone the whole evening, but he sang, switching from Zulu to English, with a subdued but unflagging energy.

The first bracket was long, musically complex, and very good. People drank quietly and listened. One person, a black woman, danced. She got up from a table a couple of songs into the bracket and moved close to the band and then danced by herself, unselfconsciously, smiling from time to time at members of the band or at her friends. During a fast final number some of the crowd cheered her on, and she got a round of applause as she went back to her table and sat down.

The beer and the quality of the music made me forget my cold, and I and my companions stayed on. The room became noisier, and considerably more people had arrived by the time the band took up their positions for the second and final bracket of the evening. This time the music was tougher, the phrasing more marked, and more of the numbers carried the rhythms and harmonies of music from the townships. The sole dancer from the first bracket was on her feet again, but this time there were others as well, in particular a white woman. She danced alongside the black woman for a while, and then began inviting others to get up and dance. The black woman joined her and together they moved from table to table, pulling people to their feet. Tshidi Mzizi and Nkapu Ranake, the two women at my table, were moving to the music and suddenly they jumped up and dragged a white woman at the next table, shy and demure-looking, to her feet. They were quickly followed by Papane and Mswazi Tsabalala, our other companion. Others jumped up, blacks dragging whites to their feet, whites dragging blacks. For a while it seemed that women invited women to dance and men simply followed the women from their table, but after a while this slight reserve broke down and men invited women and women men until everyone in the club was dancing. As an outsider I cannot be sure how spontaneous or calculated the actions of those two women who set the whole process going were, but the evening now had an exhilaration about it that was more than one gets when simply drinking and dancing to excellent music. As far as I could see everyone had become involved in some kind of conscious-unconscious celebration of the new normality, and was engaged in a profligate expenditure of trust.

Civil society is made up of groupings—the car pool, the choir—which, in the course of their everyday activities and existence, accumulate social capital. In this respect 'familiar' adult education—that is, all those non-credit courses in community adult education centres, adult learning centres, neighbourhood houses, community colleges, and other local organisations—play their part in contributing to the wellbeing and humanity of a society. Familiar adult education is a largely unsung part of our community lives. It is simply and, for the most part, unobtrusively there. Visit a town in the central west of New South Wales, some three hundred kilometres inland from the coast and there will be a small community adult education centre managed by a voluntary management committee, or a branch of a Community College, running a program of courses in arts and crafts, perhaps a language or two, a keep fit class, a yoga class, a landcare group, and perhaps an Aboriginal Reconciliation discussion group. Walk into a church hall in an inner suburb of Sydney and you will encounter 'an osteoporosis clinic' provided free of charge by a local hospital. Over a period of eight weeks two leaders and a group of some ten or so women meet weekly for an hour's theory on the management of osteoporosis and then an hour's dancing and exercise. In the 'dancing' section there is a lot of laughter, a joyfulness. Travel south down the coast road from Sydney and in a number of the towns you will find centres running courses in subjects such as computer skills, sailing, drawing and Indonesian for beginners. And walk into the building owned by the Workers' Educational Association in the centre of Sydney, and you will have a choice from over three hundred courses offered during the day and in the evening in creative writing, photography, literature, history, painting, art history, psychology, sociology, politics, current affairs, computer studies and a range of languages. This pattern is replicated in other Australian states and in many parts of the world. I suppose it is no surprise that in Britain in the nineteen eighties, under the prime ministership of the conviction politician Margaret Thatcher, who in a celebrated statement denied the existence of such a thing as society, government support for this form of adult education was severely curtailed.

Cox develops a multi-faceted concept of civil society. She draws on the ideas of American political scientist Robert Putnam (1993, 1995) who depicts a civil society made up of civic organisations. To this she adds 'the household and informal sectors which can also create social trust relationships and forms of civic wellbeing' (Cox, 1995: 21). And she extends the idea of civil society into the workplace, citing some workplace cultures that 'model open and relatively egalitarian relationships' (1995: 22).

This concept of civil society is an attractive one, but there are also some weaknesses in it. For a start it is utopian. Car pools and choirs are not necessarily conducted in social harmony; more formal civic organisations can come apart at the seams; and workplaces, while the financial control rests with management and the shareholders, can only mimic egalitarian cultures, and can only do this in the good times. The problem is that even in our everyday, local lives people can be self-absorbed, bloody-minded, and behave in ways that do not engender trust. For all our efforts we will always be objects to others' subjects, we will always live in separate 'universes', and so we will (almost) always communicate imperfectly.

A second weakness is that this trusting, essentially gentle form of civil society can only exist if the other forces that control our lives are gentle too. A civil society constructed on trust presupposes civilised state authorities that can be trusted in their turn. Even in established democracies, the impersonal nature of bureaucracies, the complexities of administrative processes and the self-interest of some duly elected political leaders make this presupposition an uncertain one.

A third weakness is that civil society comprising school fetes, theatre parties, tennis, bowls and the like conjures up a picture of a suburban lifestyle. It is a depiction that may inadvertently exclude people leading modern inner-city or alternative lifestyles.

And a fourth, and perhaps the most important, weakness is that this localised, neighbourly view of civil society appears to make a virtue of separating civil society from the economy and politics, those areas of human activity where decisions are taken daily that significantly affect ours and everyone else's futures. In this manifestation, civil society may become what is left over in our lives after the parts that really matter have been taken out.

150

These shortcomings lead others to look for 'harder', more proactive forms of civic organisation and civil society. Adult educators Peter Mayo (1994), and Allman and Wallis (1995), for example, look to Gramsci and his interpretation of the Marxist idea of superstructure. Gramsci describes civil society and the state as 'two major superstructural levels' of society (1971: 12). He sees civil society manifested in 'private' agencies, such as enterprises, educational institutions and the churches, which surround and shore up the state. He argues that this 'ensemble of organisms' provides mechanisms through which dominant groups can exercise hegemonic control over society; but that these agencies and institutions can also be sites of struggle, where we can engage in a 'war of position' in order to counter or replace the dominant hegemony (Gramsci, 1971: 229-239; Mayo, 1994: 126). If we can transform this kind of civil society we can both counter the hegemonic control it previously helped impose; and create a site for resistance against the 'direct domination' exercised by the state and 'juridical' government (Gramsci, 1971: 12). In effect we can use one major superstructural level of society against the other.

An example of a war of position can be found in the way some Australian feminists in the nineteen eighties entered the bureaucracies of the state, or took up positions in organisations like the churches, with the overt purpose of promoting feminist principles of equity from within. These femocrats managed units within major public service departments, headed up bodies like the NSW Council of Social Services, and organised pressure groups like the Movement for the Ordination of Women within the Anglican Church. Patriarchal hegemony was contested from within the organisations that in many respects were part of that hegemony. This Gramscian mode of promoting the feminist cause in Australia won praise and admiration from feminist writers abroad (see, for example, Eisenstein, 1991; Cockburn, 1991).

Other social and educational commentators (Dalton and Kuechler, 1990; Welton, 1993a: Spencer, 1995; Dalton, 1996) concentrate their attention not so much on the accumulation of social capital or counter-hegemonic struggle but on the question of alternative representation. Their interest is in activist groups such as women's groups or environmental groups or human rights groups, and the social movements of which these groups are often a part. Theirs is a civil society built on a pragmatic understanding that there are some people and some bodies that can be trusted and others that cannot. This view of civil society, too, will owe much to Gramsci and his dialectical thinking on politics, the political party and political struggle, but it draws extensively on more recent literature on community and social action and industrial relations, where action is also predicated upon a conflict of interests (Alinsky, 1971; Horton, 1990; Newman, 1995a; Foley, forthcoming).

The harder, more proactive forms of civil society do not automatically imply vigorous protest action in the streets, although they certainly do not preclude it. An organisation that would fit easily into the third kind of civil society, for example, is Action for World Development, a small but robust 'community-based ecumenical development education organisation'. AWD organised a seminar, held on a Sunday in its office in Sydney's Surry Hills and attended by some twenty people from various backgrounds, organisations and community interests, to examine the implications of GATT (the General Agreement on Tariffs and Trade) and the WTO (World Trade Organisation). Speakers were drawn from a variety of organisations including Indigenus-Philippinus, an alliance of Non Government Organisations campaigning against destructive mining in the Philippines; A SEED, an international youth organisation concerned with the effects of world trade on the environment; the Grameen Bank, which lends money to poor people in developing countries; and an organisation called Trade Winds which sells tea and coffee from estates managed by local communities in Sri Lanka and Papua-New Guinea, and which returns proportions of all sales to provide housing in those communities. The focus was not just on the exchange of information but on how to extend that information in the public domain, how to forge alliances with other activist groups, and how to take individual and group action. AWD concerns itself with matters within Australia as well, running racism awareness workshops for non-Aboriginal Australians (always conducted with an Aboriginal person present as an observer) and offering solidarity to Aboriginal people in the form of lobbying, presence at demonstrations, and vigils outside government offices or corporate headquarters. Such an organisation places itself in critical opposition to those governments and national and supra-national organisations which its members consider exploitative or unjust. AWD is small, but its work reaches into a number of countries, extending the network of people and groups concerned with promoting social justice.

Three visions of civil society emerge. One has a humanist feel to it. This form of civil society is constructed on trust, and provides sites within society where we can take action and make meaning of our lives through a variety of communal activities, without directly threatening the state or those in positions of power within the hierarchy of the state. The second derives from a structural analysis of society, and provides us with organisations and agencies as sites within which we can work to bring about radical change in the institutions and agencies themselves and in the state of which they form a part. The third is constructed out of dialectical thinking, and provides us with friends, allies and comrades with whom we can join in social action groups and social movements to pursue causes, and to combat those we judge as unjust or oppressive.

The system
In its third more proactive form, civil society can be seen as providing an alternative means of representation and action to the 'system'. The system, again, is a concept taken up and developed in the literature on critical theory, and is used to denote a combination of the processes of exchange that go to make up the economy, and the processes of political and legal control that go to make up the state. These two collections of processes combine to constrain and prescribe the way we live. In more straightforward terms we can say that the system is made up of money and power. 'The system' is sometimes interpreted as 'the state', but is a broader concept than the state, taking in *all* processes of exchange and *all* applications of power. Thus the system would include transnational economic systems, institutions and enterprises, and include such bodies as major churches, military alliances, and other kinds of political, cultural and industrial associations.

Habermas (1987: 153-5) argues that in our modern societies the system has become separated from the lifeworld. In tribal societies there was 'a high degree of correspondence' between lifeworld and system. What people intuitively believed, how they communicated, how they lived, how they exchanged goods and services, and how they collectively organised and managed themselves all coincided. In such societies it was possible to postulate a collective consciousness. Habermas admits:

> This sketch of a collectively shared, homogeneous lifeworld is certainly an idealization, but archaic societies more or less approximate this ideal type by virtue of the kinship structures of society and the mythical structures of consciousness (1987: 157).

In what he designates 'traditional societies' people's lives are organised around the state, but the state is a concentration of 'the collectivity's capacity for action'. The institutions of the state represent the interests of the people within the society, so that the system is an institutional manifestation of the lifeworld.

In modern societies, however, the system is 'uncoupled' from the lifeworld. The economic, political and legal forces become divorced from the shared lives and beliefs of people. The reification of market forces is an example. The system becomes a thing apart, and operates according to other, non-human rules.

> ... [I]n modern societies, economic and bureaucratic spheres emerge in which social relations are regulated only via money and power (Habermas, 1987: 154).

The forces that control our lives—the economy and the power structures—become alienated from us, from our everyday existence, and from the values and assumptions upon which we base our everyday existence. Worse, this dehumanised system begins affecting those underlying values and assumptions; begins 'colonising' the lifeworld.

> The thesis of internal colonization states that the subsystems of the economy and the state become more and more complex as a consequence of capitalist growth, and penetrate ever deeper into the symbolic reproduction of the lifeworld (Habermas, 1987: 367).

So we find ourselves managing and judging everyday relationships, communications, actions and events, however inappropriate it may actually be, in terms of money and power. And we find more and more of our lives subject to control by the economy and the exercise of power through the political and legal structures.

> The trend towards juridification of informally regulated spheres of the lifeworld is gaining ground along a broad front—the more leisure, culture, recreation, and tourism recognizably come into

the grip of the laws of the commodity economy and the definitions of mass consumption, the more the structures of the bourgeois family manifestly become adapted to the imperatives of the employment system, the more the school palpably takes over the function of assigning job and life prospects, and so forth (Habermas, 1987: 368).

If we accept Habermas's analysis of the uncoupling of system from lifeworld, then we can argue that civil society is a form of organisation and representation much more closely in touch with the lifeworld, and a potential site for vigorous resistance against the dehumanising influence of the system. Adult education has a role to help people learn in order to reaffirm values of cooperation and community, in order to organise themselves on the basis of trust and mutual interest, and in order to resist the colonisation of their lifeworld by the system. Adult educators have a role to help develop both the gentler side of civil society constructed on trust and the harder side constructed in action and 'a war of position' (Allman and Wallis, 1995: 135). We have a role to help develop what Welton (1995) describes as 'an autonomous and exuberant civil society' (p. 155)... in defence of 'a critically reflective lifeworld' (p. 5).

So I might argue that in the exercise at the conference, by asking the participants to acknowledge that they were committed to social justice, I was drawing attention to a set of given assumptions that they shared; that there were features of our lifeworld we needed to protect, and forces in the system we needed to oppose; and that I was hoping that these assumptions would inform the thoughts of the participants as they shared the period of silence.

Two years later I attended a meeting organised by five community workers in Sydney who called themselves the Ant Hill Mob. They wanted to express their concerns about the ways in which the state seemed to be domesticating the processes of community management, community work and community development. The worker who opened the discussion said that it had been in the coffee break immediately following the exercise at the conference that three of the five who were to become the Ant Hill Mob first began discussing what action they could take to counter this domestication.

Three cautionary tales from Australia

When I was in South Africa, although my contacts were adult and union educators, on a number of occasions I found myself talking to groups of unionists on general trade union and political matters. Over the six weeks I gradually developed a talk which, when I came to deliver it at the Trade Union Library in Capetown, I had given the title 'Three Cautionary Tales from Australia'. I talked about the competency movement in Australia and how it had been enthusiastically espoused by the unions as a way of describing work, restructuring awards and developing career paths. I discussed the advantages, but also outlined how competencies had been used to impose centralised forms of control over training and had often resulted in minimalist and second-rate training instead of more comprehensive forms of workplace education. I talked about the slogans and banners of economic rationalism and how they had become current in Australia in the discourse of government, management *and* unions. Hearing union officials talk of international best practice, benchmarks, the need to remove tariff barriers, and the beneficial effects of competition on quality—mouthing, in effect, the dominant discourse of bodies like the World Bank and the International Monetary Fund—could be interpreted, not as industrial and economic common-sense, but as an example of submission to an international capitalist hegemony. And I talked about the Australian Council of Trade Union's Accord with the Australian Labor Party over the period from 1983 to 1996 when the Labor Party was in government.

I had wondered about the alliance between the Council of South African Trade Unions, the South African Communist Party, and the African National Congress. All three organisations had been in vigorous opposition to the apartheid regime, so when Nelson Mandela was elected President and the ANC elected into the majority position in the transitional government in 1994, there was a logic for the three organisations to maintain a formal alliance. It was not for me as an outsider to comment on the alliance, but I could talk about the Accord. I pointed to a number of gains the unions and working people had made in Australia under the various negotiated and renegotiated forms the Accord took during the thirteen years of Labor government, such as a massive increase in participation by working people in superannuation schemes to which management made major contributions, and a centralised wage fixation system that, at a number of crucial stages, had served lower paid workers who in other circumstances would not have had sufficient industrial muscle to win reasonable increases in pay. But I also talked about the drop in union coverage in that period from over fifty per cent of the workforce to somewhere in the low thirties, the apparent loss of union activism in many offices and on many shop floors, the significant failure by the unions to recruit members in some of the new industries, and the stagnation or drop in the real value of wages and salaries in a number of sectors. I argued that by entering into an Accord with the Government, the ACTU had adopted a potentially disempowering role. A small union was quite clearly part of civil society. A larger union, whilst it maintained a shop floor representative structure and democratically elected branches, was part of civil society. Even a large peak body like the ACTU, while it vigorously represented the member unions and maintained a critical and, when necessary, oppositional relationship with Government, was part of civil society. But if major decisions affecting unions and their members were made at a central level, if the relationships between senior union officials and government ministers and bureaucrats became too close, then at best the peak body's role was ambivalent, and at worst it ceased being part of civil society, and became part of the system. If this were the case, when decisions were made at peak body level and passed back down the line to the unions, their branches and their members, was this not an example of the colonisation of our life-world?

16: Opposition, resistance and protest

Sleeping with the enemy may be difficult, but going into opposition has its problems as well. For a start, it is all too easy to
adopt a reactive rather than a proactive stance. If we exclude ourselves from the policy-making table, there is the danger that we
will assume that all we can do is watch and wait and, when we
disapprove of the policies and actions of those in authority,
protest. Of course we can always expend a great deal of energy
protesting and give the impression of being very busy, but our
efforts are likely to be after the event. If we do adopt this kind of
reactive opposition, then all we can really hope to do is halt some
initiative taken by the other side, and push the clock back. Rather
than a force for equitable change, we will become conservative
spoilers.

A second problem is that, if we unthinkingly conform with
recent trends, then our protest is likely to remain within certain
well-defined limits. Russell Dalton (1996: 68) notes that the
nature of protest politics has changed radically in 'advanced' societies this century. Historically, protest was often the spontaneous
outbreak of mass anger and action, the last desperate act of a frus-
trated public which challenged the existence and legitimacy of
those in power. Mobs of peasants, working class people and the
poor attacked the tax collector, overturned the governor's car-
riage, and beat up (or worse) some hapless servant wearing a
nobleman's livery. If the protest gathered strength then they
stormed the seat of government. Nowadays, however, protest in
countries like Australia is 'a planned and organised activity', with
buses ferrying people to points of assembly and marshals controlling the action. Indeed many of the people engaged in this kind of
protest may be middle class. They will be protesting in order to
affect some single piece of policy, but will have no intention of
overthrowing the established order of which, in other respects,
they are firmly a part.

A third, and perhaps the most worrying, dilemma for those of us adopting a position of opposition is that by engaging in protest of the muted, modern kind described above we may actually be serving the interests of those in power. Definitions of power seem to fall into quite distinct categories (Lukes, 1986). There are some which depict power as a resource and carry a hint of idealism in them. In these kinds of definition, power is related to people's ability to act in concert. Hannah Arendt, for example, argues that power is never the property of an individual, but belongs to a group; and that when we say that someone is 'in power' we refer to her or him being empowered by a number of people to act in their name (1986: 64). But there are other definitions which depict power as the imposition of will. Max Weber, for example, defines power as the probability that a person or a number of people will be able to carry out their own will 'despite resistance' (1968: 53). Not only is the imposition of will important in this definition but resistance is deemed a necessary adjunct to that imposition of will. Indeed, an act by the would-be powerful which was met by indifference or untroubled acquiescence might not be an act of power at all, but simply an untrammelled action. In this view of power, then, unless we go all the way to revolution and unseat and destroy the powerful, our protest can actually reinforce their status. By offering anything short of total resistance, we create the situation in which the powerful can display their power, either by refusing to budge or by magnanimously making concessions.

Unless we are very careful, our opposition can easily become domesticated. We come under the sway of a kind of 'liberal' hegemony, in which we accept uncritically that protest beyond certain bounds will threaten the system, and that to unsettle those in power will unsettle and disadvantage ourselves. In effect we take up the position of a 'friendly' opposition, a stance modelled for us in the Westminster Parliamentary concept of a 'loyal opposition'. Of course, in doing this we act on the assumption that those in power are friendly or loyal as well.

It is reasonably easy to see how such an assumption took root in certain democracies after the Second World War, and how such a hegemony was established. The nineteen fifties, sixties and seventies saw capitalism develop internationally in the form of multinational and transnational corporations and the establishment of regional trading blocks. With the wisdom of hindsight (and increased access to information) we can now see that, while lifting the material standard of living of some, this expansion set in place or accelerated the degradation of the environment in many parts of the world, the depletion or destruction of species, the exploitation of child labour, and the imposition of massive debt burdens on many countries and their populations. At the same time, however, a limited number of countries, mainly in Western Europe plus Canada, New Zealand and Australia, established or strengthened their welfare states. In these countries, to varying degrees, the populations enjoyed guaranteed minimum rates of pay at work, support in unemployment, support in old age, and access to public education and a publicly subsidised health service. In these countries, therefore, a consensus was achieved between capital, labour and the state, and some of the worst excesses of a free enterprise system constructed on greed were offset by an institutionalised system of collective controls and collective care.

The state did indeed appear to be benign, and so for the vast majority it seemed counter-productive to take protest to the point where the authorities might feel genuinely threatened. Even in 1968, when there were demonstrations in many of these welfare state countries, the governments remained in place. In May of that year in France, where the protest was perhaps the most widespread, at a crucial moment the emphasis shifted from demonstrations and riots to a national strike. Thus a potentially revolutionary situation was turned into a massive but still essentially conventional exercise in industrial action.

Of course many of the welfare states enjoyed a privileged position in the world economy based upon their histories as imperial powers or as favoured colonies of imperial powers, and so we could only maintain the belief that these states were truly benign if we kept our sights firmly fixed on conditions within our own borders, and ignored the past. But even this limited and parochial idea of the benign state has become difficult to maintain. In the past fifteen or twenty years styles of government in the democracies have changed. There has been an erosion of the collectivist aspects of our lives. Publicly owned facilities such as water and power supply and public services such as national airlines and national telecommunications systems have been wholly or partly privatised. Worse, perhaps, there has been a loss of the sense that government has a duty of care. In Australia, where for some eighteen years tertiary education was publicly funded and so was widely available on merit, fees (in a number of guises) have been reintroduced. Increasing numbers of conditions are being imposed on unemployed people if they want to draw unemployment benefits. And the government is seeking to solve some of the problems of an under-resourced health system by privileging private health funds and their associated private hospitals rather than committing itself unequivocally to a universal public health service.

If we shift our focus from government to Habermas's larger idea of a system made up of the economy and the structures of power, then the picture is grimmer. We can argue that the wielders of power have withdrawn from a shared project with the population, formerly achieved through publicly discussed forms of interventionist economic policy and well funded welfare provision, and replaced these benign forms of control with surveillance, menace and seduction. There is widespread surveillance, literally in the form of video cameras in public places, and only slightly less literally in forms such as credit ratings and computerised economic records. The adoption of a culture of restructuring and downsizing in both public and private sector organisations introduces an element of menace into people's working lives, making us, even in times of statistically proven economic growth, feel uncertain about our jobs and our futures. Governments, corporations and other wielders of power seduce us, through promotion and public relations, to live out our lives in their interests. And retailers, through insistent marketing and advertising, lure us to buy what we do not need, and did not know we wanted. Yet while the system grows less friendly, protest in the democracies remains muted. The 'liberal' hegemony prevails.

There is a fourth problem for those of us interested in mounting an effective opposition. The ideas of individualism are everywhere, in governments' rhetorical focus on the small business-person, in the idealisation of the individual entrepreneur and, in Australia, in the appeal by conservative forces to the battler. The term 'battler' used to belong to the left or popular end of the political spectrum and referred to members of working class communities who banded together to resist a developer or some other

161

force bent on interrupting or destroying their communal life. But the term has been usurped by the conservative political forces and is now used to depict as a person who when confronted by hardship and oppression, takes pride in her or his ability to 'go it alone'. In the industrial relations arena, there are open attempts by conservative forces to disempower and destroy unions, and to replace collective bargaining with individual contracts. The manoeuvre is transparent but can be horribly effective. In the company of others a protester remains part of a civil society which is constructed on a pattern of checks and balances. The sole protester becomes the odd one out, the person who is not normal. Cynthia Cockburn captures this phenomenon in her discussion of the problems facing women wanting to challenge a dominant patriarchal ideology:

> It is exceedingly difficult to break away from hegemonic ideas and counter them with other thoughts because in doing so one is made to seem eccentric, extremist, flying in the face of reality (1991: 169).

Continued resistance on your own will be seen as a repeated denial of reality, and may place you figuratively, or even literally, in the position of Michel Foucault's patient in the ward of the mental hospital. In a study of the treatment of madness in early forms of asylum, Foucault (1973: 265-273) describes how resistance to the sometimes brutal treatments was interpreted as trouble-making, and how those who persisted in their resistance were further isolated within the asylum. A patient's only hope of release lay in proving her or his 'normality' by accepting the abnormal conditions of the hospital, conforming to the abnormal rules and regulations imposed by those in control, and showing remorse. Foucault provides both a literal and a metaphorical analysis of the way in which resistance can be isolated and the person doing the resisting punished and domesticated.

Educational strategies

This last image is a dreadful one, but such situations need not arise. All of the problems and dilemmas associated with opposition, resistance and protest signalled above can be addressed. We can do this in a number of ways, and together these ways mark out a contribution adult educators can make to the struggle for a

162

just society.

First, we can help make opposition proactive by seeing it first and foremost in terms of learning. Horton adopted this approach. His avowed aim was to help people learn in the course of struggle. He would contact 'natural community leaders' at sites of resistance against racial, economic and political oppression, and invite them to attend workshops at his Highlander centre. There he would help them examine their experiences, analyse their current struggles, and plan future action. He made it clear that although this future action should help advance the participants' struggles, it should be chosen because it would lead to further learning (Peters and Bell, 1987; Moyer, 1981; Horton, 1990).

Such was Horton's commitment to learning that he even envisaged failure as positive, so long as there had been challenge and analysis (that is, action and learning).

> There's a lot to be learned from successful organisation over a specific issue, from achieving a specific victory, like preventing a building from being torn down or getting a new sewer system. However, some equally valuable learning takes place when you escalate your demands to the place where you finally lose. Now, if you don't push to the place where you might fail, you've missed a wonderful opportunity to learn to struggle, to think big and challenge the status quo, and also to learn how to deal with failure (1990: 176).

People engaging in this kind of learning-in-action, Horton argues, are likely to resist, protest and learn more creatively the next time.

Adult educators, then, have the role of asking in the planning stages of opposition: what can we learn?; in the course of the opposition: what are we learning?; and, in the aftermath of the demonstration, boycott, march or strike, what have we learnt? Wherever possible we should introduce the people we are working with to all aspects of learning, from the instrumental to essential, and help them understand the characteristics and purposes of each. Activists who learn to learn, who think about learning, and who come to understand the richness and variety of learning, will be more likely to push at the boundaries, be constantly looking for new ideas, and be eager try new processes. Theirs will be a force in constant state of creative change and, whether they have initiated the action or their action has been triggered by the actions of others, their opposition will be more likely to challenge the stability of the powerful.

Second, we can help our learners become aware of, and counter, the forces which can pull us back from the edge and render our opposition muted. To do this, we need to understand the different forms of social control—physical force, institutional control and control by ideas—and study how these can create the physical limits, the rules, and the unquestioned 'norms' that constrain us. We need to understand and explain how the 'liberal' hegemony has come into existence, and to foreground and critically examine assumptions underpinning it, such as: that capitalism is a natural mode of social and economic organisation; that democratically elected leaders will always act in the interests of the people they lead; and that people are inherently good. (Elsewhere [1994] I have argued that many have fallen prey to a naive form of humanism that holds that deep within all of us is a kind of universal human essence and that this essence is good.) We need to demonstrate how these kinds of assumption can divert us from looking at other ways of living, how they can discourage us from taking sides, and how they can prevent us from setting up effective, creative and, when necessary, aggressive oppositions.

Third, we can help people select suitable sites for resistance, opposition and protest. One approach is to help our learners examine the concepts of the lifeworld, civil society and the system, and select within which of these manifestations of society they will locate their learning and struggle. Another approach is offered by Steve Pile (1997) in a discussion of 'geographies of resistance'. He emphasises the concept of space and maintains that resistance 'not only takes place in space, but also seeks to appropriate space, to make new spaces' (p. 16). We can interpret this struggle for space both literally and metaphorically. People can struggle over the use of external physical space, as when a group of residents mobilises to claim a vacant urban allotment and turn it into parkland. But we can equally seek to appropriate the 'colonised spaces of people's inner worlds', or locate our resistance in terrains defined by social class, gender, sexuality and race. Pile argues that some resistance will be in direct opposition to forces of domination, and so located on sites dictated by those forces of domination. We protest against the construction of a freeway at the point where the earthmovers are at work, or at the construction company's headquarters, or outside Parliament house where the go-ahead to build the freeway was given. But, he suggests, resistance can also occur in 'spaces outside of power relations'.

> One possible way to remap resistance, then, is to think about the ways in which power relations are incomplete, fluid, liable to rupture, inconsistent, awkward and ambiguous. Now, spaces of resistance can be seen as not only partially connected to, but also partially dislocated from, spaces of domination (p. 14).

And this claim takes on substance when he states:

> Potentially, the list of acts of resistance is endless—everything from foot-dragging to walking, from sit-ins to outings, from chaining oneself up in the treetops to dancing the night away, from parody to passing, from bombs to hoaxes, from graffiti tags on New York trains to stealing pens from employers, from not voting to releasing laboratory animals, from mugging yuppies to buying shares, from cheating to dropping out, from tattoos to body piercing, from pink hair to pink triangles, from loud music to loud T-shirts, from memories to dreams—and the reason for this seems to be that people are understood to have capacities to change things... through giving their own (resistant) meanings to things, through finding their own tactics for avoiding, taunting, attacking, undermining, enduring, hindering, mocking the everyday exercise of power. That people can create their own ways of living—their own meanings and capacities—has forced a recognition that resistance can be found in everything (p. 14).

Fourth, we can help people decide on the most effective forms of organisation for their resistance. Pile (p. 15) recognises that his 'endless' list of forms of resistance presents a problem, and asks: 'if resistance can be found in the tiniest act—a single look, a scratch on a desk—then how is resistance to be recognised as a distinctive practice?' He suggests the answer lies in thinking through the context in which the resistance takes place and the position of people within the networks of power. As adult educators we can help our learners resolve these problems by examining different kinds of social movement, and deciding what kinds of organisation or movement they might want to establish, join or form alliances with. Social movements provide a context of people, structures and ideals within which to engage in resistance. They form, or are formed, as a response to the exercises of power and so are themselves networks of power, parts of other networks of power, and in conflict or interaction with further networks of power.

And fifth, we can help people select strategies of opposition, resistance and protest that will challenge rather than reinforce those people dominating and exploiting networks of power. Ian McAllister (1992) and Dalton (1996) discuss what they call 'participation' in the political affairs of the state, (and in doing so provide a way of categorising Pile's list of acts of resistance). They distinguish between 'conventional' and 'unconventional' participation. Conventional participation includes voting, taking part in election campaigns (as a party member or campaign worker), communal activity, and making personal contact with politicians and officials (through letter writing, phone, email or meetings). Unconventional participation includes all forms of active protest. McAllister breaks this category down into *legal protest* such as joining in boycotts and attending lawful demonstrations, *semi-legal protest* such as joining in unofficial strikes and occupying buildings, and *radical protest* such as damaging property, and using violence against people (1992: 65).

Ends and Means
These kinds of framework provide us with a gamut of actions. They remind us of the ordinary forms of civic participation available to all of us, and that these can have an effect. And they also draw our attention in a dispassionate way to different forms of protest available. But this kind of analysis goes only part of the way. For example, neither Dalton nor McAllister indicates any preference for one strategy over another, nor takes up the issue of whether we should engage in, or help others decide to engage in, the semi-legal or 'radical' (that is, illegal) kinds of protest. Adult educators working with community organisations, unions, and activist groups, on the other hand, will be helping people make these kinds of decision and so will be asking them to struggle with the age-old question of whether the end justifies the means.

The question is neither abstract nor out of date. What, for example, is the moral position of human rights activists who buy small numbers of shares in a company so that they can attend the company's annual general meeting, and then disrupt it? It could be argued that this strategy involves deception, yet their protest may draw attention to the fact that the company is abusing basic human rights in an overseas plant. What was Chris Harvey's moral position when he talked to some difficult course participants about thieves on a building site having their fingers broken? At one level it was a *non sequitur*, but at another it was menace. And what is the moral position of the environmentalists who drive metal spikes into felled trees waiting to dragged to the timber mills? In one celebrated case (Foley, 1991), such an incident marked the turning point in a campaign that saved a rain forest; and yet a power saw hitting one of those spikes could have maimed or killed the operator.

To deal with the moral issues of opposition, resistance and protest, we need to tell stories. These stories should show good people grappling with complex moral issues. They should be stories that challenge, that will make us think. They should be the kinds of story that enable us to ask our learners: 'Well, what would you do?':

From 1991 to early 1998 Gordon McColl worked for the International Confederation of Free Trade Unions—Asian Pacific Regional Organisation (ICFTU-APRO). The ICFTU, of which the Australian Council of Trade Unions is a member, plays a coordinating, developmental and educational role for trade unions in countries all over the world. McColl was based in Singapore and his concerns were with the protection and promotion of human rights, particularly within or related to workplaces, in the Asian-Pacific region. His interest—what drives him, in fact—was the fight against the use of child labour.

McColl had some success in an area of north Pakistan where there are a large number of brick kilns that use children. The children come into virtual slavery along with their families. At some stage in the past the parents, or even the parents of the parents, borrowed money to meet an obligation or to avert a crisis. They contracted to work in order to pay off the debt, but this proved impossible, since the interest alone was as much as the couple could earn. In order to meet these contracted obligations, everyone in the family is forced to help, and the family becomes, in effect, the property of an employer. Whole families live at the kilns and work together, infants placed to one side in swaddling and everyone else from toddler-age up squatting on the ground in the heat, using hand-held moulds to shape hundreds upon hundreds of clay bricks per day. Bonded labour is officially illegal in Pakistan but continues to be a fact of life for many thousands of families.

McColl was appalled by what he saw and found people who were equally concerned in a Pakistani peak union body. Together they formulated a strategy to secure the release of the children from the brick kilns in one particular area. Although it took time, commitment and political skill to implement, the concept was simple. They found the necessary funding—to cover transport, books, uniforms and a small allowance for the families—to enable some forty children to go to school, and they then put legal, moral and other kinds of pressure on the kiln owners to let the children attend. One of McColl's Pakistani union comrades had won a Danish trade union award for contributions to humanity, and he used this money and some other small donations to build two additional rooms to the school so that two class rooms became four. McColl is modest about his own role, suggesting that he was just one of many contributing to the success of the campaign, but I did see a video—shown to me by someone else who wanted McColl's contribution recognised—which showed McColl being greeted at an event attended by hundreds of villagers, and surrounded by children proudly wearing their new school uniforms. Some in the crowd were holding up large banners with McColl's portrait on them. Under his portrait were the words: 'Gordon McColl—Long Live'.

When I talked to McColl about the campaign he told me about the union officials in the peak body. They were, he said, remarkable people, dedicated to fighting for the rights of people to live and work with some kind of dignity. One official with whom he worked closely had spent time in prison under both democratic and military regimes for his political views and activities, and had been beaten and tortured. His and his comrades' support had been crucial, and the actions of this official in particular had saved the project.

An owner had tried to defeat the strategy by moving families to another kiln hundreds of kilometres away. The children of these families were at school one day and gone the next. The official was a Pathan with tribal as well as union contacts. Shortly after the children and their families were removed from the region, the kiln owner's son was kidnapped. The kiln owner received a message which said: 'You have stolen my children, so I have kidnapped yours. Your son will be well looked after but if you do not bring the families back, you will never see him again.' The families were transported back, the children resumed classes, and the kiln owner's son was returned.

McColl had worked as a union official and then as a union trainer in Australia, before taking up his post with the ICFTU. He has stories to tell of strikes at abattoirs in the Australian outback, of fatalities from fires in Chinese factories and, again in north Pakistan, of an industrial dispute settled by an exchange of gun fire. He has example upon example of the pettiness, the selfishness, the callousness and, in the case of fires in locked buildings and the rape of bonded women labourers, the out and out criminality of employers. He has a way of pinpointing ironies, and when he does he tips his head forward and to one side, rests it lightly against his hand, looks up at you, and mutters: 'Jeez'.

Of course McColl could not have freed those children on his own. He needed the help of the ICFTU, the Pakistani peak union body, local unionists, and, although he may have refused their help had he known what they intended to do, those Pathan contacts of his Pakistani comrade. Indeed McColl argues that it is essential for any activist intervening from the outside to have the support of local activists, and for these local activists to have the final say. This highlights a sixth way in which adult educators can contribute to effective opposition, resistance and protest, and that is to help people understand and combat the individuation of resistance. We need to help ourselves and others learn how to join together in order to enhance the power and effectiveness of our protest. We need to help people understand the concept of civil society and see it as a site for learning and action. We need to promote the idea of civil society as an ever-changing amalgam of groups, organisations and movements of very different sizes and fields of influence. This larger concept of civil society encompasses a group of four parents concerned with a neighbourhood creche, a local sports club with hundreds of members, a union with over a hundred thousand members, and a council of churches representing congregations in their millions. We need to help people engage in complicities, form alliances and enter into solidarities in this kind of civil society, and to see the formation of connections as a potential act of resistance in itself.

Section 7: The adult educator

17: Role models

New York is a city I can take for about five days. After that I want to leave. All those things people say about the place crowd in on me: the ceaseless noise of sirens, the distressing juxtaposition of wealth and poverty, the remorseless pace, and, for a Sydneysider like me, the oppressive straightness of the streets. But like a legion of others, in those first few days before the urge to flee overtakes me, I find the place exciting. Being there has a vividness. The best and the worst in the world elide. The preposterous nature of the place makes me think.

I had gone to the United States to attend a conference in Kansas City Missouri, and once it was over I travelled to Chicago and then on to New York to see colleagues in the field of adult education. However, I must also admit that I was really in New York to see my daughter who was living and working there. She was not free during the daytime so, after having completed my professional visits, I was left with a couple of days to fill. I was already growing edgy. I had visited museums and galleries but now went looking for a theatre matinee to attend, as much to get out of the crowds and into an enclosed and comfortable space as to see a play. I wandered the streets around Times Square looking at the theatres and the billboards carrying excerpts of reviews and found a theatre where *The Tempest* was playing, with Patrick Stewart in the role of Prospero. I knew of Stewart by name, had seen him perform in a TV role, and was fascinated by the idea of casting him as one of Shakespeare's most complex and powerful characters. I bought a ticket and went to see the play.

The production was full of shifts of pace, garish, loud, wistful and subtle. All the performances were first rate but the two movers and shakers—Prospero and his servant-spirit Ariel—were supreme. Ariel was played by a woman (which I have always felt was right) called Aunganue Ellis and her performance was a combination of mystery, rebelliousness, joy and, in the magical banquet scene, staggering ferocity. Stewart gave a dynamic performance (no aged figure clutching a staff here!), constructing his character around the warring emotions of a love for the people and spirits on his island, and a terrible, smouldering anger. There is a pivotal moment in the play when Ariel asks Prospero: 'Do you love me, master?' In this production a sullen Ariel walks away, spins on her heel and, in a mercurial shift of mood, fires the question across the width of the stage. Prospero, committed to releasing Ariel when she has completed her tasks, stares back in rage, and anguish. Master and spirit. Love and anguish. Father and daughter. New York had performed its magic.

Back in Australia when I was required to prepare a paper on my thinking and writing about adult education, instead of turning to the conventional educational literature, I used the play and Stewart's interpretation of Prospero as my starting point. I argued that Prospero is, in effect, an adult educator and, as many of us do in this trade, he adopts a number of guises. He is the scholar-recluse, alone with his books, developing ideas and theories. He is the moralist pedagogue, given to straightforward instruction. In this he is superbly successful with his daughter Miranda but a failure with Caliban, the 'salvage and deformed slave'. He is the consummate experiential educator. He sets up situations—the whole course of the play, in effect—in which Alonso, the King of Naples, Sebastian, Alonso's brother, Ferdinand, Alonso's son and Antonio, the usurping Duke of Milan, have to face challenges, deal with problems, be tested and learn from those experiences. He is a skilled dialogic educator. In this guise he helps Alonso, Antonio, and Gonzalo, 'an honest old Councellor', reflect on and learn from past events and from the parts they played in those events. He is the facilitator, setting up pageants and performances, and then helping the observers draw understanding about their own condition through debriefing and commentary: 'We are such stuff as dreams are made on... ' And he is the activist educator. By intervening in the lives of others, he brings about change in the social and political domains of his time.

The play depicts a struggle between base nature and high moral quality, and Prospero employs learning in this struggle. He can only achieve learning at an instrumental level in Caliban, who learns the skills of language but makes use of that language to curse in. In Miranda and Ferdinand, Prospero promotes affective learning, and tries to pace the couple's encounter so as to help them develop a real love, that is, real and full communication, in place of a sudden infatuation. And in Alonso he promotes a kind of critical learning that results in a moral transformation. Indeed, the idea of transformation is captured in Ariel's song 'Full fathom five...' and symbolised in Ariel's transition from a spirit imprisoned in a cloven pine, to Prospero's servant, to a spirit of the air, finally, fully emancipated from the shackles of her former existence.

Prospero uses conflict openly to generate learning and promote change. He helps people move from conflict towards reconciliation, but the reconciliation is achieved without romanticism. Alonso and Gonzalo are genuinely reconciled with Prospero, but Sebastian and Antonio are only reluctantly brought to accept their loss of power and prospects. Some enemies are rendered allies and even friends but others, for all the constraints they may be placed under, will remain enemies and must be carefully watched. In this particular production Patrick Stewart portrayed Prospero as an eccentric and passionate learner and educator, driven by an anger at injustice, a belief that the world could be a better place, and a readiness, given the opportunity, to intervene in order to shift people towards his view of the world. I liked the way his Prospero used differing techniques with different people to inform, persuade, prompt, encourage and, with the furious assistance of Ellis's incandescent Ariel in the banquet scene, shock and confront.

But that is the point. I like the Prosperos in our trade. I like adult education that confronts, that puts a case, that takes sides, and sets out to cause change. I like adult education that is driven by a touch of anger. I think I have always acted on this understanding of adult education, but it has taken me some time, and encounters with a number of remarkable educators, in order to recognise and articulate the understanding at all fully.

A personal story

In 1971 I took up the full-time post at Addison Adult Education Institute in inner London which would lead to my meeting Maeler. Amongst the Institute's five hundred or so courses was one called 'The Sociology of Race', consisting of ten weekly meetings, each presented by a visiting expert in the field of race relations.

The course seemed removed from the social confusion of our part of London and so the next year with the encouragement of Terry Jackson, the Vice Principal, I set up a course which used all black speakers, put a black point of view, and was called 'Black Experience'. This course and another entitled 'Alternative Societies' attracted good enrolments and some publicity, and so during that year and subsequent years we set up courses on women's liberation, gay studies, housing, civil liberties, welfare rights, alternative education and a number of other subjects or issues, all of which were openly one-sided or pushed a particular line.

Alongside courses in keep fit, dressmaking and French for Beginners, we were running a program described in the press as 'a radical night school'. However, looking back I can see that the courses were not as radical as the Daily Mail portrayed. Most were actually inward-looking. The title 'Black Experience' is a giveaway. A number of the courses focussed on the experience of a particular group itself. They were about being black and living in London, or about being a woman, or being gay.

A few years later I was asked by a member of the London Irish community to follow the same principle of the one-sided course and to set up a course on Irish Studies. Given the bombings and sectarian murders in Northern Ireland, I was tempted to retreat into the protection of principles such as objectivity, balance and academic detachment, but both the Addison Institute and the London Working Men's College, to which I moved at the time of the request, went ahead and ran a course that put a view of the events in Ireland well out of kilter with mainstream, mainland views. However, once again with the advantage of hindsight, I can see that the course conformed with the standard adult education procedure of starting with the self. It was about Irish history and Irish politics—that is, about the Irish experience. While there was a lot in this course and the others I have mentioned about the oppressed, there was not too much about the oppressors.

I returned home to Australia and in 1984 took up a post as a trainer for the Australian Trade Union Training Authority. In this job I was training people who had a clearly identifiable, institutionalised opposition—in the form of management. Further, this opposition was not always distant or abstract but manifested itself in managers, office supervisors, senior executive officers, senior public servants and politicians—actual bosses the participants often encountered on a daily basis. For the full length of any course, the trainer and the participants could engage in an anti-management rhetoric. It was the knowledge that we all had an opposition which motivated the learning and gave participants, drawn from different parts of the country and from a whole variety of industries and unions, a sense of common purpose and solidarity. The courses were one-sided, pro-union in every possible respect, and intended to be just that. And yet again something was missing. The courses may have been aimed at helping unionists effectively stand up to management, but for the most part they were focussed on unionism, on the skills and knowledge needed to be better unionists, on the experience of being unionists.

When I joined the University of Technology, Sydney in 1989 I witnessed something of the same kind of common purpose and solidarity with two other groups. I found myself ostensibly tutor of a group which consisted of seven women, all feminists, some of them senior femocrats, doing a Graduate Diploma in Adult Education course. I say 'ostensibly tutor' because there were moments when the women appeared to forget my presence, or ignored me, and got on with a kind of learning that was different from other courses and kinds of learning I had been involved in. The focus shifted from the experience of being women within a patriarchal society to a hard and uncompromising examination of the patriarchal society itself. The act of oppression became the object of study. My other teaching included leading seminars on a course for Aboriginal adult educators. Here I found that as teacher or facilitator I could make choices about the program design based on the assumption that the participants were part of a struggle and that they had an opposition in the uncaring, unthinking or prejudiced white majority. We would sift through mainstream educational theory, looking for ideas and methods which would be of use in Aboriginal contexts and communities. But the opposite also happened and we found ourselves looking for ideas and methods in the mainstream theory that might be inappropriate or inimical to the interests of Aboriginal people.

As a university person I had time to write, and it was when I was writing about particular changes in trade union education and training (1993, 1994) that I began to really understand the significance of the different educational experiences I have described

177

above. In the early nineteen nineties there was a lot of talk about joint training—that is, training unionists and representatives of management together. This came about as part of the push for consultative mechanisms in the workplace. The argument that flowed from this was that if management and unions were going to meet together to consult, they should attend training for these consultative processes together. I had been quickly hostile to the idea, and now understood why.

Management and unions have conflicts of interest. Both parties are interested in increasing production, but each will want a larger share of the benefits of that increased production: management in the form of increased profits and dividends; unions in the form of increased wages and improved conditions. Andy Banks and Jack Metzgar (1989) argue that management is always interested in increased productivity—that is, production for less expenditure; while unions are only interested if it benefits their members. If management can increase productivity while downsizing the workforce—sacking people, we used to say—it will.

Union members on a consultative committee are still representatives of their colleagues and should see themselves as protecting and promoting their members' interests. If unions are going to share, consult, and cooperate with management, they need to study management in order to gauge management's competence, to examine management's values and motives, and to establish the degree to which management can or cannot be trusted. This kind of learning simply cannot be done in partnership with management because *management itself is the object of study*. Really effective learning for action is not when we start from our own experience but when we start by examining the values, the motives, the actions and the experience of the people holding us back. Adult education for social justice will be oppositional, and the learning within that educational activity will be best constructed around an analysis of conflicts of interest and a definition of the oppositional forces in those conflicts. Learning for change is done by defining the enemy.

Friends and colleagues

Along the way towards this realisation I have worked with adult educators who engaged in this kind of teaching and learning. Together they provide a living background to the story I have just told, and together they provide a range of models.

Terry Jackson's life, in a sense, was a case study in a particular kind of English adult education. He had started life as a steel-worker in Rotherham, become a union activist, then shop steward, attended Workers' Educational Association classes and union courses, gained admission to Ruskin College Oxford, and gone on to gain a degree. He joined the Workers' Educational Association as a tutor-organiser in the Midlands, before coming to London to the post of Vice Principal at Addison Institute. Jackson and I spent a lot of time talking about adult education. I was excited by the 'radical' courses we were setting up and Jackson both channelled me the resources to make the courses happen and made me give them a sharper political edge. Jackson's concept of adult education was informed by a working class culture, and had its origins in the independent working class education of people like Thomas Cooper and William Lovett in the first half of the nineteenth century (Kelly, 1970; Peers, 1972). More than twenty five years after those conversations with Jackson, and on the other side of the world, I enjoy teaching about the bitter debate in Britain in the eighteen twenties and thirties between the supporters of the mechanics institutes who advocated 'useful knowledge', and the working class radicals like Cooper, Lovett and Benjamin Ward from the Chartists, the cooperative movement and the trade unions, who advocated 'really useful knowledge' (Johnson, 1988).

Jacques Compton coordinated the 'Black Experience' course. He was from Grenada in the West Indies, and he conducted his course with good humour and great erudition, either giving the sessions himself or chairing sessions given by guest speakers. Over ten weeks he and his guests catalogued and analysed the experiences and conditions of black people from the days of slavery to the colonial days in the West Indies to the period of immigration from the West Indies to Britain after the Second World War to contemporary Britain. Compton was the first person I saw conduct a course which was relentlessly one-sided and which relentlessly sheeted home the blame. He had a way of presenting the most terrible of facts with a chuckle that both lightened the moment and communicated his condemnation and dismay.

Marsha Rowe and Rosie Boycott, founding editors of the magazine *Spare Rib*, ran a course at Addison in 1973 called 'Women and Men', and then another the following year called 'Women's Liberation'. They arranged the group in a large circle, a couple of layers deep, and then sat at different points in the circle. There was no centre of authority in the room, but two points from which questions were sometimes asked and information sometimes given. Boycott sat back, relaxed, and Rowe leant forward, intense. They listened hard, and when they spoke they provided information not as an end in itself but as a tool to help elucidate a point or to identify another issue.

Peter Newell was the Education Officer of the National Council of Civil Liberties and I asked him to organise a ten-meeting course on Civil Liberties. He conducted the course but during it revealed that he had moved from the NCCL to set up White Lion Street Free School in Islington, London. I visited the school, and together we planned a course on 'Alternative Education', which was run at Addison Institute in the latter part of 1973. White Lion Street Free School was a living experiment in alternative education where the focus was not on subjects or issues but on the learners, their individual wants and needs, and the wants, needs and interests of their social class. Through Newell I began seeing adult education as an alternative.

As the seventies progressed my job changed to include an 'outreach' or community element. Outreach workers were being appointed to other London adult education institutes and we met together regularly. Nell Keddie was one of these. She came into adult education from a previous career as an academic where she had edited an influential sociological text *Tinker, Tailor... The Myth of Cultural Deprivation* (1973). Reading that book, conversing with her and hearing her speak at meetings made me aware of traps in ideas such as 'need' and 'disadvantage', helped me understand social class in cultural as well as political terms, and helped me appreciate how one class could, through the control of institutions and ideas, impose its culture on another. Keddie provided an intellectual framework within which to begin understanding the confusing and disordered business of trying to identify and then respond to people's interests and demands. She helped me begin understanding the degrees to which I and others doing similar community education jobs were agents of the state, and the degrees to which we were not. Keddie's intellectual rigour was evident in her teaching. She never hurried a response. She

180

would pause and consider, then speak softly and with force. To be with her, therefore, was to share her thoughts.

It was in this period that I also met Head. There is an irony in that I was one of the people (Newell was another) who encouraged Head to enter the adult education service, but that once appointed he quickly became a kind of adult education mentor to me. He had been a Methodist minister, had spent some time in West Africa, and had been the General Secretary of the Student Christian Movement of Great Britain and Ireland. When I met him he had just written *A Free Way to Learning* (1974) in which he examined alternatives to schooling. Head went to work as an outreach worker in a neighbouring adult education institute to mine and we met regularly, helped with each other's programs of courses, and set up a joint project to respond to the unemployed in our two areas. It was in this project that I watched Head display his respect for the learner. We had canvassed unemployed people in our institutes' patches using leaflets, notices and personal contacts, and called a meeting for a Tuesday morning. Only three unemployed people turned up to the first meeting and I wondered whether we should go ahead. But Head never hesitated. For the three who were there, this might be important. Head opened the session just as he would have if there had been twenty people present and, although it is impossible to prove, it is my belief that this meeting and subsequent meetings and activities we organised helped one of those initial three avoid sinking into homelessness and perhaps madness. Head moved after two years to the City Literary Institute. As part of his job there he worked with some single homeless people in central London, and wrote about the experience in an article 'Education at the Bottom' (Head, 1977). The article is the critical commentary of an educator working subtly and humanly within a Freiran framework, gradually shifting a group of people from a state of dispirited fatalism to a state of critical consciousness. It is also the story of action. Following Head's intervention in their lives (or was it invasion? he asks) the group composed a letter protesting against some of the indignities forced on them by authorities. 'What you have done,' the letter says, 'is to turn us into hostel dwellers, and forced us to adopt a way of life you disapprove of.' Some of the group formed a housing cooperative, gained use of several short-life properties, and so were no longer homeless.

181

Ivan Gibbon was the tutor of the 'Irish Studies' course held at the Working Men's College in 1980. He was a tall man and softly spoken. He would attach a map of Ireland to the board behind him and although the room was small and the group only some fifteen or so, sometimes he would stand next to the map to speak so that the map served as a kind of statement. His style, however, was inclusive and he encouraged people to explore the apparently intractable situation that was Northern Ireland with great frankness and honesty. His knowledge of the subject was vast, and it seemed that this provided a kind of bedrock upon which people felt able to test and exchange differing views.

Trevor Blackwell and Jeremy Seabrook approached the College and asked whether we could house and advertise a course for them, which we did in conjunction with the Extra Mural Studies Department of the University of London. They called the course 'The Unmaking of the Working Class?', and the question mark at the end of the title gives a clue to their approach. Rather than imparting knowledge, Blackwell and Seabrook set about generating knowledge. Both of them were published authors and, with the cooperation of the group who enrolled, they began developing and testing ideas for a book they subsequently published in 1985.

Michael Costello was my mentor during my first few months in the Australian Trade Union Training Authority in 1985. I co-trained with him on a number of courses and so learnt the trade. The courses focussed on skills needed by union activists, such as negotiating, grievance handling, conducting meetings, problem-solving, advocacy and the like, and Costello trained participants in these skills in an apparently straightforward way, drawing on his own experience as a union official. However Costello read philosophy 'as a pastime', and his interest in choice and the moral dilemmas associated with choice was evident in the structured exercises he wrote. One exercise required the shop steward participants to represent a member who had removed materials from a worksite. Removing small amounts of material was a perk of the job, accepted by both management and workers, but this member had removed more than was 'normal'. How would the participants represent their member, and save his job? How, for a start, would they define his actions? Was this a matter of established custom and practice, or was it a matter of theft? (Costello told me he named the member in the exercise Alf Ayer after the philosopher A. J. Ayer.) Costello would show a film, construct an exercise, or light on a problem during a discussion, fix the group in his gaze, and ask: 'What would *you* do?'

Phil Drew was Director of the Trade Union Training Authority's Clyde Cameron College, and I co-trained with him extensively there on residential courses from 1985 to 1989. Drew, more than any other educator I have worked with, has formed a clear understanding of his relationship to the participants in a course. He employs democratic processes and demonstrates an extraordinary respect for the learners as union members, but retains a non-negotiable authority to conduct training that promotes union policy. He sees his contract with the union organisation taking precedence over any contract he might have with the participants as learners. This means that when he uses role play or other kinds of structured exercise, he does so to promote union development first and personal development a very distant second. This means that he has developed a very particular style of presenting information. Drew will start a session by asking questions, standing thoughtfully by the whiteboard. He will record, often in single words, some of the answers he receives, but not all. There is none of the humanist adult educator's respect for all contributions here. Drew judges answers according to their value to the subject in hand, to the union, and to the union's struggle. Gradually a dynamic develops. The terms upon which answers will be accepted become clear and people become eager to contribute. Lots of ideas, information and opinions are volunteered. But always Drew remains in charge, pausing, considering, accepting or rejecting replies, adding in his own ideas and taking the session in the direction he wants it to go. Watching Drew conduct one of his 'interactive information sessions' is to see a professional in full control of his moment.

Three adult educators stand out in the literature as models for the activist adult educator. These are Freire, Horton and Thompson. I have written about each of them in two other contexts (1993, 1994) so will content myself with a quote from each. Together these quotes provide a discourse of adult education as opposition.

Freire (1972b: 72-73) describes the forces his educational work is pitted against:

The Right in its rigidity prefers the dead to the living; the static to the dynamic; the future as a repetition of the past rather than as a creative venture; pathological forms of love rather than real love; frigid schematization rather than the emotion of living; gregariousness rather than authentic living together; organization men rather than men who organize; imposed myths rather than incarnated values; directives rather than creative and communicative language; and slogans rather than challenges .

Horton (Moyer, 1981) recognises that educators in opposition must face up to the possibilities of violence, and in doing so must take sides:

I know that in a class-structured society violence exists and the victims are the poor. And I'm not going to stand back when they try to devise ways of doing things and not try to help them work out their own ways of doing it.

And Thompson (1983: 54), writing about her work at the Southampton Women's Education Centre, talks of education in opposition constructed on anger:

Growth through anger, focused with precision, can be a powerful source of energy, serving progress and change. Anger expressed and translated into actions in the service of women's visions and women's futures can be a liberating and strengthening act of clarification, for it is in the painful process of this translation, that we identify who are our genuine allies and who are our enemies.

Others whom I might put forward as models, such as Gordon McColl, Jillian Nicholson, Astrid von Kotze and Sithando Ntshingila, you have already met.

184

18: Counter-cultural adult educators

I have used a commitment to education as opposition as a criterion for identifying people who might serve as models for adult educators. However, commitment does not mean that the people I have described were unnecessarily earnest, as Compton's chuckle would attest, or Drew's wry smile, as he pauses and considers a response, lets the tension build and then, to the delight of the participants, adds the response to the white board. But to make the point in a little more detail I want to describe one more course and two of the people involved in it. Again I am delving some way into the past, but there is a reason for this which I will try to explain.

In 1971 with the help of a friend I set up a course at Addison Institute called 'Alternative Societies'. The course came at an interesting time. The student riots, the rock concerts in Hyde Park and at Woodstock, flower power, Haight-Ashbury, and the plethora of underground press that marked the sixties were mostly over but still vivid in the memory. In Australia and the USA the anti-Vietnam war campaigns were growing in force and anger. In the UK community action groups were proliferating. Counter culture and community action seemed to provide alternative ways of looking at and dealing with the world. The course attracted some fifty people before enrolments were closed, and they made an interesting sight, some dressed in velvet and beads, queuing alongside members of dressmaking and keep fit classes in the school cafeteria at tea break on Wednesday evenings.

The friend was Andrew Fisher. He had no experience in adult education but was a perfect coordinator and facilitator of the course. He had been involved closely in *Oz Magazine*, which during the second half of the nineteen sixties had been the mouthpiece of the counter-cultural movement in London. As a result he had contacts throughout the counter-cultural organisations that proliferated in London, and was able to invite leaders and luminaries as speakers. He had a first degree in law and a post graduate degree in international law, and this training was evident in his ability to draw the diverse strands of the course together and to keep some of the wilder speakers on track. He was widely read in socio-political and counter-cultural literature, so that from time to time he was able to provide a theoretical grounding for some of the ideas promoted by speakers or canvassed in class discussion. And by virtue of his alternative lifestyle, he brought to the class an anarchic sense of inquiry, an openness to new and extravagant ideas, and that cheerful irreverence for all givens that made the counter culture so attractive.

Fisher and I are both Australians, and we invited Richard Neville, another Australian, to speak on the Alternative Societies course. Neville was one of the editors of *Oz Magazine* and a recognised figure in the international counter-cultural movement. He has written books, including *Playpower* (1971) and *Hippie Hippie Shake* (1995), dealing with the counter culture of the sixties. These contain vivid description and shrewd analysis, but in my experience it is as a speaker that he has had the most impact. As editor of *Oz Magazine*, Neville was charged with publishing obscene material, and defended himself at the Old Bailey. The trial is recounted by Tony Palmer in his book *The Trials of OZ* (1971). The book, better than most, captures the flavour of the counter-cultural ideas of the time, and has examples of Neville in eloquent full flow. At the Alternative Societies course Neville spoke passionately and illuminatingly about other ways of thinking and living, and I particularly remember his analysis of the mechanical and spiritually unproductive way most work, even so-called intellectual work, was organised. At the time he spoke he was on bail pending an appeal against a conviction. He was in excellent form, articulate and full of iconoclastic good humour. But even if his talk had been lacklustre it would not have mattered. The trial, his conviction, the shearing of his hair in gaol and his application to appeal had all received national publicity in the UK, and Neville had become a public figure, a symbol, an image.

The Alternative Societies course was exciting, and seemed unique. However, as I have already indicated, it was a product of its time; and the wisdom of hindsight enables me to see that it reflected an intellectual trend already well under way. In the late

186

nineteen sixties and the nineteen seventies we talked of alternative societies or counter cultures. Theordore Roszak, seen by some as the 'resident philosopher' of the counter culture, depicted the resistance by young people in North America in the nineteen sixties as a rejection of the rationalism of the enlightenment, and as an attempt to find other, sometimes older and more traditional, ways of living and relating to our world:

> For all its frequently mindless vulgarity, for all its tendency to get lost amid exotic clutter, there is a powerful and important force at work in this wholesale willingness of the young to scrap our culture's entrenched prejudice against myth, religion and ritual. The life of Reason (with a capital R) has all too obviously failed to bring us the agenda of civilised improvements the Voltaires and Condorcets once foresaw (1971: 145-146).

And he argued that we needed to re-establish the magical in our intellectual lives:

> Our habit in the modern west—especially in the academy—is to denature all symbols on contact, the better to keep them isolated at a cerebral level... There is prodigious scholarship on myth, ritual, religion and rite, mostly by experts who have never lived their way into these things for a moment... So there are ways of knowing and ways of knowing, and if there is any magic to be found in the great sacramental symbols of human culture, it is certain our orthodox way of knowing will never find out (1973: 140-141).

Another major voice seeking alternatives in the seventies was that of Robert Pirsig. In *Zen and the Art of Motorcycle Maintenance* (1976) he captured the moment between the fading force of the counter-cultural discourse, and a new kind of intellectualism based on an informed and sceptical kind of self-examination and a return to older philosophical values. He attacked our Western European habit of analysing concepts by breaking them down into their component parts—'this dumb, ritual of analysis, this blind, rote, eternal naming of things (p. 365)'—and he promoted a pre-intellectual 'Quality' as the source of all subjects and objects (p. 250), a cause of meaning of our lives. In a sense Pirsig's whole book is an examination of Quality, but in one passage he describes Phaedrus, one of the writer's personae in the book, reflecting on the need for a new spiritual *rationality*—in which the ugliness and the loneliness and the spiritual blankness of dualistic technological reason would become illogical. Reason was no longer to be 'value-free.' Reason was to be subordinate, logically, to Quality, and he was sure he would find the cause for its not being so back among the ancient Greeks, whose mythos had endowed our culture with the tendency underlying all the evil of our technology, the tendency *to do what is 'reasonable' even when it isn't any good* (p. 363).

In what constitutes a direct challenge to some of the ideas that have shaped our Western European culture, Pirsig seeks to rehabilitate the Sophists, those much maligned philosophers who preceded Plato, Aristotle and, more particularly, Aristotelean logic. Throughout the book Pirsig combines the techniques of fiction, autobiography and analysis, and through the personae of Phaedrus and the 'I' of the narrator makes use of two sometimes dissonant voices. In an extraordinary passage (pp. 358-385) he takes the reader into a philosophy tutorial filled with repressed intellectual conflict, out on to the highways on a motorcycle, into a township of lonely people, and into libraries along with Phaedrus in search of other interpretations of the pre-Socratic philosophers. He argues that Plato, with Aristotle hard on his heels, set out to discredit the Sophists; and in the course of his search Pirsig gradually uncovers the Excellence or Quality or Good he believes was taught by the Sophists. This Excellence or Quality or Good can be apprehended and acted upon but carries none of the Platonic idea of an ideal or an immortal truth, nor the Aristotelean concepts of form or substance, and so defies conventional definition.

> The Good was not a form of reality. It was reality itself, ever changing, ultimately unknowable in any kind of fixed, rigid way (p. 383).

Pirsig decries the loss of this Excellence as a source. In burying the Sophists and adopting the ideas of Plato and Aristotle, he argues, we developed the scientific capability to build empires, manipulate nature, and create power and wealth; but in return for this we

> exchanged an empire of understanding of equal magnitude: an understanding of what it is to be part of the world, and not an enemy of it (p. 382).

The term 'counter culture' had associations with the period of flower power in the sixties, and as that period rapidly dated so the term became less current. As the seventies progressed the terms 'post-structuralism' and, a little later, 'postmodernity' entered the language, and writers associated with these concepts such as Jacques Lacan, Michel Foucault, Jean-Francois Lyotard and Jean Baudrillard began to have an influence beyond the academy and beyond their native France. Lacan and Foucault had been writing during the sixties and the influence of their ideas had been felt in the student riots in Paris in May 1968 and, through the widespread influence of those riots, in the various manifestations of the counter-cultural movement in other parts of the world. There was a time lag between the publication of Foucault's earlier work in French and then in English, yet ideas have an uncanny way of travelling and while the Alternative Societies course made no reference to Foucault or Lacan, the course nonetheless reflected something of Foucault's thinking on the plurality of resistances, his analyses of knowledge and power, and his study of the inculcation in people of self-imposed conformity. Perhaps the course also reflected something of Lacan's questioning of conventional ideas of identity as a stable set of characteristics, and his proposal that we actually 'get knowledge of what we are from how others respond to us' (Sarup, 1993: 12).

Lyotard, in *The Postmodern Condition* rejects totalising theories and stresses the fragmentation of society and the self. Art, morality and science have become separated. In the place of wisdom there is the accumulation of computerised data, and in the place of learning there is the commodification of knowledge.

> Knowledge is and will be produced in order to be sold, and it is and will be consumed in order to be valorized in a new production: in both cases, the goal is exchange. Knowledge ceases to be an end in itself, it loses its 'use value' (1984: 4-5).

In place of 'grand narratives' such as the Enlightenment, Lyotard sees a multiplicity of discourses without coherent connections. At one point he defines 'postmodern' as being an 'incredulity towards metanarratives' (1984: xxiv). He argues that we struggle in an agonistic environment using various discourses or 'language games' that observe different rules. Because these conflicting discourses are governed by different rules, there is no way of judging between them. It is as if in one language game we

189

are playing chess, and each utterance we make is a like a move, and in another language game we are playing tennis where each utterance is a like a racket stroke. There is, as Bauman argues, no overarching or 'supracommunal' authority to which we can appeal.

> Instead, the post modern perspective reveals the world as composed of an indefinite number of meaning-generating agencies, all relatively self-sustained and autonomous, all subject to their own respective logics and armed with their own facilities of truth-validation (Bauman, 1992: 35).

Since Lyotard accepts that communication is like point-scoring, he rejects Habermas's ideal of consensus achieved through discussion, arguing that 'such consensus does violence to the heterogeneity of language games'. Invention, he maintains, is born of dissension; and the fragmentation implicit in postmodern ideas of knowledge, society and self 'refines our sensitivity to differences and reinforces our ability to tolerate the incommensurable' (Lyotard, 1984: xxv).

Baudrillard adds to this extraordinary mix of ideas. In his earlier work written in the late nineteen sixties and early seventies he argues that consumption has replaced production as the major activity upon which we construct society, rank people and things, create codes, and make meaning of our lives. From the mid-seventies on he examines the way we have divorced image from reality in this consumer society, and made our world one of simulations. To explain his concept of simulation, he compares a person who feigns illness, with another person who simulates illness and in doing so actually produces some of the symptoms of the illness.

> Thus, feigning or dissimulating leaves the reality principle intact: the difference is always clear, it is only masked; whereas simulation threatens the difference between 'true' and 'false', between 'real' and 'imaginary'. Since the simulator produces 'true' symptoms, is he or she ill or not? The simulator cannot be treated objectively as ill or not ill (Baudrillard, 1988: 168).

Baudrillard argues that in our late twentieth century world we are assaulted by images which exist as themselves and have no other meaning. We accept the signifier, reject the signified, and enter a kind of 'hyperreality'. More and more we accept the play of images, simulacra and vicarious encounter made available through mass media and modern technology as 'real', in place of the direct experience of an event. In such a world the distinctions between reality and illusion are lost, and both reality and illusion go unchecked. In Baudrillard's vision, for example, theme parks do much more than provide us with entertainment.

> Disneyland is presented as imaginary in order to make us believe that the rest is real, when in fact Los Angeles and the America surrounding it are no longer real, but of the order of the hyperreal and of simulation (1988: 172).

It is the world we inhabit *outside* our theme parks which has become the illusion.

There was something of all this in that magical Alternative Societies course. A number of the texts I have referred to or quoted from above were written after the event, but in the event itself, in the form the course took, in the behaviour of those involved, in the attitudes displayed, in the ideas exchanged, and in the events that followed, there were features that Robin Usher and Richard Edwards (1994: 10) see as contributing to the condition of postmodernity. There was an evident 'breakdown of the faith in science and rationality' as a universal and value-free source of knowledge. There was 'a questioning of the modernist belief in a legitimate and hence legitimising centre upon which beliefs and actions can be grounded'. And, most significant for the course, the 'lack of a centre and the floating of meaning' were 'understood as phenomena to be celebrated rather than regretted'.

The blurb advertising the course promised contributions from:

> Women's Liberation and Freedom Movements, BIT (the underground information service), the Arts Lab Movement, Agit Prop, representatives of both city and rural communes, black communities, Free Communication groups, Black and White Panthers, Yippies, Release (to talk about the role if any of drugs), the underground press (various editors who will put forward the philosophies of their papers, e.g. Oz, It, Friends, etc.), the underground network (Vision), underground film-makers.

From the beginning of the course there was an air of excitement, elation even, at being in a classroom (the course was in a building occupied by a secondary school during the day) studying such a subject. This excitement was present throughout the course in the involved and at times emotionally charged discussions, and it reached its peak on the evening Neville spoke, an event that more than anything was a celebration of the other, the different, the alternative. The speakers presented widely varying views, with the only really unifying feature being a rejection of any totalising authority. Some of the speakers were as promised in the course blurb but a number, by the nature of their lifestyles, proved difficult to pin down to definite dates. Very early on Fisher, as the coordinator of the course, took to announcing various possibilities at the end of each meeting and asking the group for their preferences and sometimes their help in finding an appropriate speaker. The course was advertised as a ten-meeting course to be held in the first term of the academic year, but some thirty five of the group decided to go on into second term. By this time the course had developed a life of its own. Fisher still acted as facilitator, but the group took over responsibility for the content. The second term started with a member of Recidivists Anonymous speaking on alternatives to prison. During the following week a member of the group attended an RA group meeting in a prison and two others visited a hostel set up by RA for recently released members. At the second meeting the class met three ex-prisoners, and at the third meeting the strands were drawn together in a discussion and a report. The term continued with the group investigating the cases put by the women's movement, and then by People Not Psychiatry. The group decided to go on into third term, but now in an entirely autonomous form. They chose their own topics, organised their own activities, including a weekend away at a conference centre. They discussed education, environment, sexual mores, and meditative and dietary disciplines. And when the third term was over a group of some fifteen continued meeting in a pub nearby. Some worked an allotment, and a number became founding members of a welfare rights action group which ran an information stall on Saturdays in Shepherds Bush market, took up cases with local authorities, and campaigned for the protection and improvement of welfare and civil rights. Among these was Andrew, the photographer.

Most exhilarating about the course was the fact that it brought together a large group of people who quickly committed themselves to examining ideas without prejudice. They were ready to hear speakers arguing for the abandonment of totalising ideas like

Capitalism and Marxism, yet were ready to talk about holistic concepts that anticipated Pirsig's discourse on Quality. They could entertain the ideas of a Reichian therapist in one session, the politics of Black Power in the next, and the deliberate disconnectednesses of an alternative film-maker in the next. There were echoes or anticipations of Foucault in their examination of the worlds of psychiatry and prisons, of Lacan (or, more directly, the psychologists R.D. Laing and David Cooper) in their discussions of the person, of Lyotard in their rejection of grand narratives and their readiness to accept a variety of sometimes mutually exclusive discourses, and of Baudrillard in their examinations of the media and their conscious delight in the semiotics of Neville's presence and presentation.

19: Looking for postmodern adult educators

A number of theorists have examined the implications of the ideas of postmodernity for adult learning, and from the late nineteen eighties onwards a postmodern discourse in adult education has begun to emerge. Among these theorists are Westwood (1991), Usher and Edwards (1994), Bagnall (1994), Briton (1996) Usher, Bryant and Johnston (1997) and Tisdell (1998). Usher and Edwards argue that postmodernity does not indicate the ending of an epoch of history or constitute a movement. Of the term 'postmodernism' they say:

> Perhaps it is best understood as a state of mind, a critical, self-referential posture and style, a different way of seeing and working, rather than a fixed body of ideas, a clearly worked out position or a set of critical methods and techniques (1994: 2).

At another point in their text, Usher and Edwards make reference to Baudrillard's concept of the hyperreal and talk of the postmodern in terms of experience:

> To be postmodern is to experience the world in a way and to an extent in which it has not been experienced previously, by participation and immersion in its images. It is to recognise that experience is not a direct representation of the world, but is itself a construct, an outcome of discursive practices (1994: 199).

And they celebrate change:

> Rather than being seen as a problem or a source of error, the fluidity of the world and its constantly changing images are identified as pleasurable, as something to be enjoyed(1994: 199)

Robin Usher, Ian Bryant and Rennie Johnston pick up on Lyotard's concept of incredulity and talk of postmodernism providing the intellectual resources that enable us to critique, that is to be incredulous of, aspects of our lives which we nonetheless continue to live with. We may need science but...

Postmodernism enables a questioning of the scientific attitude and scientific method, of the universal efficacy of technical-instrumental reason, and of the stance of objectivity and value neutrality in the making of knowledge claims. This is not so much a matter of rejection but rather of recognising that these are claims not truths, claims which are socially formed, historically located cultural constructs, thus partial and specific to particular discourses and purposes (1997: 7).

This attitude of incredulity, they argue, will involve 'self-critique and a dissolving of self-certainty' (p. 7):

The modernist search for a true and authentic self and the fulfilment of a pre-given individual autonomy gives way to a playfulness where identity is formed (and 're-formed') by a constantly unfolding desire that is never fully or finally realised. The unified, coherent and sovereign self of modernity, the firm ground for the fixing of identity, become a multiple and discontinuous self, traversed by multiple meanings and with shifting identity (p. 10).

Together, Usher and Edwards, and Usher, Bryant and Johnston argue that postmodernity involves a new state of mind, mood or attitude, a new kind of critique, a new way of experiencing the world, a new idea of what is real, and a new concept of the self. These are extraordinary claims and would lead the reader to expect that they and other authors making these claims would go on to outline new kinds of adult education, cite case studies, and suggest new ways of going about helping people learn. Yet the texts listed above remain for the large part theoretical. They discuss the various ideas and discourses of postmodernity and use them as ways of understanding contemporary contexts, but give few examples or case studies of educational practice. Nowhere can I find a portrait of a postmodern educator, or evidence that such a person exists. Usher and Edwards do discuss the increased legitimacy given to experiential learning 'as a condition of and for the postmodern' (1994: 196), yet experiential learning in its most pervasive form is a thoroughly humanist and therefore modernist project, concerned with the examination of a self conceived as a single entity. And Usher, Bryant and Johnston in their book entitled *Adult Education and the Postmodern Challenge* (1997) give over more than a chapter to a discussion of the ideas and practice of Schon. But Schon's ideas of reflection in and on practice (1983) are located within the modernist project of professional and corporate management procedures. Schon recognises the uncertainties and confusions (the swamp) of much of human life, but seeks ways of managing well within that environment and of bringing parts of that environment under control. Usher, Bryant and Johnston subject some of Schon's text to a form of discourse analysis, so perhaps could be said to be applying a postmodernist form of analysis, yet their conclusion that Schon's own analysis lacks reflexivity owes more to critical theory than postmodernism.

Derek Briton in his *The Modern Practice of Adult Education: A Postmodern Critique* (1996: 99-119) formulates the concept of 'a postmodern pedagogy of engagement', yet when examining the implications for practice of this concept he resorts to generalised exhortation. He argues, for example, that the case he has put 'means the security and certainty of scientific rationality has to be relinquished', that 'it means acknowledging that adult education is a sociohistorical and political practice, not a range of techniques and instrumental methodologies devoid of human interest', and that 'ultimately, it means coming to terms with post-ideological or post-hegemonic forms of adult education practice, with adult education as a pedagogy of engagement' (p. 116). In a postscript, Briton frankly acknowledges his silence on educational practice. He says that he fully intended ending his book with a chapter on the practical application of his ideas to teaching and learning but for the time being has decided not to.

> I find myself struggling, however, to think and write about these practical concerns in a way that does not subjugate them to the abstract and decontextualised ideas that have come to dominate lived experience... (p. 121).

Elizabeth Tisdell (1998) does give an example of practice. Drawing on her experience 'as a postmodern or poststructuralist feminist adult educator' (p. 148), she recounts how she and a student negotiated a final assessment task for a masters level class on adult development. She uses the example to examine her 'positionality' as a white woman instructor backed up by institutional authority, but despite her use of the postmodern concept of position, the example would appear to be that of a teacher and student engaging in critical self-examination in a conventional, that is, modernist, university setting.

Tisdell argues that 'poststructuralist feminist pedagogies' foreground the positionality of those involved; deconstruct dichotomies and emphasise 'the connections between'; problematise the notion of truth; and envisage identity as always shifting. She acknowledges the strong connections with critical theory, but I would go further and argue that some of the features she identifies derive directly from dialectical analysis or critical theory and owe little or nothing to postmodern discourse. Emphasising what mediates opposites sounds very much like a dialectical process; while examining the influences that contribute to one's positionality, and problematising truth may both be part of a postmodern pedagogy but they are equally tools of critical thinking.

Amongst the purposes and strategies of poststructuralist feminist pedagogies Tisdell cites working for change and 'giving voice' to marginalised groups. Again, these are ideas that sit equally well, if not more appropriately, within the modernist project of social and political emancipation.

The postmodern discourse in adult education can be frustrating. It collects together exciting ideas and poses significant challenges (such as Tisdell's aims, for example), but where are the applications of these ideas and challenges? I can find courses *on* postmodernity or postmodernism, but few if any courses, activities, or examples of learning that *are* postmodern. When stripped of some of the verbiage used to describe them, the few examples given by writers on postmodernity in adult education seem to fall within the humanist, corporatist or critical traditions.

Again I find myself thinking of the Alternative Societies course, and accept that I must to go back to 1971 in my own experience in order to find anything in practice that has a resonance with this postmodernity discourse. Of course an appeal to my own experience proves nothing at all but it does excite my doubts about the applicability, the relevance and ultimately the value of these ideas.

So I can mount a thoroughly 'modernist' criticism of the postmodern discourse on adult education. The discourse does not accord with reality. It is generated by a group of thinkers dealing in the abstract at a time when adult education on the ground, in the forms of continuing education, human resource development, and industrial training, is becoming ever more obviously the servant of the state or corporate world, at a time when the design and delivery of these kinds of adult education are dominated by the mechanistic principles of competency-based training, and at a time when adult education is increasingly subject to forms of validation and surveillance of curriculum by centralised accreditation bodies that are part of the state or the system.

The trouble is that the postmodernity discourse contains such a multiplicity of ideas and allusions that it is often easy to find within it apparent explanations for trends or events. Recently in Australia universities have been rewriting courses into flexible or distance or self-managed mode, developing packages and programs that enable students to study off-campus in a variety of ways. We could draw upon the imagery of decentredness and 'dedifferentiation' (Usher, Bryant and Johnston, 1997: 23) to describe and 'explain' this new diversity of forms. We could draw on the ideas of consumption and desire to explain the new relationships of these distance students to the providing universities. But if we look at the forces behind this development, we see that the Federal Government has reduced funding to universities and, in line with its other policies, is placing pressure on universities to generate their own income through competitive marketing of their courses. This competition leads to wasteful duplication and, in some cases, distance learning packages that can be no more than pale imitations of the courses offered on campus where teachers and students can work together, negotiate curriculum, generate knowledge, and perhaps occasionally share moments of wisdom. While the new forms of provision making use of a variety of print and electronic media might be open in some superficial way to a postmodern analysis, the forces driving these developments have much closer affinities to a raw and old-fashioned capitalism.

I can also mount a criticism of this postmodern discourse on adult education from within the discourse itself. These writers have constructed a language game of their own, with its own rules and its own parameters, and with no connection with other language games. Once one takes up the postmodern language game, one takes up a way of thinking and arguing that becomes satisfying in itself and appears to have a kind of recurring resonance and meaning. One can delight in the disorder, the lack of logic. Within this language game one can say:

> Instead of only one truth and one certainty, we are more ready to accept that there are many truths and that the only certainty is uncertainty (Usher, Bryant and Johnston, 1997: 210).

In other language games this statement would be regarded as nonsense. As Eagleton, whom I quoted in an earlier chapter, so acerbically pointed out, across the world there are moves to fundamentalist ideologies where vast masses of people cling to single unquestioned and unquestionable 'truths'. Worse, however, is the apparent implication in the Usher, Bryant and Johnston statement that we are more ready to accept a world without any moral certitudes, without any ideas, any causes that might help us direct our thoughts and our actions. Their view may hold at the outset of our lives, but as we develop into social beings and make meaning of our lives, some of us (many, I hope) find that concepts such as community and equity 'work'. They become true, take on a supertruth, and so become principles we strive to abide by. That there are multiple truths and endemic uncertainty may be an acceptable position to adopt in the postmodern language game, but in the language game of real life we need a number of moral certitudes. For some of us it would be difficult to accept that a commitment to consumerism is no more or less certain, or true, than a commitment to social justice.

We could argue that writers on postmodernity in adult education have constructed their own hyperreality, an imaginary adult education disconnected from the adult education the rest of us engage in. Indeed there is an irony in the fact that these writers *talk* about postmodernity, yet do not use postmodern forms for their texts. They write in conventional academic prose and their texts are devoid of the kinds of experimentation with typeface, layout, structure or genre we can find in some forms of late twentieth century literature (or, as I pointed out in an earlier chapter, in the work of Laurence Sterne). Indeed some writers on postmodernity and adult education make clear statements at the outset that, although they are writing on postmodernity, they are resisting any attempt to be postmodern or to produce a postmodern text. In one case the justification for this inconsistency is typical of the postmodern language game:

> Our own attitude to the postmodern is itself ambivalent. At one
> level, we agree with Couzens Hoy (1988) that in order to be con-

sistently postmodern, one should never call oneself a postmodern. There is a self reverential irony about this which we find ludically apt in encapsulating our relationship as 'authors' to this text. Accordingly, we shall not, and do not at any point, call ourselves 'postmodern'. Are we then being consistently postmodern and is this what we seek to convey to our readers? Not necessarily, because who, after all, wants to be consistent? (Usher and Edwards, 1994: 3)

I do not believe that the postmodern discourse has translated well from French into English. Or perhaps I should say, it has not translated well from the French *culture*. At a social occasion in France a break in the flow of conversation is simply not tolerated. There must be talk, and the instant a possible break threatens, other speakers intervene. Talk, be it a serious exchange or the parry of witticisms, is the thing. Whether the speakers believe what they are saying or not, let there be discourse. And let the discourse be clever, have shape, and challenge the minds of everyone involved in the conversation. The world of ideas *qua* ideas has a place in everyday life and serves an important social purpose, providing a base for communicative interaction. The participants in the conversation are, after all, people from a culture that reveres its thinkers, and who can turn out on the streets in their tens of thousands to mourn the death of a philosopher.

Foucault, with each of his major books, broached an entirely new subject and made little or no reference at all to his previous works. Lyotard's *The Postmodern Condition* covers a vast intellectual landscape in a remarkably short text. Baudrillard plays with and conjures up a multiplicity of ideas in his writings. Luce Irigaray (1991) writes a dialogue with Nietzsche on the subject of water! These people are using language, playing with ideas, consciously exploiting form and text. They are being particularly French, and their discourse has both a logic within itself and a social purpose rather like the dinner party conversation in which talk is preferable to silence.

Writers in English can miss the point. They take the ideas too earnestly. By locating their discussion within a conventional textual format, they lay themselves open to modernist criticisms of the kind I have levelled at them above. They miss, or ignore, or fail to understand that the French are engaged in a kind of intellectual game that reinforces the life and cohesion of a society.

And they come adrift morally. They exult in the uncertainties, inconsistencies and multiple truths; and they miss, or ignore, or fail to appreciate that their French counterparts are writing within a culture that has the moral reference points of a majority doctrinal religion (still hugely significant in French society whether actually believed in or not), and a pervasive philosophical tradition built on the primacy of rational thought.

With the French context in mind, we can better understand the wit in Baudrillard's description of Disneyland and Los Angeles. We can understand Foucault's lengthy and harrowing description of torture in the opening pages of *Discipline and Punish* (1995) as the work of a merciless raconteur. And we can see Irigaray's lyrical mixture of analytical discourse, poetry, fiction and philosophy as an elated and challenging exposition. Each in her or his own way is 'talking' in order to make us *think*. But there is no obligation for our thinking to remain in that rarefied context. When we put on our coats and leave the group at the bar or the dinner table and go out into the winter streets of Paris, we take those thoughts back into a fairly harsh and imperfect modern reality.

Viewed in this way the postmodern discourse offers little substance but it does make us think. It serves as a reminder that we need imagination, that from time to time we must break free from tradition, and that we need to take intellectual risks. This 'French' approach assumes that we retain a moral base to our intellectual adventure and so, while playful, it is not frivolous or daft. After all, if we are to be fully human we need to be able to imagine the climb.

I have already suggested that the moments when the writers on postmodernity in adult education make sense for me are when they draw not so much on postmodern ideas but on critical theory or other modernist ideas. Since the postmodern discourse is such a grab-bag of ideas, this happens from time to time. Briton (1996) draws his arguments to a close by identifying what he calls 'critical postmodernism' and then going on to discuss 'a postmodern pedagogy of engagement' (pp: 94-98). To support his ideas he draws on writers such as Vaclav Havel and Eduard Lindeman, two thinkers committed in their different ways to the pursuit of that modernist emancipatory concept of social justice. The irony is that only in the section on Havel does Briton come at all close to describing educational *practice*, and this practice is critical, not postmodern, practice.

By the same token, some people describe the film *Bladerunner* (Scott, 1982) as postmodern. The term was used in reviews and publicity when the 'director's cut' was reissued in 1992. Donovan Plumb (1995: 180) notes that 'the fragmented and alienating cultural landscape' in *Bladerunner* has affinities with some of Baudrillard's predictions of the future. Yet for me the pivotal moment in the film is when one of the replicants puts her arm gently, menacingly, around the genetic engineer's shoulders and says: 'I think, Sebastian, therefore I am'. This is a highly verbal, highly modernist moment, signalling wryly to the audience that, however extravagant the futuristic imagery may be, the film neither depicts, nor is part of, a hyperreality. The images are neither 'delinguistified', 'de-differentiated' nor 'de-politicised' (to use some postmodern jargon). They have meaning, and the film is steeped in our traditions of western thought. It is a debate about being and not being, a study of the value of life, an examination of experience, and, in the climactic roof top scene, a hymn to the choices we have and the choices we make.

20: A critical adult educator in action

Critical adult educators are easier to find. Recently I attended an afternoon of a two-day meeting of workers from the NSW Tenants Advice and Advocacy Services. These are people funded through a program coordinated by the Tenants's Union of NSW and who advise, represent, and promote the interests of boarders, caravan park residents, and tenants in private and public housing. The group of about thirty workers had spent the morning demonstrating at an event attended by the state government minister responsible for housing. Their purpose had been to draw the minister's attention to the pressures being placed on tenants by the increases in rents occurring or likely to occur as a result of Sydney hosting the Olympic Games. Back in a training room at a community centre the group of workers spent the first session of the afternoon reviewing what had happened at the demonstration.

The session was led by Gael Kennedy, the Tenants' Union training officer and she had placed several large sheets of paper on the walls of the room carrying quotes she had gathered from members of the group about the wisdom or otherwise of this kind of demonstration. These opinions differed greatly, with some arguing that it was inappropriate and potentially self-destructive to demonstrate against a minister of a government providing funding to the Tenants' Union, and others arguing that their first responsibility was to tenants which inevitably involved challenging government. Gael opened the session by inviting those whose views were expressed on the sheets of paper to elaborate, and a long discussion followed, involving analysis and self-analysis, attacks and counter-attacks. Gael occasionally intervened, using overhead transparencies carrying quotes from documents and the literature of social action. In this way during the course of an hour and a half the group examined different approaches to their work and the differing values that underpinned these approaches.

Were they agents of the state, or activists? Could they be both? Were they working for a better deal for tenants within a system, or challenging the system? What were their ideals? Were those ideals achievable? If not, did they become a hindrance? If so, then how far were they prepared to go to achieve them?

The session was not a neat affair, and it came to an end rather than a conclusion. Some of the exchanges had been vigorous, and in the aftermath one member asked for time in the presence of the whole group to apologise to another member for certain statements she had made in the heat of the discussion. The apology was accepted, and this was possible because the search for different understandings and different recognitions had been carried out within a context of pragmatic alliance typical of organisations that make up the harder forms of civil society. Some may have been angered by others; some may have disliked others; but all present shared a sufficient number of ideals to be able to work together to provide an alternate kind of representation.

Critical theory has been through the hoops. The people gathered together by the Institute at Frankfurt in the nineteen twenties were left wingers, a group of intellectuals influenced by Hegel and Marx. They were Hegelian in that they drew on his ideas of dialectical analysis, and sought to develop a critique constructed on the idea of the moving subject, the person who achieves both self-knowledge and knowledge of the world through reflection and action, through praxis. This kind of self-reflection is transformative for the individual in that it allows the person to come to know her or himself at an ever higher level of consciousness; but it is also 'reflection in history' and so transformative in the political or social sense:

> The ancient assumption that the purpose of reflection was for knowledge itself, allied with the further assumption that pure contemplation was the proper end of the human subject, was replaced by another end of reflection also derived from classical thought, but with its own peculiarly modern twist: theory when allied with praxis has a proper political end, namely social transformation (Rasmussen, 1996: 12).

They were Marxist in that they saw this praxis located in the workers' movement, and saw their critique as a way of uncovering knowledge otherwise ignored or suppressed by the capitalist

204

classes. In fact their open association with Marxist thought in those early years earned the institute the student nickname 'Cafe Marx' (Jay, 1996: 43).

With the rise of fascism in the thirties, the splintering of the workers' movement in Germany, and the advent of Stalinism in Russia, some of the thinkers associated with the institute began questioning the working class as the major and legitimate source of knowledge through action. This shift away from a concern with a revolutionary critique was further exacerbated by the fact that the institute was relocated from Germany to New York in the thirties when the Nazis came to power, and the members of the institute worked in the USA in a form of social and intellectual isolation, continuing to write in German and having only minor contact with American intellectuals (Jay, 1996). Their concern, expressed by Horkheimer in an essay entitled 'Traditional and Critical Theory' in 1937, focussed more on the concept of theory itself. Critical theory as opposed to traditional theory was still linked with social justice and a concern for reasonable conditions of life, but now the attention was on a critique of the ahistorical reification that takes place in much scientific theory-making. Horkheimer maintained that a radical reconsideration was needed 'not of the scientist alone, but of the knowing individual as such' (Rasmussen, 1996). Thus the concern shifts to a study of the way knowledge, theory and ideology are constructed, and to an examination of reason.

Theodor Adorno and Max Horkheimer were the most prominent figures associated with the Institute in the late thirties and into the forties and it is not surprising, given their isolation, the war, and the moral and physical destruction occurring in the country they had left, that their thinking was pessimistic and betrayed a loss of faith in the transformative force of reason. In a jointly written book, published in 1947 and entitled *Dialectic of Enlightenment*, they identify a paradox in the concept of enlightenment. They argue that as reason, in the search for enlightenment, broke free from its religious, mystical and magical influences, it became just as much a tool for social control as for emancipation. Rasmussen expresses the problem in this way:

> Enlightenment, which harbors the very promise of human emancipation, becomes the principle of domination, domination of

nature and thus, in certain hands, the basis for domination of other human beings (1996: 23).

Reason as it expressed itself in the development of scientific knowledge and inquiry in western societies became 'instrumental reason', whose concern was self-preservation through control and repression. Adorno and Horkheimer found themselves in a kind of intellectual cul-de-sac.

In the early nineteen fifties the institute was re-established in Franfurt, and Horkheimer, Adorno and others returned. The institute had been invited back, and so once again had a position within the intellectual life of the country and community where it was located. This regaining of position and prominence was marked by the fact that the institute, its members and their work came to be known as 'the Frankfurt School'.

Along with this rehabilitation came attempts to break free from the self-defeating nature of Horkheimer and Adorno's analysis of enlightenment, and to find again a positive and emancipatory role for critical theory to play. Adorno attempted this by turning to art. Art is a form of cognition. It has intelligibility and so can be said to be rational. But the rationality is of another kind, an expression of a form of reason that is not instrumental. Moreover, a work of art is non-identical in character. As a result, art can be a medium of truth yet be free from the dangers of generalisation and reification. And, in expressing suffering, a work of art can anticipate the removal of that suffering. As a result, art can signal emancipation.

Another way out of the cul-de-sac is to be found in the work of Habermas. In his earlier work, culminating in his book *Knowledge and Human Interests*, first published in 1968, Habermas develops his ideas on knowledge constitutive interests. As we have already seen, he postulated that there were three domains in which different kinds of human interest lead us to generate knowledge. These domains have come to be referred to in commentaries on critical adult education as 'instrumental', 'interpretive or communicative' and 'critical or emancipatory'. In this representation of knowledge-generation Habermas relegates instrumental reasoning to only one of three domains, and revives interest in knowledge of other kinds and other orders being generated in the interpretive and critical domains.

In a sense these three domains or 'tripartitions' recur through Habermas's later work (Dallmayr, 1996: 85-87), providing a framework within which to engage in critique and analysis not only of knowledge-generation but of human interaction, values, and social and political organisation. Thus parallels to the categories of instrumental, interpretive and critical generation of knowledge can be seen in the way academic disciplines can be categorised into the physical sciences (such as geology), the descriptive social sciences (such as sociology) and the critical social sciences (such as psychoanalysis). We can see human interaction respectively in terms of subject-object, subject-subject, and subject-to-itself. We can identify the modern value spheres of science, ethics, and self-expression. And we can identify objective, social and subjective worlds.

In his later work Habermas takes the interpretive or communicative domain as the major locus for praxis, and formulates his ideas of the ideal speech situation and communicative action. In doing this he maintains the critical theorists' search for social justice and 'reasonable conditions of life', but shifts the focus from a concern with reasoning and knowledge-generation to a concern with discourse and communication. There is no such thing as pure reason. Rather, reason is tied up in language, and so 'enmeshed' in communicative action and the lifeworld upon which communicative action is premised.

> As an incarnate faculty embroiled in real-life situations, reason cannot simply soar above or cancel space and time, but is always somehow 'in-the-world'. Similarly, given the linguistic character of reason—its inability to be denuded of language—there cannot be a 'pure' or purely rational language, but only an 'interlacing' or 'tensional mixture' of opacity and clarity, of real and ideal elements of discourse (Dallmayr, 1996: 86).

In his search for elements of ideal discourse, Habermas promotes the concept of criticisable validity claims. Each time we make an utterance, whether explicitly or implicitly, we make three validity claims: to truth, rightness, and truthfulness. Each of these claims is criticisable because it can be tested by a yes/no response, and each of these claims again has a relation to the three domains of knowledge-generation. The claim that our utterance is true can be redeemed by reference to instrumental reasoning. The claim that our utterance has rightness, that is, that we have a right or the authority to make the utterance, can be tested with reference to our experience in the social world, our relationships, our ethics, and our position within the organisation of society. And our claim to truthfulness, that is, our claim to sincerity, can be redeemed by reference to our personal integrity, our consistency, and our accordance with the values of the lifeworld we share with the listener.

Communicative action provides another view of praxis. Knowledge is generated through discourse-in-action. Communicative action provides another kind of ideal, in the form of uncoerced consensus. And communicative action provides new tools for critique in the form of validity claims that can be used to test every utterance.

For all its twists and turns, critical theory has a number of constants. Its concerns are with justice, reason and critique (Forst, 1996). We develop an understanding of reason in order to apply critiques that will distinguish truth from ideology, and so allow us to create a more just world. Underlying all forms of critical theory is the understanding that emancipation begins when we have come to understand how the knowledge, values and ideologies that constrain the way we think have come into being. For it is once we have understood the history of our thinking, that we can change it. For Rasmussen (1996:12):

> Critical theory derives its basic insight from the idea that thought can transform itself through a process of self-reflection in history.

And for Welton (1995: 14):

> Critical theory is a theory of history and society driven by a passionate commitment to understand how ideological systems and social structures hinder and impede the fullest development of humankind's collective potential to be self-reflective and self-determining historical actors.

It is easy to romanticise. In one sense the session Gael Kennedy conducted with the NSW Tenants Advice and Advocacy Services was simply a debriefing following the demonstration. But Kennedy is an experienced adult educator with an understanding of critical theory and we can also see how that understanding influenced the way she conducted the event. She created a kind

208

of praxis by encouraging reflection on the morning's action and by seeking decisions about further action from the group. She encouraged self-reflection by placing viewpoints on large pieces of paper and asking the holders of those views to speak. By offering additional information through her own interventions and through the use of overhead transparencies, she helped locate this self-reflection in history. By placing conflicting viewpoints on those large pieces of paper, she encouraged discussion and debate—reasoning and critique—of the values that underpinned the participants' work. And in the knowledge that all present were committed to the concepts of equity and justice, she sought to help those present achieve an uncoerced consensus.

This consensus was not achieved and the session ended with at least one participant aggrieved by things said. However at the start of the next session the apology was offered and accepted. The participant who had given offence had made reference to certain political events in another country. She said she hoped the other participant would understand that, while her comments may have been inappropriate to the matter in hand, she had made them in the course of a debate about sincerely held views. A form of reconciliation was achieved by an appeal to truth, rightness and truthfulness.

21: Adult educators for social justice

One can understand a group of German thinkers in the nineteen thirties, faced with the apparent mass acquiescence to Nazism, doubting the idea of any one particular social class being the source of knowledge through struggle or the agents for social transformation. One can understand them in the forties, when science and technology were being used to create massive war machines, doubting the rationality of the enlightenment and seeing instrumental reason as a force for control and 'masterly enslavement' (Marcuse, 1964: 25). One can understand those in the Frankfurt School in the nineteen fifties and sixties wanting to develop critiques that would dissociate truth from ideology, and to understand how and why knowledge was generated. After all, they had some unsettling case studies of 'truths' accepted by whole sectors of a society in their recent history which, now that the madness had subsided, were self-evidently nonsense. And one can understand how in the communications era of the seventies and eighties they would shift their attention away from cognition, with its implications of certainty, to language, with all its ambiguities and relativities; from the business of coming to know, to the process of reaching understanding.

However, there are problems in all these phases of critical theory. If our purpose is to engage in a constant critique of ideologies, then it will be difficult to adopt a belief system or vision of our own. This problem seems particularly obvious in Habermas's theory of communicative action. If we take ideology to mean 'the science of ideas' then Habermas provides us with the framework of knowledge constitutive interests within which to examine ideas and how they come into existence. If ideology has its more everyday meaning of 'a body of doctrine', then Habermas provides us with ways of critiquing and judging an ideology by testing the validity claims made by anyone expressing that ideology. If by ideology we mean 'a way of living', then Habermas offers us a way of understanding and critiquing social organisation against his framework of the lifeworld, civil society and system. But when we set about forming our own conclusions about the world, or arriving at our own set of ideals, Habermas has less to offer us. He may have his own vision, to be found, perhaps, in his concept of a consensus to be achieved through ideal speech; but for the idealist/pragmatists amongst us, that is, for adult educators concerned with social justice, achieving consensus is not enough. We need to know what that consensus will be about. We need to know upon what moral and political principles it will be based. And we need to know who has the political power to coerce or influence or inveigle or berate or negate and so influence the 'consensus' to their own ends. (Indeed there may be those who, along with Lyotard, will argue that invention is born of dissension, and that seeking consensus will be counter-productive.)

When Habermas talks of the uncoupling of the system from the lifeworld, he recognises inequalities of power. Yet when he talks of achieving consensus through communicative action, he seems to be assuming that everyone involved will be in a sufficiently strong position to challenge and test the validity claims of everyone else. This is an assumption we and others engaged in learning in action can never make. By its very nature, critical theory post 1937 offers frameworks for analysis, tests to be applied, and processes to be used; but uncertain political content.

There has been a major attempt in the literature of adult education to reintroduce that substance and to interpret critical theory in strongly political terms. It is *In Defense of the Lifeworld: Critical Perspectives on Adult Learning*, (1995) edited by Welton, and contributed to by himself, Mezirow, Collins, Hart and Plumb. In the opening chapter Welton states the political nature of the book's project:

> Critical theory holds out the promise of enabling us to specify concretely with practical intent how we can think of all of society as a vast school; it also helps us to understand how a global society ruled by predatory corporations and dominated by 'technocratic' or 'instrumental' rationality, is consciously structured to block, constrain, and contain societal-wide and historically deep collective enlightenment, empowerment and transformative action (p. 12).

Welton contributes two chapters. In the first he examines the origins of critical theory and traces some of the shifts of thinking in the Franfurt School. In the second he develops his argument, which I have already referred to in an earlier chapter, about adult education's role in countering the colonisation of our lifeworld by the system.

Mezirow further develops and refines his transformation theory of adult learning. In doing so he addresses the problem of the ideal nature of Habermas's consensus (echoing Turner's argument for the description of an ideal society):

> Discourse [in order to arrive at a consensus] has sometimes been misunderstood and discounted as a patently unattainable ideal in a real world in which individuals of different races, sexes, classes, and degrees of power are historically so unequally benefited educationally, economically, politically, and socially. The impact of these realities obviously so distort communications and the process of rational discourse as to make the ideal seem an unrealistic assumption because it is never encountered in real life. What is important is that ideals be understood as indispensable to enable us to set standards against which to judge performance and to provide us with goals and a heuristic sense of direction (pp. 53-54).

Collins charts the move in adult education towards professionalisation and away from the idea of adult education as a social movement. He describes the resulting reification of the ideas of self-direction, the de-skilling of educators, and the commodification of adult education in the form of standardised packages that, ironically, gain their legitimacy from andragogical ideas that education should be learner-centred, individualised and self-paced. He links these aspects of andragogy to the 'fairly recent manifestation of behaviorist influences' to be found in competency-based education, outcomes-based education and human resource development. These manifestations of adult education serve 'system world imperatives' rather than drawing on the lifeworld of the learners. In the workplace, therefore,

> ... with the alignment of HRD and the corporate ethos and modern adult education practice, adult education abandons all confidence in the collective capacity of ordinary men and women *to organize* industrial production, distribution and delivery of services. It fails to engage with the moral-political problem of what

gets in the way of ordinary men and women realising the potential which resides in the collective *competence they already possess*. Hence the anomaly within modern adult education, of *directed* self-directed learning (pp. 87-88).

Mechthild Hart focuses on the question of work, and hers is the contribution in the book that applies, rather than explicates, critical theory. She sets out to dissociate truth from the capitalist, racist and patriarchal ideologies that govern work and people's attitudes to work. Through reference to research and social, political and economic analysis she demonstrates how certain ideas about women, minorities and immigrants in the North American workforce have come into being, and whose interests these ideas serve. She mounts an attack on the scientific rationality that results in a world of work with its 'deadly fixation' on the bottom line, and on 'ever faster, ever more efficient, and ever more risky technology'. And she is critical of the individual self-sufficiency which has become the 'prime insignia of professionally defined good adult education', and which can occur in the guise of education for personal empowerment or personal transformation. She analyses how women's association with child-rearing has been used to denigrate their role in the workplace and relegate them to lower paid and casualised work; and she turns this argument on its head, promoting the concept of 'motherwork' and the values and practices inherent in it as a way of reconnecting the system of work and education with the collective issues of life and survival.

Plumb is the last of the contributors to the main section of the book. He takes another tack, and provides a critique of critical theory from a postmodern perspective. He maintains that postmodern thinking challenges the concept of culture upon which critical adult education is constructed. Culture is no longer understood as the 'distinct location for symbolic reproduction' but as a commodity. Knowledge, ideas and other cultural elements are no longer generated to meet broadly shared human interests, but for a multitude of specific purchasers to buy. These changes in the way we understand, generate and employ culture can be depicted in a number of interrelated ways. Culture has been 'de-differentiated'. Distinctions have been blurred or removed between high and low art, between art and experience, and between systematic interpretation and random and immediate apprehension. Culture has been 'delinguistified'. There has been a shift from language to image, undermining the role of rational discourse. Culture comes to us as immediate images that seduce, rather than as validity claims open to appraisal.

> Consumers are motivated to watch TV, listen to CDs, change fashions simply because it feels good, not because it makes sense (p. 175).

And this kind of culture has been 'de-politicized'. Such an understanding of culture has no place for ideas and ideologies, and so provides no site for hegemonic and counter-hegemonic struggle. Culture in this postmodern form is no longer a 'key site for social contestation'.

Plumb's contribution to the book both follows the rule and provides the exception. Like the other contributors he is influenced by key figures in the formation of critical theory. For example, in preparing the ground for his comparison of critical and postmodern concepts of culture, he draws on Marx's ideas of use value and exchange value, and on Habermas's differentiation between system and lifeworld and his theory of communicative action. But Plumb departs from the other contributors in the way he draws on postmodern writers such as Baudrillard and Lyotard in order to question and extend the ideas taken from Marx and Habermas. Like the other contributors he acknowledges and condemns the depredations of capitalism. But he differs in the way his text implies that postmodernity is a current social reality, rather than one amongst other frameworks for analysis and understanding within a capitalist or late capitalist world.

The book—a project engaged in by five prominent adult educators—is a strong political statement, in that it sets out to counter the instrumentalism that dominates adult education theory and practice in many educational arenas in many countries. And it provides an example of critical theory in practice, in that the authors not only use critical theory in their social and educational analyses but apply their own principles of critique to themselves. In a final section of the book each takes up and responds to points the others have made in their substantive chapters. In this section, for example, Welton questions Mezirow's learning theory, suggesting that he isolates 'the individual' from 'the structure', whilst Mezirow, as if to disprove this very point, demonstrates an acute awareness of context and structure in his spirited criticism of his fellow authors' reliance on European sources for critical theory, and he lists a convincing number of critical thinkers and activists from North American and elsewhere to make his point.

The book, then, makes an important contribution to the literature in the field. And yet I find it disappointing on two counts. The first is that there is little case study. Although educators making use of critical theory and practice can be found, few appear in these pages. Some are named, but their practice is not described or analysed. Theory floats free from any closely observed practice and in this respect the authors are in danger of laying themselves open to criticisms similar to those applied to postmodern theories of education.

The second count on which I find the book disappointing is that it really only deals with part of the story. In this respect, the book falls victim to a weakness in Habermas's differentiation between system and lifeworld. In chapter 15 I separated discussions of the lifeworld and the system with a discussion of various interpretations of civil society, taking my cue from Jodi Dean who argues that 'civil society mediates between the lives of social members and the state and economic systems' (1996: 221). I was in fact proposing *three* differing concepts, with civil society providing alternative forms of organisation and representation to those in the lifeworld and those in the system. Habermas recognises this form of buffer in terms of 'the new resistance and withdrawal movements reacting to the colonisation of the lifeworld' (1987: 396), but sees these arising 'along the seams between system and lifeworld' (p. 395). As this phrase suggests, Habermas departs from his clear espousal of 'tripartitions' and for the most part sees system and lifeworld as a duality: two social constructs in complex interrelationship. As a kind of shorthand, Collins (1995) refers to Habermas's 'lifeworld/system differentiation'.

In chapter 6 I argued that the class system may be less easy to recognise in these high-tech, 'post industrial' days but was still there in the forms of social groupings with profoundly conflicting interests. I maintain that Habermas's lifeworld/system differentiation obscures the existence of class, and in this he continues to reflect the Frankfurt School's retreat from class analysis in the nineteen thirties. I also maintain that because a number of the authors of *In Defense of the Lifeworld* accept the lifeworld/system differentiation, the book as a whole plays down the question of class.

We can still perceive the influences of a class analysis in Habermas's concept of the system. The system comprises power and exchange and we can easily populate it with senior executive officers, senior politicians, senior police officers, superannuation fund managers, and so on. Clearly we must concede that politicians in many countries are democratically elected, and fund managers, in theory at least, represent and therefore are responsible to the members of the fund; but it is undeniable that a class exists made up of people who exercise control over money and operate in the upper levels of structures of power. These people still constitute a 'ruling class', 'the bosses', people who put profit first, the manager-beneficiaries of capitalism.

In differentiation to the system, however, Habermas postulates the lifeworld, and this concept is far less easy to populate. In adopting the idea of the lifeworld Habermas has abandoned a class analysis, and taken up an abstract idea which he presents metaphorically as a 'web' or a 'background' of shared values, assumptions and symbolic understandings. This makes it difficult to see the system and the lifeworld in any kind of encounter, let alone in conflict, since the system is reasonably substantial and contained, while the lifeworld is abstract and almost infinite.

What is more, if we define the lifeworld as the vast background of givens upon which we base communication, then in some senses at least the lifeworld is shared by everyone, including those benefiting from the system. And if we define the system in terms of power and the economy, then in a sense everyone is implicated in it. Plumb addresses this conundrum when he talks of the relationship between the system and the lifeworld:

> Whereas the lifeworld becomes reliant on the economic sub-system for material reproduction, the economy also remains dependent on the capacities of the lifeworld for symbolic reproduction (1995: 164).

Such a symbiotic relationship plays down the existence of conflicts of interests and throws into question the injunction that we should defend the lifeworld. Who exactly will we be fighting against? Where will we construct the ramparts? Can we really defend a *background*?

These doubts lead me to go looking for writers on adult education who will provide detailed case study and so locate their theory in a time and a place; and whose discussions of these case studies will take account of social class. This is not some nostalgic yearning for a traditional working class, but I do want to find theorists and practitioners who recognise that there *are* social classes, and that these social classes are defined by matters such as work and the absence of work, language, gender, sexual preference, race, history, culture and belief. I want writers who recognise that some social classes will want to exercise control over others, and that some of the other classes will want to struggle against that control. I want to find adult educators who construct their thinking and practice on a recognition of the fact that, despite the complexities of our contemporary world, we still live in social groupings which have different, and conflicting, practical, ideological and moral interests.

Adult educators drawing upon class analysis do exist (and Hart and Welton are amongst them). In a major study of education and work, Hart (1992) analyses the devaluation and exploitation by capital of women, immigrant and Third World workers. Mayo (1994, 1997) examines Gramsci's ideas of hegemony, culture and class, and the work of Freire. Freire himself (1972a, 1972b, 1976, 1985, 1994), of course, examines education and oppression in terms of class and culture. Ettore Gelpi (1979, 1985, 1992) formulates his ideas of lifelong education as a system, practice and tool to be employed in the struggle to correct the unequal divisions of wealth and labour between rich and poor countries. Frank Youngman (1986) draws on Marxist theories of political economy and historical materialism in his analysis of adult education and development. And Allman and Wallis (Allman, 1987, 1988; Allman and Wallis, 1990, 1995) talk unambiguously about education for socialism.

My search for adult educators who not only draw upon class analysis but also ground their analyses in detailed case study takes me to Lotz in his collaborative writing with Welton, and to Jane Thompson, Griff Foley, Fred Schied and Linda Cooper.

I have already mentioned Welton's historical studies, and his work with Lotz on Father Jimmy Tomkins, Father Moses Coady and the Antigonish movement. Lotz and Welton write about farmers and fisherfolk, about working class priests, and about learning in the poorest part of Canada. Inherent in their descriptions and analyses is a recognition of social class, and they chart Tompkins' and Coady's careful manoeuvring of their project along a middle road between the Communism and Fascism of their times. I have referred elsewhere (Newman, 1993, 1994) to the work and writing of Thompson. She has described and analysed the learning engaged in by working class women at the Women's Education Centre in Southampton, England in the nineteen eighties, and more recently at Ruskin College, Oxford. Her educational work takes account of, and seeks to redress, the still glaring social, political and economic inequalities between classes; and she locates her class analysis within an uncompromising feminist analysis. And I have referred elsewhere (Newman, 1994) to the writing of Foley. He has drawn various themes in his writing together in a forthcoming book, grounding his analysis of informal learning in an eclectic range of case studies which includes a green campaign, neighbourhood houses, and a mining community in Australia; campaigns by women in North America and in Brazil; workplace and industrial relations in Australia and overseas; and the Zimbabwean struggle for independence.

Foley puts the case for his use of case study. We can interpret history, he argues, as a continual struggle between groups seeking to dominate, and groups resisting that domination. Learning, whether it is the unlearning of oppressive ideologies or the learning of 'insurgent' and emancipatory ones, is central to this struggle. These kinds of learning are complex and contradictory, and are best understood through descriptions of concrete situations, and of how people make sense of those concrete situations; that is, through accounts which, after Geertz (1988), convey a sense of 'being there'. By recounting and analysing case studies Foley sets about constructing a theory of adult education that 'both explains and enables action'.

Foley recognises that learning can also be 'dominative', reproducing oppressive relationships and ideologies. To better understand and avoid these dangers, he examines the global context within which his localised case studies take place, arguing that the economic restructuring of the past twenty five years, ostensibly undertaken for the benefit of all, has in fact been a reorgani-

218

sation of capitalism. And in the course of a discussion of work reorganisation he issues this challenge:

> Do we as adult educators choose to work with and for, capital, by accommodating ourselves to, with whatever qualifications and continued rhetorical resistance, the language and techniques of workplace restructuring which is so clearly driven by the interests of capital? Or do we take the far more difficult path of striving to develop forms of education which really serve the interests of working people? (Foley, forthcoming)

Foley's writing contains a class analysis, which he applies directly in his discussions of capitalism and which is evident in the way he talks unambiguously of, and so expresses solidarity with, 'working people', 'ordinary people', 'the uncommon common people' (a term he quotes from Horton), and 'the working class'.

Schied (1993), too, talks unambiguously of working class people. He argues that in the USA adult education has been defined in institutional terms. Histories of adult education have by and large been histories of adult education organisations, and so have paid little attention to the extraordinary amount of non-formal and informal education and learning taking place in people's working, community and family lives. In particular, he argues, 'workers' education has, until recently, been seen as either peripheral to the study of adult education or simply not discussed' (p.149).

Schied redresses this lack by providing a detailed case study of the lives, events, emotions, pleasures, and hardships of the German-American working class community in Chicago during the nineteenth century. He describes the informal learning and education which took place at picnics and festivals, in bars and saloons, through German language newspapers and publications, through German language theatre, in the libraries, reading rooms and lectures provided by a wide variety of associations, in discussion and debating societies, through workers' clubs and workers' unions, and through political activity and action.

The case study takes up the four main chapters of the book, to which Schied adds an afterword. In this he sets about reconceptualising adult education history in the USA. He links workers' education with current radical non-formal and informal education. Such current practice is not without antecedents. It is informed by history, of which nineteenth century workers' education is a major part. In this section Schied makes little reference to his case study, so that the case study and the afterword stand in a kind of contrapuntal relationship, separate but hugely significant to each other by virtue of their juxtaposition.

Schied's work is important for at least two major reasons. The first is that in arguing that social class be given due weight in analyses of adult education, he uses a concept of social class that extends beyond one defined by people's relationship to production. Schied depicts class as groups of people deriving their commonality not only from shared experiences of work and relationships to the means of production, but also from shared cultures, histories, communities, languages and ethnicities. He reminds us that a social class can be made up of people who as individuals may have differing ways of earning their living and different places in the structure of an economy yet who will come together in cultural and political action.

A second major reason why Schied's work is so important is that he uses a historical case study and educational analysis in this 'contrapuntal' way to inform debates about current theory and practice of adult education. Schied draws on his personal story to explain:

> For me [history] was always a *lived* experience. From my status as a refugee in Austria, to my family's displaced person status in the U.S., I was always conscious that I lived in a historical present. That is, the present as not only shaped by history, but the past as always present in everyday life (p. 2).

While I was in South Africa I had a sense of people living history in the way Schied describes. For many, their talk and their actions were informed by the years of apartheid and the recent lifting of apartheid. And because the political and moral world they now lived in was so utterly different, many of the actions they took, whether big or small, broke some kind of new ground. Even in the course of living out the routine parts of their lives, people seemed to be encountering new experiences and challenges daily and so were actually *making* history.

Cooper (1998) captures this sense of history in her analysis of the shifts in union and worker education in South Africa. She argues that there are two conflicting discourses. The first derives from the history of the black union movement from the early nineteen-seventies to nineteen ninety, a period in which the unions formed, engaged in industrial action, grew in size and number, developed national structures and peak bodies, and became major participants in the political struggle to defeat the apartheid regime. This discourse, Cooper argues, draws on workers' collective experiences of oppression and exploitation and 'views the purpose of education as one of empowerment and social transformation' (1998: 143).

As the unions themselves developed structures, so some of the worker education within the union movement took on the structured forms of courses, seminars and workshops. But throughout this period, Cooper tells us, worker and trade union education also took place at meetings, rallies and *siyalalas* (gatherings where workers debated political and industrial issues late into the night); through art exhibitions, workers' theatre (of the kinds described by von Kotze), performance by workers' choirs, and poetry readings (inspired by people like Qabula); through newsletters, union newspapers, calendars, pamphlets and booklets; and in the course of strikes and other forms of workers' resistance.

In certain respects the working class Cooper depicts is a recognisably industrial one, defined by their work in factories making use of production-line modes of work organisation. But her depiction has affinities with Schied's in that it is also defined by race and culture and language, by the township communities in which the workers live and from which they have to travel in order to work, and by the unique contemporary political context.

The second discourse on workers' education, Cooper argues, is one which has emerged since 1990, the year when Nelson Mandela was released from prison, and South Africa began working its way towards its first democratic elections. In this period, and particularly since the 1994 elections, the black trade unions have moved from being an oppositional force in a political struggle to partners in many of the processes of government. Union representatives have found themselves on tripartite bodies, helping formulate and then implement government policies. In the case of worker education, these policies have included the establishment of the South African Qualifications Authority and the development of a new National Qualifications Framework. This new discourse, Cooper argues, is derived from outside the labour movement:

> The dominant meaning associated with worker experience and knowledge is being transformed from that of a shared resource (a source of knowledge and a guide to action) which can be drawn upon in order to advance collective interests of the working class, into the notion of 'experience' as a commodity which is individually 'owned' and can be exchanged for a qualification in order to compete with other workers on the capitalist labour market, and in the struggle for individual upward mobility and 'career paths' (1998: 152).

Cooper maintains that practices and thinking associated with political struggle survive, 'and in some places thrive', and she cites the continued use of the discourse of struggle in union debates, the political nature of questions raised by workers in seminars and workshops, and research that indicates that many workers 'most deeply value' democratic and critical practices in their education and training. In much the same way as Foley does, Cooper challenges educators to find the conditions in which the more radical, transformative approaches to worker education might contest the 'hegemonic knowledge practices' currently underwriting the newer discourse.

When I was in South Africa I led a session of a course for community adult educators being run by Cooper and her colleague Janice McMillan at the University of Capetown. Under apartheid, the university had been an almost wholly white institution. The eighteen or so participants attending the course were black while Cooper, McMillan and I were white, so revolutionary change had taken place in one respect but not in another. A couple of days later Cooper and McMillan were going to visit three course participants at a community and welfare centre where the participants were voluntary workers, and they asked me to come along. They picked me up at my temporary lodgings on the hillside just below the university campus, and we drove down and out of the white suburb, on to the plain and, after some fifteen or twenty kilometres, into the sprawling township of Khayelitsha.

I had visited Soweto and Sharpeville when I was based in Johannesburg, and Cato Crest camp outside Durban, but I was still struck by the immensity of the township, the lack of vegetation, the rows upon rows of matchbox houses, the dust from the unsurfaced roads, and the unremitting harshness of it all. For the visitor from the comfortable places I normally inhabit, the crowded, cluttered, heavily populated, disordered landscape of endless, low-lying constructions might have come from a work of science fiction. As if to reinforce this impression, there were bizarre anomalies. To get there we had driven along a modern freeway. Once into the township we got briefly lost. We were looking for a petrol station, at which we were to turn right, but found two in sight of each other, both modern self-service facilities with covered forecourts. The tilted covers, supported by thin metal stanchions, stood higher than the surrounding buildings so that the petrol stations, like two sentinels, dominated the landscape.

Once we had found our bearings, we drove to a community health clinic where Cooper and McMillan met with the coordinator. Beside the clinic was a cargo container donated, I learnt, by a shipping company and converted into a radio station. We were shown through a small door in the side of the container, and found ourselves in the antechamber to the broadcasting studio. On the other side of the glass panel in the studio itself an announcer played township music, introduced with a patter in a language I did not understand but which had the familiar swoops of intonation and extravagant emphases of the universal disc jockey.

From the clinic we drove to a building that housed a number of community agencies. The building, like all the others around it, was a single storey construction made out of cement bricks. In one of the offices we found the three participants, and a long-time community activist with whom they were working. The six South Africans talked of the problems in this area of the township and the perennial struggle for funding while I sat silent. I had nothing to contribute. The differences in the standards of living between the suburb in Capetown I had left that morning (and the suburb in Sydney I had left a couple of months earlier) and here were so great that I could not imagine where anyone would start in order to repair the inequities.

I was still in Capetown the following week, and Cooper told me that Kholeka Ndamase, one of the three participants we had visited, wanted to talk with me after class. The two of us met in Cooper's office, and Ndamase asked me if I could suggest ways of identifying needs to which she and her volunteer colleagues might make an educational response. She said she was still uncertain how she should make a start.

We looked at each other. Did she have friends and allies, I asked. Well, yes, her two colleague volunteers, the activist coordinator I had met, and some others. There was a white board on the wall and I suggested we indicate these people on the board, and draw lines between them where the relationships were strong. What governed those relationships? Friendship? Family? Common experience? Beliefs? We wrote in one of two factors that mediated the relationships. Did those allies and friends have other contacts and allies themselves? We wrote in a few, and drew some more lines. What organisations did some of these figures on the board relate to? We wrote up a couple of examples, drew lines, and identified what mediated the relationships. So far, the people and organisations identified seemed to be allies. Were there any organisations or groups that she saw as likely to obstruct the things she and her friends and allies might want to do? This was a bit more difficult, but we put up one or two agencies that seemed indifferent to community initiatives, drew some lines to other agencies, and thought about what mediated those relationships. The whiteboard began looking untidy, but we could see some contacts that might be usefully reinforced, some new alliances to forge and, in some of the factors mediating some of the relationships, one or two issues emerging.

It was late afternoon and Ndamase had to go so our discussion had been reasonably brief. After she left, I sat for a while. We had not got very far. I was still overwhelmed by the dimensions of the township, the apparently intractable nature of the challenges facing everyone living there, and the awful gap between the different South African realities. Out of a kind of desperation I had used a form of analysis that hinted at class and conflict, but it had been all too brief and I had been all too oblique in the way I had gone about it. A few days later I flew out of Capetown and on to Europe and the next stage of my six months study leave.

Some eighteen months later there was a possibility that I might get to South Africa again. In the end I was unable to go and I wrote to Cooper telling her this. In her reply there was a postscript saying that Ndamase would be disappointed. When

Cooper had told her that I might be visiting Capetown again, Ndamase had said that if I did manage to get there she would like to tell me about the literacy training program for women that she and her two volunteer colleagues were working to establish.

Section 8: Intervention and struggle

22: Learning and morality

In that production of *The Tempest* I saw in New York Patrick Stewart gave an inspired performance. But giving him the role of Prospero was an inspired piece of casting as well, since for a number of years Stewart had played Jean-Luc Picard, the captain of the Starship Enterprise in the TV series *Star Trek: The Next Generation*. I always liked the way Stewart portrayed Picard as a man with a strong morality which new situations continually challenged. The TV series has its origins in the counter culture of the late sixties. The first series of *Star Trek* was a downmarket, popular expression of the rejections of conventional rationalism, and the revelling in image that found an intellectual expression a little later in Lyotard and Baudrillard. Shakespeare's *The Tempest*, in its turn, is like a piece of science fiction and Prospero, like the captain of the Starship Enterprise, presides over a place where beings from different worlds are brought together and where extraordinary events occur. In this piece of casting, the fantasies of Shakespeare and of a popular TV program coalesced.

For me the casting worked. For his Prospero Stewart could draw on an ancient past inhabited by legends and fairies, and on a fantasy/science fiction future, on Romance, Renaissance and modern pop culture, on great literature and the moral simplicities of pulp television. And once I had accepted the association with Picard in the character of Prospero, I found other associations with the television series in other features of the production: in the sometimes garish use of lighting, in the flowing, slightly hippie-like shift that Ariel wore, and in the fact that, just as people were beamed up and down in the television series, so in the play spirits dissolved into air, into thin air.

In my reflections on the play I have enjoyed seeing Prospero/Picard as a model for the adult educator. Prospero/Picard operates in a world of contradictions. There are different forms of power, some rational and explicable, and some more mysterious.

There is love. There is loyalty. There is violence and there are enemies. But people can and do change. And sometimes that change will be more than the acquisition of a new skill or a new piece of knowledge or some slightly adapted attitude. It will be 'a sea-change into something rich and strange'. Prospero/Picard, motivated by a vision of a just and reasonable world, intervenes in the lives of other people, sometimes effectively, sometimes imperfectly but always humanly, in an attempt to help them learn.

Freire intervened in the lives of peasant villagers, shanty-town dwellers and tenement dwellers in Brazil in the early nineteen sixties and, when he was exiled from Brazil after the military coup in 1964, in Chile. Through the use of study circles and literacy circles he sought to help people move from a naive or 'magical' or fatalistic consciousness to a critical one, a sea change he described as *conscientization*. He sought to help his learners claim and recount their own experience, cease being people to whom social history happened, and become people who consciously lived within, and played a part in *creating*, their own histories. Central to his project was the use of authentic rather than inauthentic language. Through teaching and learning processes which included carefully coded drawings, and dialogue and discussion, Freire sought to help people see and describe the world around them in their own terms rather than in the terms given or dictated to them by those in power. 'To exist, humanly,' he said, 'is to *name* the world, to change it (1972a: 61).'

Freire's ideas have been written about, analysed, interpreted, extended and put into practice in many parts of the world. He challenges the 'banking' concepts of education which privilege the experts and their expert bodies of knowledge; and he expresses his respect for the learners and their own experience and cultures, describing them as *learner-teachers* and the educators working with them as *teacher-learners*. He talks openly of the oppressed and the oppressors, and sees teaching and learning as being of central importance within a revolutionary process he names as 'cultural action for freedom'. His work is admired, indeed revered, by educators and activists committed to principles of social justice.

For my own part, however, when I came to read Freire's writings I was ready to be critical. I had been prepared by Michael

Costello who, in a conversation when we were both working as union trainers, had pointed to what he maintained was a significant inconsistency in Freire's discourse. Freire advocated that the educator should respect the learners' experience and culture, yet by encouraging the development of a critical consciousness he appeared to be mounting an attack on the beliefs in magic and superstition that formed a significant part of the Brazilian peasant learners' culture. This, Costello maintained, did not betoken respect but rather a desire on Freire's part to impose his way of thinking on others.

Youngman argues that Freire's 'entire method' is dependent on a theoretical position. He describes Freiran educators in Brazil using an image to help learners examine themes such as transforming nature, labour and capital, and agrarian reform. He goes on:

> It is by no means predictable that a discussion of a plough should raise the question of labour and capital, for example, unless the teacher was committed to considering prevailing relations of production as problematic (1986: 177).

Being a union trainer, I no way condemned Freire for wanting to push a particular line, but it did make me sceptical of some of the ideas he espoused in his writing. How, for example, could he use sophisticated methods and the resources of a range of university professionals, set out to change some of the most basic assumptions according to which his peasant learners lived out their lives, and yet describe the dialogue upon which he based his method as a *horizontal* relationship (1976: 44) between teachers and learners? There is nothing horizontal in a relationship where one party decides on, and is far more expert in, the methods that mediate that relationship.

This concern in turn influenced the way I interpreted Freire's concept of praxis. Part of Freire's genius was to understand that the process of naming the world could be a revolutionary one. 'Once named,' he wrote, 'the world in its turn appears to the namers as a problem and requires of them a new naming' (1972a: 61). So, to construct an example from Freire's idea, if an educator works with a group of shanty-town dwellers in order to help them see, that is, really take note of, the water flowing down the centre of a street, they will name the water as dirty and therefore undesirable. If they rename it as sewage, now it is not only undesirable but evidence of the bureaucratic neglect of the district. If they rename it as a feature of the district that the authorities would never let occur in wealthier suburbs, it becomes an example of injustice. In this process of naming and renaming, the learners come to see their world not in terms of givens to be uncritically accepted but in terms of problems to be addressed. As the learners think, so they must act.

Yet, if this educational process is valid, and as powerful as it seems, then by intervening in the learners' lives and using techniques that make them name their world, the educator may be impelling the learners into kinds of action those learners may never otherwise have engaged in. In some cases the image may not be so much that of learners gently but firmly taking hold of their own lives, but of a group of people being hurled into the flow of social history. Again, despite the rhetoric of respect, there seemed to be a hint in this particular discourse that the learners' specific considerations might take second place to the educator's political vision.

These doubts meant that I was ready and willing to be affronted by Freire's comparison of animal awareness with human consciousness. In the opening passage of the essay 'Cultural Action and Conscientization' in *Cultural Action for Freedom* (1972b) Freire states that animals are

> incapable of objectifying either themselves or the world. They live a life without time, properly speaking, submerged in life with no possibility of emerging from it, adjusted and adhering to reality (pp. 51-52).

And a little further on he says:

> By their characteristic reflection, intentionality, temporality and 'transcendence', men's (sic) consciousness and action are distinct from the mere *contacts* of animals with the world. The animal's contacts are a-critical; they do not go beyond the association of sensory images through experience. They are singular and not plural. Animals do no elaborate goals; they exist at the level of immersion and are thus a-temporal (pp. 52-53).

This passage (and a similar one in *Pedagogy of the Oppressed*) annoyed me for a superficial reason. How, I asked myself, would he know? And it troubled me in a much more serious way. Was

Freire not in danger of demeaning the poor, the oppressed, the exploited, the hungry by implying that their naive or magical consciousness was akin to some kind of 'animal' state? When he talked of existing 'humanly' as an ideal, was he implying that some of the people he worked with were sub-human? If this were so, then he was appallingly wrong. Once it became even a remote possibility, McColl tells me, those bonded workers in the brick kilns, living under makeshift shelters slung between piles of fired bricks, some of them with no idea of their ages, were desperate for their children to go to school. They may have had little hope for themselves, but they had a definite vision of the future for their children

Writing this book has drawn me back to this passage about animal consciousness, and now I read it in a different way. To explain why, I need to talk about the process of writing, and then return to the way we might interpret the word 'animal'.

Freire's *Pedagogy of the Oppressed* and *Cultural Action for Freedom* occupy a special place in the literature of adult education. They have been published and republished throughout the world, passed from hand to hand in places where they were banned, carried about like handbooks by activists, and pored over and analysed by academics. They are, as Welton somewhere describes them, 'hallowed texts'. It is easy, therefore, to forget that at the time Freire was writing them he may well have gone through the common doubts and agonies of the writer, struggling with words, structure and meaning, unsure at times of exactly what he wanted to say, or of how to say it, or of exactly *why* he was trying to say it.

We write for different reasons. Sometimes it is to say something we are absolutely clear about. Sometimes it is to express doubt and to examine the significance and nature of the doubt. Sometimes it is to test an idea by seeing whether it actually can be contained in the written word. Sometimes it is a process of research and discovery in which we write out half-formed ideas in order to see whether they will grow and change. And sometimes it is to express our joy or deal with our dismay.

If we speculate on the process of writing for a moment, then we need to remember that Freire was writing after the trauma and dislocations of being arrested, seeking asylum and going into exile, that he was writing within the revolutionary climate (of

233

right wing coups, and left-wing resistance) of Latin-America in the nineteen sixties, and that he was writing in the intellectual climate of radical questioning already finding expression in Sartre, Lacan, Foucault, Roszak and many others. If we bear these factors in mind, then it seems reasonable to read some passages in Freire as tentative rather than expository, as forms of questions in themselves, as an intellectual search rather than exegesis or polemic. So the passage comparing animal awareness to human consciousness can be read not so much as statements but as opening hypotheses. How does he know? Well, he does not know, but is proffering a comparison (that has antecedents back as far as Aristotle) which he hopes may carry an element of supertruth in it and serve as a useful analogy in his political analyses later in the text.

We need also to remember that Freire was a practising Catholic (Taylor, 1993: 21), and that Brazil, in which he grew up and worked until the age of 43, and Chile, where he went into exile and worked and wrote during the nineteen sixties, were both Catholic countries. Commentators on Freire make reference to his Catholicism. Taylor (1993: 34-35) argues that readers of Freire's work 'will find references to Aristotle side by side with arguments from French sociology, traditional Catholic theology explained by radical Protestantism, and descriptions of cultural poverty or oppression enlightened by international Marxism and Jewish mysticism'. Kirkwood and Kirkwood (1989: 32) refer to Freire's Latin American Catholicism, suggesting it may be different from the Catholicism known to their mainly British readers. Mayo (1997: 367) notes that Freire described himself as 'a man of faith', and maintains that the radical religious organisations which made their presence felt in Brazil in the 1950s and 1960s influenced the development of Freire's ideas.

As Taylor and other commentators indicate, Friere's writing does draw on an extraordinarily wide range of sources: Aristotle in his comparison of alienating consciousness (*doxa*) with critical consciousness (*logos*); Hegel in his historical and cultural analyses; Marx in his analyses of domination, of conflict of interests, and of the construction of consciousness through work; Jean-Paul Sartre, Che Guevara, Julius Nyere and many others. To such an eclectic list of influences, we might be tempted to add Catholicism as just one more. But Freire's Christian beliefs are more pervasive than that. Indeed, Youngman questions the use of 'eclecticism' to describe Freire's theoretical position.

> In fact, it should perhaps be described as syncretism (i.e. the adding of other elements to a religious belief) because Freire is first and foremost a Christian (1986: 186).

Certainly, Freire's Christian beliefs, drawn from both conventional Catholicism and liberation theology, are a major if not the dominant influence in his language, in many of the ideas he canvasses, and in his manner of argumentation. For example, we can hear echoes of the liturgy in the sometimes incantatory style he adopts, as evidenced in the passage quoted in an earlier chapter: 'The Right in its rigidity prefers the dead to the living...(1972b: 72-73)'. We can sense elements of a biblical nominalism in his concept of 'naming the world' and his reverence for 'the word': 'Men are not built in silence, but in word, in work, in action-reflection (1972a: 61)'. We can see elements of the Christian idea of forgiveness in his concept of cultural synthesis (1972b: 146-150). We can see Christian virtues in his advocacy of a dialogue based on faith, hope, humility and trust (1972a: 62-65). And, perhaps most remarkable of all, we can see him adopting an unabashedly spiritual form of argumentation. In a passage early in *Pedagogy of the Oppressed* Freire aligns teachers with the revolutionary leadership, and students with the oppressed (p. 44). In a later passage where his discusses domination, he draws on the image of resurrection, arguing that:

> ... in the revolutionary process there is only one way for the emerging leaders to achieve authenticity; they must 'die', in order to be reborn through and with the oppressed (p. 103).

The use of this image so central to Christianity is no momentary matter. In another text (1985: 122) he repeats and develops his thesis that people who commit themselves to the oppressed need to 'experience their own Easter'.

Freire almost invariably ties Christian concepts in with others. So when he suggests we are defined 'in word, in work, in action-reflection' he is combining concepts which are linguistic, Marxist, and spiritual. Or to take another example, Freire uses dialectical analysis to examine oppression and the struggle against it: the oppressed and the oppressors are each defined in terms of their relationship to the other, so that if the oppressed free themselves they negate the relationship upon which the oppressors base their existence, and so 'free' the oppressors as well. Into this somewhat intellectual argument Freire drops a very Christian idea:

> Yet it is—paradoxical though it may seem—precisely in the response of the oppressed to the violence of their oppressors that a gesture of love may be found (1972a: 32).

I find myself in an ambivalent position here. I believe Freire is unsuccessfully mixing language games. In some kinds of religious discourse the idea of salvation through death and resurrection may have a meaning. But employed in another language game, concerned with debate about liberatory education, for example, such ideas make little sense. I realise I am touching on matters debated over the years by many, but I simply cannot accept that the language used to describe miracles and evoke leaps of faith is appropriate or useful to discuss the development of political consciousness. And yet, perhaps paradoxically, if I recognise that Freire's religious beliefs are not just one more influence but actually pervade his texts, then I can read his reference to animal awareness in another light, and so interpret his concept of conscientization in a way I find much more useful.

In Christian discourse human beings have souls and animals do not. In some Christian discourse this soul is an object of struggle, as is evidenced in the idea of the evangelist or missionary 'saving souls'. In this kind of discourse the soul is the seat of our morality, and since animals do not have souls, they lack the potential for a moral life that human beings can have.

If I take this tack, then I can interpret the 'animals' Freire describes at the outset of the essay 'Cultural Action and Conscientization' as unmoral beings. And if I go trailing through the essay looking for the people this analogy may refer to, then I find myself back at the passage: 'The Right in its rigidity prefers the dead to the living; the static to the dynamic; the future as a repetition of the past rather than as a creative venture; pathological forms of love rather than real love; frigid schematization rather than the emotion of living...'(1972b: 72-73). The 'animals' Freire refers to are not the oppressed, upon whose potential for change he bases all his writing, but the oppressors in all their brutish

236

rigidity. This passage is all the more significant because in writing it Freire liberates himself from that conventional Christian need to see our enemies as objects requiring our love, and simply sees them as enemies. This compelling application of moral judgement is in line with a liberation theology which advocates that Christians express their faith in a struggle for social justice within the concrete realities of this world rather than prepare through individual devotion for a next one. This passage may carry the echoes of a liturgy but the meaning is clear, and in the text surrounding this particular passage the language games are not mixed.

This reading of Freire's text helps me interpret the concept of conscientization. It places it apart from other concepts such as meta-cognition, critical consciousness, and perspective transformation. Conscientization is a process in which we pass through a number of stages, from a naive consciousness to a critical consciousness to a *moral* consciousness. In using the term, Freire is writing about moral learning.

I have always felt there was something dispassionate about the concepts of meta-cognition, critical consciousness and perspective transformation. In various ways they imply that we develop a kind of personal monitor. This other part of us enables us to stand back from the world we are immersed in, and examine how we absorb data and process it in order to come to know; or how we recognise such concepts as the lifeworld and develop the ability to foreground and analyse parts of that lifeworld; or how we come to understand and reorder the collections of values and assumptions that constrain the way we think, feel, and act. By allowing the religious element in his thinking to enter and pervade his texts, Freire is signalling that conscientization is the development of a moral consciousness, in which we achieve the levels of meta-awareness implied in the other concepts but also come to know what we understand as good and bad—and take sides with what we have decided is good. The Right in its rigidity prefers the dead to living, and we will side with the living.

Freire speaks in the language of his own culture and religion, but does not proselytise. He alerts me through the use of religious allusions, images and style to the moral nature of his ideas on education for conscientization, but nowhere does he require me to take up his religious faith. So I can recognise the moral implication of commitment implied in his Easter image, yet reject the notion of dying in order to 'be reborn again with the beings who were not allowed to be' (1985: 123) as an inappropriate metaphor upon which to base my social, political or moral action. I am white and middle class and living in a developed country and I am not going to become one with black or working class or majority world people in the mystical manner implied in the Easter experience. Perhaps, however, I can help myself and others understand and review the moralities we use to make judgements, choose the sides we want to be on, and express our commitment through moments of complicity, pragmatically negotiated alliances and, if those alliances work, enduring solidarity.

It may be dangerous to over-intellectualise, or mystify, the concept of conscientization. It is a process by which we come to understand the values which motivate and govern our thinking and actions, and which help us judge what is good and bad. Perhaps there may be no need to try and construct elaborate moral theories to explain what is good or bad, or devise discrete language games in which to elaborate those theories.

Bauman argues that 'morality is not safe in the hands of reason', and that 'what makes the self moral' is

> that unfounded, non-rational, unarguable, no-excuses-given and non-calculable urge to stretch towards the other, to caress, to be for, to live for, happen what may (1993: 247).

Jarvis examines the implications of Bauman's definition for adult education:

> Morality, which is universalisable, is pre-knowledge and lies beyond cognitive reason. It is about desire and, paradoxically, we are faced with an almost unresolvable problem—the education of desire—since desire as we understand it lies beyond the realm of education. ... People have to want to work for [a better society] even when it means subsuming their own interest to the benefit of the whole. They have to desire it—and that is something they alone can do and all that education for adults can do is to act as teachers with different social movements helping them to present their own arguments, but then leaving it to people, as autonomous and authentic members of a learning society, to reflect upon their experiences and—perhaps—to re-orientate their desires and their acts (1997: 165).

Jarvis is describing the role of the liberal adult educator who, at an essential moment, stands apart from the learners. But I want to promote a more activist and interventionist role and to do this I must express a fundamentally different belief.

Morality is *not* pre-knowledge. We come by our moral sense through living, and we have a role in helping ourselves and others do this living well. Moral learning is the process whereby we foreground our consciences, and give them space to develop. It does not involve the use of reason in its limited scientistic sense, but it does involve achieving a complete and passionate consciousness, and the continual making of radical choices.

23: Turning back the dark wind

I asked Gordon McColl much the same question as I had put to Tas Bull about how he had learnt his morality. We were sitting in McColl's flat in Singapore, it was late at night, and we had been talking for a long time. McColl may not have felt like answering in any detail, but I probably got the answer he would have given me anyway. 'We are good' he said, 'because it is good to be good.'

I had arranged my flights so that I could stop over for three days in Singapore and see McColl. He is a friend and former colleague, but I also wanted to interview him about his work. We talked about the campaign against the use of child labour in the brick kilns in north Pakistan and some other projects; and he gave me a training package for a five-day residential course for trade union educators entitled 'Integrating trade union and other human rights into trade union training', which he had designed for use in the Asian-Pacific region. The package included a timetable, objectives for each session, session plans, activities, trainers' notes, case studies, and handouts.

The course starts with a case study of the violation of workers' rights. This is an all too familiar story of workers lawfully demonstrating, being arrested, imprisoned and tortured and, upon their release, finding that they have been dismissed for having been absent from work. The course builds from this opening case study, taking the participants through sessions on national laws, the International Labour Organisation and trade union rights; methods of analysing violations of rights; economics and the theories of development; women's rights as a trade union issue; the development of problem solving models; planning a 'rights reporter network'; and, finally, preparing and presenting reports on rights and the violation of rights. The course meets the classic Tylerian criteria of continuity, sequence and integration: each session flows into the next, reiterating basic principles of trade union and other human rights in the workplace; each session

240

builds on the previous one, dealing with increasingly complex issues and developing higher levels of skill; and the course as a whole is integrated into the lives of the learners and the concerns of their unions through the use of exercises, the last of which is devoted to putting into place an actual project in the region.

Some years ago I was one of two trainers running an occupational health and safety course for union representatives and we visited a glassworks on the southern side of inner Sydney to conduct a mock hazards-identification inspection. The other trainer was leading the group, which meant I was able to fall behind at one stage and watch one particular worker swabbing out a mould with a sponge and rod. The mould closed, molten glass filled it, the mould opened and a bottle slid out. At that moment, the worker swabbed out the open mould, the mould dropped shut and the process was repeated, over and over and over again.

I have always liked seeing professionals at work, be they a glass worker, a dancer, or the lead guitarist, head bowed, playing that silvery solo. True 'professionals', whether they are paid for their activities or not, are in full control of their moment, able to make the right choices, and morally, intellectually and, even in the moment of supreme effort, somehow physically at ease. Of course, the examples I have just given are of people we can easily observe. But sureness, control, and the ability to make the right choices are the marks of any professional. These qualities were evident in the way McColl had designed the training package, and in his demeanour in that video he did not want me to watch of the celebrations in the village in north Pakistan. To watch him being greeted by the villagers and workers, surrounded by some of the children he had helped get released from the brick kilns, and talking with his Pathan comrade, was to watch an activist-educator in full control of his moment.

Certainty, ease, sureness of decision may mark their actual performance, but all professionals can have doubts beforehand, and afterwards many will feel they could have done better. Perhaps these doubts and disappointments are also marks of the true professional. McColl was only too aware that what had been achieved in north Pakistan was minuscule when compared to the massive and often unchecked exploitation of child labour in other parts of the region and in other parts of the world. It was clear from the way he spoke that he sometimes felt a terrible dismay.

Just six weeks later I was sitting in a community centre in the black township of Khayelitsha, confronted by the disparities and inequities in South Africa, and feeling my own dismay.

Dismay is a powerful emotion. For a moment we are confronted, swept by 'that dark wind' blowing from our futures that Camus' *Outsider* (1954) felt. But dismay is a short lived emotion. It brings us up short, then galvanises us into action. Faced with the shattered plate on the floor, we stare, then act. Confronted by a problem, we experience the full horror, the enormity of it, then act. We flee, adapt, or take up the challenge and defy the future we have just seen.

David Deshler, who was visiting our Faculty from Cornell University, met with a group of participants from a course I was coordinating. The participants were community adult educators and social activists. Some were in stressful jobs and one or two were close to burnout. As happened occasionally, the discussion took a pessimistic turn and Deshler found himself listening to a catalogue of local, national and international woes: the attacks on community and welfare services; the continued failure to address the demands and rights of the indigenous population; the apparently relentless shift to the right in politics; the flow of wealth from 'south' to 'north'; the increase in debt of the poorer countries. The mood became sombre, to the point where one participant expressed her dismay: 'But the problems are too big!' Deshler's reply was rapid, apparently spontaneous, and broke the negative mood of the session, setting the scene for an exchange of examples of education in action. 'Just because the challenges are big,' he said, 'doesn't mean we give up the struggle.'

Of course he is right. Wherever we look we can find examples of people making choices, taking control of the moment, and turning back the dark wind. Ndamase and her two volunteer colleagues plan a literacy project for women. McColl and his colleagues bring action and education together in a fight for children's rights. A youth worker employs the ideas of Boal in an inner city suburb. Thousands of clothing trades workers go out on strike. And all these years later I can still recall that wonderful, shocking defiance in Maeler's regard.

Bibliography

Adorno, T. and Horkheimer, M. (1979) *Dialectic of Enlightenment*, Verso, London

Alinsky, S. D. (1971) *Rules for Radicals: a Practical Primer for Realistic Radicals*, Random House, New York

Allman, P (1987) 'Paulo Freire's education approach: a struggle for meaning' in Allen, G. et al (eds) *Community Education: an Agenda for Education Reform*, Open University Press, Milton Keynes

Allman, P. (1988) 'Gramsci, Freire and Illich: their contribution to education for socialism' in Lovett, T. (ed.) *Radical Approaches to Adult Education*, Routledge, London

Allman, P. and Wallis, J. (1990) 'Praxis: implication for "really" radical education', *Studies in the Education of Adults*, Vol. 22, No. 1

Allman, P. and Wallis, J. (1995) 'Gramsci's challenge to the politics of the left in "Our Times"', *International Journal of Lifelong Education*, Vol. 14, No. 2

Arendt, H., 'Communicative power' in Lukes, S. (1986) (ed.) *Power*, Blackwell Publishers, Oxford

Bagnall, R. (1994) 'Postmodernity and its implications for adult education practice' in *Studies in Continuing Education*, Vol. 16, no. 1

Banks, A. and Metzgar, J. (1989) 'Participating in management: union organising on a new terrain' in *Labor Research Review*, Vol. VIII, No.2

Baudrillard, J. (1988) (ed. Poster, M.) *Jean Baudrillard: Selected Writings*, Polity Press, Cambridge

Bauman, Z. (1992) *Intimations of Postmodernity*, Routledge, London

Bauman, Z. (1993) *Postmodern Ethics*, Blackwell, Oxford

Best, S. and Kellner, D. (1991) *Postmodern Theory: Critical Interrogations*, MacMillan London

Blackwell, T. and Seabrook, J. (1985) *A World Still to Win: The Reconstruction of the Post-War Working Class*, Faber and Faber, London

Boal, A. (1979) *Theatre of the Oppressed*, Pluto Press, London

Boud, D., Cohen, R. and Walker, D. (1993) *Using Experience for Learning*, The Society for Research into Higher Education and Open University Press, Buckingham

Boud, D., Keogh, R. and Walker, D. (1985) *Reflection: Turning Experience into Learning*, Kogan Page, London

Boud, D. and Walker D. (1990) 'Making the most of experience', *Studies in Continuing Education*, Vol. 12, No. 2

Briton, D. (1996) *The Modern Practice of Adult Education: A Post-Modern Critique*, State University of New York Press, New York

Brown, A. (1979) *Groupwork*, Heinemann, London

Camus, A. (1954 [1942]) *The Stranger [L'Etranger]*, Vintage Books, New York

California Newsreel (1978) Film: *Controlling Interest*

Chomsky, N. (1992) *Deterring Democracy*, Hill and Wang, New York

Cockburn, C. (1991) *In the Way of Women: Men's Resistance to Sex Equality in Organisations*, ILR Press, Cornell, Ithaca

Cohen, J. (1985) 'Strategy or identity: new theoretical paradigms and contemporary social movements', *Social Research*, Vol 52, No. 4

Collins, M. (1991) *Adult Education as Vocation: A Critical Role for the Adult Educator*, Routledge, New York

Collins, M. (1995) 'Critical commentaries on the role of the adult educator: from self-directed learning to postmodern sensibilities' in Welton, M. (ed) *In Defense of the Lifeworld: Critical Perspectives on Adult Learning*, State University of New York Press, New York

Cooper, L. (1998) 'From "rolling mass action" to "RPL": the changing discourse of experience and learning in the South African labour movement' in *Studies in Continuing Education*, Vol. 20, No. 2

Cousens Hoy, D. (1988) 'Foucault: modern or postmodern' in Arac, J (ed) *After Foucault: Humanistic Knowledge. Postmodern Challenges*, Rutgers University Press, New Brunswick

Cox, E. (1995) *A Truly Civil Society: 1995 Boyer Lectures*, ABC Books, Sydney

Crane, M. (1987) 'Moses Coady and Antigonish' in Jarvis, P. (ed.) *Twentieth Century Thinkers in Adult Education*, Croom Helm, London

Dallmayr, F. (1996) 'The discourse of modernity: Hegel, Nietzsche, Heidegger and Habermas' in Passerin d'Entreves, M. and Benhabib, S. (eds.) *Habermas and the Unfinished Project of Modernity*, Polity Press, Cambridge

Dalton, R. (1996) *Citizen Politics*, Chatham House Publishers, New Jersey

Dalton, R. and Kuechler, M. (1990) (eds.) *Challenging the Political Order: New Social and Political Movements in Western Democracies*, Polity Press, Cambridge

Dalton, R., Kuechler, M and Burklin, M (1990) 'The challenge of new movements' in Dalton, R. and Kuechler, M. (Eds) *Challenging the Political Order: New Social and Political Movements in Western Democracies*, Polity Press, Cambridge

Dean, J. (1996) 'Civil society: beyond the public sphere' in Rasmussen, D. (ed.) *The Handbook of Critical Theory*, Blackwell Publishers, Oxford

Diani, M. and Eyerman, R. (1992) *Studying Collective Action*, SAGE Publications, London

Dreyfus, H. L. and Rabinow, P. (1982) *Michel Foucault: Beyond Structuralism and Hermeneutics*, University of chicago Press, Chicago

Eagleton, T. (1991) *Ideology: An Introduction*, Verso, London

Eisenstein, H. (1991) *Gender Shock: Practicing Feminism on Two Continents*, Beacon Press, Boston

Ferrara, A. (1996) 'The communicative paradigm in moral theory' in Rasmussen, D. (ed.) *The Handbook of Critical Theory*, Blackwell Publishers, Oxford

Field, L. (1990) *Skilling Australia*, Longman Cheshire, Sydney

Finger, M. (1989) 'New social movements and their implications for adult education' *Adult Education Quarterly*, Vol. 40, No. 1

Foley, G. (1991) 'Terania Creek: learning in a green campaign', *Australian Journal of Adult and Community Education*, Vol. 31, No. 3

Foley, G. (forthcoming) *Learning in Social Action: A Contribution to Understanding Informal Education*, Zed Books, London

Forst, R. (1996) 'Justice, reason and critique: basic concepts of critical theory' in Rasmussen, D. (ed.) *The Handbook of Critical Theory*, Blackwell Publishers, Oxford

Foss, D. and Larkin, R. (1986) *Beyond Revolution: A New Theory of Social Movements*, Bergin and Garvey, South Hadley, MA

Foucault, M. (1970) *The Order of Things: an Archaeology of the Human Sciences*, Tavistock Publications, London

Foucault, M. (1973) *The Birth of the Clinic: an Archaeology of Medical Perception*, Tavistock Publications, London

Foucault, M. (1988) *Madness and Civilisation: A History of Insanity in the Age of Reason*, Vintage books, New York

Foucault, M. (1995) *Discipline and Punish: The Birth of the Prison*, Vintage Books, New York

Freire, P. (1972a) *Pedagogy of the Oppressed*, Penguin, Harmondsworth

Freire, P. (1972b) *Cultural Action for Freedom*, Penguin, Harmondsworth

Freire, P. (1976) *Education: The Practice of Freedom*, Writers and Readers Publishing Cooperative, London

Freire, P. (1985) *The Politics of Education: Culture, Power and Liberation*, Bergin and Garvey, Massachusetts

Freire, P. (1994) *Pedagogy of Hope: Reliving Pedagogy of the Oppressed*, Continuum, New York

Geertz, C. (1988) *Works and Lives: The Anthropologist as Author*, Stanford University Press, Stanford

Gelpi, E. (1979) *A Future for Lifelong Education; Vol 1, Lifelong Education: Principles, Policies and Practices*, Manchester Monographs

Gelpi, E. (1985) *Lifelong Education and International Relations*, Croom Helm, Beckenham, Kent

Gelpi, E. (1992) 'Scientific and technological change and lifelong education', *International Journal of Lifelong Education*, Vol II, No. 4

Goldstuck, A. (1994) *Ink in the Porridge* Penguin Books, London

Gramsci, A. (1971) (eds. Hoare, Q. and Smith, G. N.) *Selections from the Prison Notebooks of Antonio Gramsci*, International Publishers, New York

Habermas, J. (1972) *Knowledge and Human Interests*, Beacon Press, Boston

Habermas, J. (1984) *The Theory of Communicative Action*, Vol 1, Polity Press, Cambridge

Habermas, J. (1987) *The Theory of Communicative Action*, Vol 2, Polity Press, Cambridge

Habermas, J. (1990) *Moral Consciousness and Communicative Action*, Polity Press, Cambridge

Hart, M. (1992) *Working and Educating for Life : Feminist and International Perspectives on Adult Education*, Routledge, New York

Hart, M. (1995) 'Motherwork: a radical proposal to rethink work and education' in Welton, M. (ed.) *In Defense of the Lifeworld: Critical Perspectives on Adult Learning*, State University of New York Press, New York

Head, D. (1974) *Free Way to Learning*, Penguin, Harmondsworth

Head, D. (1977) 'Education at the Bottom' in *Studies in Adult Education*, Vol. 9, No. 2

Heron, J. (1989) *The Facilitator's Handbook* Kogan Page, London

Heron, J. (1993) *Group Facilitation: Theories and Models for Practice*, Kogan Page, London

Hills, B. (1998) 'The financial monster that tried to eat Australia', newspaper report in *The Sydney Morning Herald*

Hoare, Q. and Smith, G. N. (eds.) (1971) *Selections from the Prison Notebooks of Antonio Gramsci*, International Publishers, New York

Holford, J. (1995) 'Why social movements matter: adult education theory, cognitive praxis and the creation of knowledge' *Adult Education Quarterly*, Vol. 45, No. 2

Horton, M. (1990) *The Long Haul* Doubleday, New York

Irigaray, L. (1991) *Marine Lover of Friedrich Nietzsche*, Columbia University Press, New York

Jarvis, P. (1987a) *Adult Learning in the Social Context*, Croom Helm, London

Jarvis, P. (1987b) (ed.) *Twentieth Century Thinkers in Adult Education*, Croom Helm, London

Jarvis, P. (1997) *Ethics and Education for Adults*, NIACE, Leicester

Jay, M. (1996) 'Urban flights: The Institute of Social Research between Franfurt and New York' in Rasmussen, D. (ed.) *The Handbook of Critical Theory*, Blackwell Publishers, Oxford

Johnson, R. "Really useful knowledge" 1790—1850: memories for education in the 1980s' in Lovett, T. (ed.) (1988) *Radical Approaches to Adult Education*, Routledge, London

Johnston, H. and Klandermans, B (1995) *Social Movements and Culture*, University of Minnesota Press, Minneapolis

Kaye, M. (1996) *Myth-makers and Story-tellers : A Guide for Effective Managers*, Business & Professional Publishing, Sydney

Keddie, N. (1973) *Tinker, Tailor... The Myth of Cultural Deprivation*, Penguin, Harmondsworth

Kelly, T. (1970) *A History of Adult Education in Great Britain*, Liverpool University Press, Liverpool

Kemmis, S. and McTaggart, R. (1982) *Action Research Planner*, Deakin University Press, Victoria

Kirkwood, G. and Kirkwood, C. (1989) *Living Adult Education: Freire in Scotland*, Open University Press, Buckingham

Kolb, D. (1984) *ExperientiaL Learning*, Prentice-Hall, Englewood cliffs, New Jersey

Kotze, A. von (1988) *Organise and Act: the Natal Workers Theatre Movement 1983-1987*, Culture and Working Life Publications, University of Natal, Durban

Kuechler, M. and Dalton, R. (1990) 'New social movements and the political order: inducing change for long term stability' in Dalton, R. and Kuechler, M. (eds.) *Challenging the Political Order: New Social and Political Movements in Western Democracies*, Polity Press, Cambridge

Kumar, K. 'The post-modern condition' in Halsey, A. H., Lauder, H., Brown, P. and Wells, A. S. (eds.) (1997) *Education: Culture, Economics and Society*, Oxford University Press, Oxford

Laclau, E. (1987) 'Class war and after' in *Marxism Today*, April

Lotz, J. and Welton, M. R. 'Knowledge for the people: the origins and development of the Antigonish movement' in Welton, M. (1987) (ed.) *Knowledge for the People: The Struggle for Adult Learning in English-speaking Canada*, 1828-1973, OISE Press, Toronto

Lotz, J. and Welton, M. R. (1997) *Father Jimmy: Life and Times of Jimmy Tompkins*, Breton books, Wreck Cove, Cape Breton Island

Lukes, S. (1986) (ed.) *Power*, Blackwell Publishers, Oxford

Lyotard, J-F. (1984) *The Postmodern Condition: A Report on Knowledge*, Manchester University Press, Manchester

McAllister, I. (1992) *Political Behaviour: Citizens, Parties and Elites in Australia*, Longman Cheshire, Melbourne

McGivney, V. and Murray, F. (1991) *Adult Education Development: Methods and Approaches from Changing Societies*, National Institute of Adult Continuing Education, Leicester

McIlroy, J. and Westwood, S. (1993) (eds.) *Border Country: Raymond Williams in Adult Education* National Institute of Adult Continuing Education, Leicester

McIntyre, J. (1996) 'On becoming a meditator: reflections on adult learning and social context' in Willis, P. and Neville, B. (eds.) *Qualitative Research Practice in Adult Education*, David Lowell Publications, Melbourne

Mandela, N. (1994) *The Struggle is My Life*, Mayibuye Books, University of Western Cape, South Africa

Marcuse, H. (1964) *One Dimensional Man: Studies in Ideology of Advanced Industrial Society*, Routledge and Kegan Paul, London

Mayo, P. (1994) 'Synthesizing Gramsci and Freire: possibilities for a theory of radical adult education', *International Journal of Lifelong Education*, Vol 13, No. 2

Mayo, P. (1997) 'Tribute to Paulo Freire (1921-1997)', *International Journal of Lifelong Learning*, Vol. 16, No. 5

Mezirow, J. (1981) 'A critical theory of adult learning and education', *Adult Education*, Vol. 31, No. 1

Mezirow, J (1991) *Transformative Dimensions of Adult Learning*, Jossey-Bass, San Francisco

Mezirow, J. (1994) 'Understanding transformation theory' *Adult Education Quarterly*, Vol 44, No. 4

Mezirow, J. (1995) 'Transformation theory of adult learning' in Welton, M. (ed.) *In Defense of the Lifeworld: Critical Perspectives on Adult Learning*, State University of New York Press, New York

Mezirow, J. (1996) 'Contemporary paradigms of learning', *Adult Education Quarterly*, Vol. 46, No. 3

Mezirow, J. (1998) 'On critical reflection' *Adult Education Quarterly*, Vol. 48, No. 3

Mezirow, J. and Associates (1990) *Fostering Critical Reflection in Adulthood*, Jossey Bass, San Francisco

Morphet, A. 'A biographical introduction' in Turner, R. (1980) *The Eye of the Needle: Towards Participatory Democracy in South Africa*, Ravan Press, Johannesburg

Moyer, B. (1981) Television program: 'The adventures of a radical hillbilly', *Bill Moyer's Journal*, WNET, New York

Neville, B. (1989) *Educating Psyche: Emotion, Imagination and the Unconscious in Learning*, Collins Dove, Melbourne

Neville, R. (1971) *Playpower*, Paladin, St. Albans

Neville, R. (1995) *Hippie Hippie Shake: the Dreams, the Trials, the Love-ins, the Screw-ups... the Sixties*, William Heinemann Australia, Port Melbourne

Newman, M. (1993) *The Third Contract: Theory and Practice of Trade Union Training*, Stewart Victor Publishing, Sydney

Newman, M. (1994) *Defining the Enemy: Adult Education in Social Action*, Stewart Victor Publishing, Sydney

Newman, M. (1995a) 'Adult education and social action' in Foley, G. (ed.) *Understanding Adult Education and Training*, Allen and Unwin, Sydney

Newman, M. (1995b) 'Locating learning in social action' *Social Action and Emancipatory Learning*, Seminar Papers, School of Adult Education, University of Technology, Sydney

Palmer, T. (1971) *The Trials of OZ*, Blond and Briggs, London Kegan Paul, London

Peers, R. (1972) *Adult Education—A Comparative Study*, Routledge and

Peters, J. M. and Bell, B. 'Horton of Highlander' in Jarvis, P. (1987) (ed.) *Twentieth Century Thinkers in Adult Education*, Croom Helm, London

Pile, S. 'Introduction' in Pile, S. and Keith, M. (eds.) (1997) *Geographies of Resistance*, Routledge, London

Pirsig, R. (1976) *Zen and the Art of Motorcycle Maintenance*, Corgi, London

Plumb, D. (1995) 'Declining opportunities: adult education, culture, and postmodernity' in Welton, M. (ed) *In Defense of the Lifeworld: Critical Perspectives on Adult Learning*, State University of New York Press, New York

Poster, M. (1988) (ed.) *Jean Baudrillard: Selected Writings*, Polity Press, Cambridge

Putnam, R. (1993) *Making Democracy Work: Civic Traditions in Modern Italy*, Princeton University Press, New Jersey

Putnam, R. (1995) 'Bowling alone: America's declining social capital' in *Journal of Democracy*, Vol. 6, No. 1

Qabula, A. T. (1989) *A Working Life Cruel Beyond Belief*, National Union of Metalworkers of South Africa

Qabula, A. T. (1995) 'It has been such a long road' in *South African Labour Bulletin*, Vol. 19, No. 6

Rasmussen, D. (1996) (ed.) *The Handbook of Critical Theory*, Blackwell Publishers, Oxford

Resnais, A. (1966) Film: *La Guerre est Finie*

Rogers, C. (1970) *Encounter Groups*, Allen Lane, London

Rogers, C. (1983) *Freedom to Learn for the 80s*, Charles E. Merrill, Columbus

Roszak, T. (1971) *The Making of a Counter Culture*, Faber and Faber, London

Roszak, T. (1973) *Where the Wasteland Ends: Politics and Transcendence in a Post-Industrial Society*, Faber and Faber, London

Sartre, J-P. (1947) Play: *No exit (Huis clos)*, A. A. Knopf, New York

Sartre, J-P. (1976) *Being and Nothingness*, Methuen, London

Sarup, M. (1993) *An Introductory Guide to Post-structuralism and Postmodernism*, University of Georgia Press, Athens

Saunders, S., Sheehan, M., Egg, M., Townsend, B., and Bassan, J. (1994) 'Learning, politics and the women's refuge movement', *Unpublished Paper*

Schaafsma, H. (1995) 'Understanding and facilitating change in the workplace' in Foley, G. (1995) (ed.) *Understanding Adult Education and Training*, Allen and Unwin, Sydney

Schied, F. M. (1993) *Learning in Social Context: Workers and Adult Education in Nineteenth Century Chicago*, LEPS Press, Northern Illinois University

Schon, D. (1971) *Beyond the Stable State: Public and Private Learning in a Changing Society*, Maurice Temple Smith, London

Schon, D. (1983) *The Reflective Practitioner*, Temple Smith, London

Schutz, A. (1967) *The Phenomenology of the Social World*, Heinemann, London

Scott, R. (1982) Film: *Bladerunner*

Shakespeare, W. *The Tempest* in Kermode, F. (1954, 1994) (ed.) *The Arden Shakespeare*, Routledge, London

Spencer, B. (1995) 'Old and new social movements as learning sites: greening labor unions and unionizing greens', *Adult Education Quarterly*, Vol. 46, No. 1.

Taylor, P. V. (1993) *The Texts of Paulo Freire*, Open University Press, Buckingham

Tennant, M. and Pogson, P. (1995) *Learning and Change in the Adult Years*. Jossey-Bass, San Francisco

Thompson, J. (1983) *Learning Liberation: Women's Response to Men's Education*, Croom Helm, London

Tisdell, E. (1998) 'Poststructural feminist pedagogies: the possibilities and limitations of feminist emancipatory adult learning theory and practice' in *Adult Education Quarterly*, Vol. 48, No. 3

Tuckman, B. (1965) 'Developmental sequence in small groups', *Psychological Bulletin*, No. 63

Turner, R. (1980) *The Eye of the Needle: Towards Participatory Democracy in South Africa*, Ravan Press, Johannesburg

Usher, R. and Edwards, R. (1994) *Postmodernism and Education*, Routledge, London

Usher, R., Bryant, I and Johnston, R. (1997) *Adult Education and the Postmodern Challenge*, Routledge, London

Weber. M. (1968) *Economy and Society: An Outline of Interpretive Sociology*, Bedminster Pres, New York

Welton, M. (1987a) '"Vivisecting the nightingale": reflections on adult education as an object of study' *Studies in the Education of Adults*, Vol. 19, No. 1.

Welton, M. (1987b) (ed.) *Knowledge for the People: The Struggle for Adult Learning in English-speaking Canada*, 1828-1973, OISE Press, Toronto

Welton, M. (1991a) 'Shaking the foundations: the critical turn in adult education theory', *Canadian Journal for the Study of Adult Education*, Vol. V, special issue

Welton, M. (1991b) 'Dangerous knowledge: Canadian workers' education in decades of discord', *Studies in Adult Education*, Vol. 23, No. 1.

Welton, M. (1991c) *Towards Development Work: The Workplace as a Learning Environment*, Deakin University Press, Victoria

Welton, M. (1993a) 'Social revolutionary learning: The new social movements as learning sites' in *Adult Education Quarterly*, Vol 43, No. 3.

Welton, M. (1993b) 'The contribution of critical theory to our understanding of adult learning' in Merriam, S. (ed.) *An Update on Adult Learning Theory*, Jossey-Bass, San Francisco

Welton, M. (1995) (ed.) *In Defense of the Lifeworld: Critical Perspectives on Adult Learning*, State University of New York Press, New York

Westwood, S. (1991) 'Constructing the future: a postmodern agenda for adult education' in Westwood, S. and Thomas, J. E. (eds.) *Radical Agendas? The Politics of Adult Education*, National Institute of Adult Continuing Education, Leicester

Wilkinson, P. (1971) *Social Movement*, MacMillan, London

Willis, P. (1998) *Inviting Learning: An Exhibition of Risk and Enrichment in Adult Education Practice*, PhD thesis, University of Technology, Sydney

Youngman, F (1986) *Adult Education and Socialist Pedagogy*, Croom Helm, London

Index